MW01006160

Colonialism and Resistance in Belize

Essays in Historical Sociology

by O. Nigel Bolland

CUBOLA BOOKS / BELIZE

Published by:
Cubola Productions
35 Elizabeth Street
Benque Viejo del Carmen
Belize, C.A.

First Published 1988
Second Revised Edition, 2003
6th Revised Edition, 2016

Copyright © 2003 by Cubola Productions

ISBN 968-6233-04-0

Printed and bound in Mexico

Contents

7   Foreword

10   Preface

11   Acknowledgements

Part I: The Early Settlement, Slavery, and Creole Culture

17   1. The Social Structure and Social Relations of the Settlement in the Bay of Honduras (Belize) in the 18th Century

50   2. Slavery in Belize.

78   3. African Continuities and Creole Culture in Belize Town in the Nineteenth Century

Part II: Colonization and the Maya in the Nineteenth Century

101   4. The Maya and the Colonization of Belize in the Nineteenth Century

128   5. Alcaldes and Reservations: British Policy Towards the Maya in Late 19th Century Belize

Part III: Labour Control, Resistance, and the Labour Movement since Emancipation

159   6. Labour Control and Resistance in Belize in the Century after 1838

172   7. The Labour Movement and the Genesis of Modern Politics in Belize

Part IV: Decolonization and Nationhood

199   8. Ethnicity, Pluralism and Politics in Belize

224   Bibliographical References

233   Index

Foreword

The historiography of the British Caribbean has always displayed an imbalance in the geographic coverage of the region, with Belize being one of the more under-researched areas. Since the 1970s, O. Nigel Bolland and others have worked consistently to redress this imbalance. It was within this context that Bolland's *Colonialism and Resistance in Belize: Essays in Historical Sociology* was welcomed by the academy when it first appeared in 1988. The republication of this collection of his essays, with a revised last chapter which brings the collection up to date, will turn the spotlight once more on the study of what scholars have termed the "circum-Caribbean region".

In this revised collection, Bolland, combining his knowledge of history, sociology and cultural studies, in a state-of-the-art interdisciplinary strategy, explores the experiences of Belizeans in all their multidimensionality. The essays cover aspects of a colonial and post-colonial society in the centuries after the initial British settlement in the Bay of Honduras in the mid-17th century, up to and beyond independence from Britain in 1981. Over this long period, important themes in the social history of Belize are explored: the dispossession of the indigenous Maya, the colonial rivalry with Spain, the forced relocation and enslavement of Africans, the establishment of British economic and socio-political hegemony, the formation of the modern Belizean state and post-colonial economic and socio-political developments. In the process, Bolland weaves a story of contested terrain among rival parties: the British and Spanish, the British and Maya, the enslaved and their enslavers, the British settlers and their own metropolitan government, and finally the different ethnic groups in multi-ethnic, post-colonial society.

Although Bolland does not set out to write a strictly historical account, he does succeed in giving much-needed historical micro data on the social structure and social relations of the settlement in the Bay of Honduras in the 18th century; slavery in Belize, showing the impact of economic and cultural factors on the slave system; African continuities and Creole culture in Belize Town in the 19th century; the implications of the Maya presence in the history of Belize; British policy towards the Maya and Maya resistance to British domination. He also examines labour control and resistance since emancipation, stressing the continuities between slavery and post-emancipation society. He forces us to view transition in modes of domination rather than seeing a distinct boundary between slavery and freedom. The detailed discussion of the labour movement serves to locate Belize within the wider Caribbean context of worker insurgency and the impact of the 1930s labour movement on the socio-political history of the region. The ideologies that drove the labour movement, most notably Garveyism, were as pronounced in Belize as in other parts of the Caribbean, including Jamaica, Marcus Garvey's island home. Indeed, while the work is focused on Belize, it also touches on the experiences of the wider Caribbean, showing the similarities and differences even among territories colonized by the same European powers. For example, in his explication of the economic history of Belize, Bolland demonstrates the inapplicability of the sugar plantation economy model that has been a staple of the British Caribbean historiographical tradition; for timber (first logwood and then mahogany) not sugar, was the *raison d'être* of this settlement.

In the new chapter, Bolland problematizes the meaning of the constructed and contested category of 'ethnicity' in Belize, especially its relationship to culture and the way its fluid nature affects what is defined as 'national culture'. Traditionally, in culturally heterogeneous societies, culture is often linked to a specific ethnicity; but in Belize, as the problems of mixture, immigration and emigration redefines ethnic groups and changes constantly their percentage in the population, the perception of what is 'national culture' and who is the 'dominant' ethnic group, also changes. In addition, internal demographic changes have resulted in many Belizeans being multi-cultural and multi-lingual; so that there is no direct and easy fit between ethnic groups and cultural markers. There is also no outright ethnic base to any political party, though this does not mean that people have no ethnic allegiances. But ethnic differences (and the potential for ethnic conflict) have not become institutionalized or legitimized politically. This becomes clearer as Bolland rehearses M.G. Smith's plural society model, tests/contests its applicability to Belize and tries to theorize an alternative model. In so doing, he engages in much-needed comparative analysis, facilitating an engagement with the question of why some societies, like Guyana, have institutionalized cultural pluralism as structural pluralism in the public domain while others like Belize, have not.

Bolland adopts a 'world systems' approach to study the themes in the history of Belize; for his rationale is that development in any country is conditioned by its place in the world division of labour, not only its internal forces and external relations with the colonial power. Thus, he tries to blend the social structure/system with the social action approach so that he pays enough attention to human agency in the plotting of their history. He does this through dialectical analysis which enables him to explore and make sense of the mutually dependent relationship between structure and agency. Dialectical analysis, in other words, allows Bolland to look at conflict and resistance as part of the colonial reaction to colonialism. In this regard, it falls within that tradition of scholarship quite noted in the 1980s and 1990s of focusing on people's agency as a way of suggesting that colonialism and forms of exploitation are not passively received/accepted by the colonized. The book's overarching ideological standpoint, then, is that despite the impact of colonialism, internal developments and global socio-economic forces, Belizeans have struggled to improve their situation socially and materially and to carve out an autonomous nation state. Of course, the society is still in a constant state of change, affected by internal and external forces; it is not static.

Inevitably, in a collection of essays written as individual articles and chapters over a period of some 30 years, some overlap is unavoidable. But careful editing by the author has kept this to a minimum. This revised collection of essays will now take its place on the shelves of scholars of Caribbean history, alongside Bolland's other works, the most recent being *The Politics of Labour in the British Caribbean*, published in 2001.

Verene A. Shepherd
Professor of Social History
University of the West Indies
Mona, Jamaica

Preface

The following essays, except the last one, were written during a period of sixteen years, between 1971 and 1987. During this time I published several other studies of Belize but this selection of essays possesses a certain theme and treatment that distinguish them from my other books. My intention is to make this collection accessible to a wider audience in the Caribbean than may have studied Belize hitherto.

In the process of selecting this collection I have identified some broad topics that are important in the social history of Belize and have grouped the essays accordingly. In editing the essays I have sought to reduce the repetition that would be apparent if they were republished uncut, but I have minimized revisions in order to retain the original tone of the essays. I have replaced the essay that ended this collection when it was first published with a more recent one, first published in 1999, that addresses the same topic, namely ethnicity and politics in Belize.

Acknowledgements

I have accumulated many debts during the years I have spent studying colonialism and the Caribbean.

First, I wish to acknowledge my debts to Peter Worsley and Ivar Oxaal, two of the fine teachers I had at the University of Hull, whose intellectual stance and commitment continue to inspire me. The former encouraged and shaped my interest in colonialism and the Third World and the latter focussed it on the Caribbean.

I wish to acknowledge the institutional support and the intellectual stimulation that I received from my colleagues and students at the University of the West Indies where I was a Research Fellow between 1968 and 1972. Without that support my interest in problems of colonialism and development in the Caribbean would probably have remained underdeveloped. I also gratefully acknowledge the support of Colgate University, in particular the Research Council and the Dean of the Faculty, for providing finance for numerous research efforts and a generous fellowship during 1987 when I prepared this manuscript.

Over the years I have benefited from the assistance, which I have too often taken for granted, of the staff of several libraries and archives, including the National Archives of Belize in Belmopan, the General Registry and the National Collection in Belize City, the Public Records Office, the British Library, the Library of the Institute of Commonwealth Studies, and the Royal Commonwealth Society Library in London, the Library of the University of the West Indies in Jamaica, and the Case Library at Colgate University. To all the helpful and skilful people in these institutions, I extend my thanks.

Specifically, I wish to acknowledge that the essays in this book have been published elsewhere and are reprinted here with permission.

Chapter 1, "The Social Structure and Social Relations of the Settlement in the Bay of Honduras (Belize) in the 18th Century;" appeared in the *Journal of Caribbean History* 6 (1973), and is published here with the permission of the editor.

Chapter 2, "Slavery in Belize;" first appeared in the Journal of Belizean Affairs 6 (1978).

Chapter 3, "African Continuities and Creole Culture in Belize Town in the Nineteenth Century;" was first published in *Afro-Caribbean Villages in Historical Perspective*, edited by Charles V. Carnegie, and is reprinted with the consent of the African-Caribbean Institute of Jamaica.

Chapter 4, "The Maya and the Colonization of Belize in the Nineteenth Century," was first published in *Anthropology and History in Yucatán*, edited by Grant D. Jones (Austin: University of Texas Press, 1977; copyright © 1977) and is reproduced here with permission.

Chapter 5, "Alcaldes and Reservations: British Policy Towards the Maya in Late Nineteenth Century Belize," was originally published in *América Indígena*, Vol. 47, No. 1 (1987) and is published here with the permission of the Head of the Research Department, Instituto Indigenista Interamericano.

Chapter 6, "Labour Control and Resistance in Belize in the Century after 1838," first appeared in *Slavery and Abolition*, Vol. 7, No. 2 (1986). It is reprinted by permission from and published by Frank Cass & Co., Ltd., 11 Gainsborough Road, London Ell IRS.

The author and publishers wish to thank Macmillan Publishers Ltd. for permission to reprint Chapter 7, "The Labour Movement and the Genesis of Modern Politics in Belize," from Malcolm Cross and Gad Heuman, editors, *Labour in the Caribbean: From Emancipation to Independence*.

Finally, Chapter 8, "Ethnicity, Pluralism and Politics in Belize," was first published in *Identity, Ethnicity and Culture in the Caribbean*, edited by Ralph R. Premdas, and is reprinted by permission of the School of Continuing Studies of the University of the West Indies, St. Augustine, Trinidad.

I thank Ellen Peletz for professionaly drawing the maps in Chapters 3 and 5.

I also wish to acknowledge my intellectual debt to Grant Jones, Ken Post, Assad Shoman, and Arnold Sio, for the examples and criticisms they have contributed over many years, though I have too often been unable to meet their exacting standards. Other friends who have made helpful comments on my efforts, including some of the essays included here, are Malcolm Cross, Gad Heuman, Sidney Mintz, Rebecca Scott, Mary Turner, and Gary Urton. Although I have not been able to deal adequately with the suggestions of all my critics, these essays, for which I alone remain responsible, are much the better for their efforts. To all these good people, then, and to my other colleagues and friends, students and secretaries, informants and librarians, who are too numerous to mention individually, I wish to express my genuine gratitude.

Finally, I thank my wife, Ellen Bolland, for her careful reading of my manuscripts and her perceptive criticism of my ideas. She has frequently made me clarify my thoughts and improve my prose, so these essays owe a great deal to her.

This book is dedicated to the memory of my mother, Joan Bolland, for her great love and humanity.

Abbreviations in the notes

BA refers to the Belize Archives, Belmopan.
CO refers to the Colonial Office records, Public Records Office, London.
GRB refers to the General Registry, Belize City.

Part 1

The Early Settlement, Slavery, and Creole Culture

1. The Social Structure and Social Relations of the Settlement in the Bay of Honduras (Belize) in the 18th Century

Introduction

At the time this article was written in 1970, the history of the people of Belize[1] had not been written. Histories of "British Honduras" have all, to a greater or lesser degree, taken the view that the history of the country, a British settlement for about two hundred years until 1862 when it was declared a Colony, is a minor aspect of British colonial history. The chief topics in such histories are the relations between the British settlers and the neighbouring Spaniards, the problems posed for colonial administrators by the anomalous constitutional position of the settlement, and the development of the country's legislature, courts, and other institutions of British origin. Above all there is the legal dispute over territorial rights which has, significantly, for so long been defined as the concern of Britain and Guatemala, rather than as an object for the self-determination of the Belizean people. Though it is obviously true that British colonialism is a major factor in Belizean history, it should not follow that the only important historical matters are those which concern the British.

When the people of Belize are considered their story usually begins with the assumption that the original inhabitants, the Maya, deserted the area long before the arrival of the British who occupied an uninhabited land. The story goes on to describe the hearty British settlers, buccaneering types, who worked alongside and earned the devotion of their slaves (who were really slaves in name only) and who ruled themselves with a primitive but pure democracy, the Public Meetings.

Together the masters and slaves worked, it is asserted, in mutual affection and to mutual benefit, and together they drove away the scheming Spaniards who sought to destroy their society. Such a colonially-oriented version of Belizean history is not an academic creation, but is a story which pervades and affects the thinking of many contemporary Belizeans about themselves with the force of a myth. Some people who are aware of the mythical nature of the story are yet unwilling to dispel it. This article is merely a preliminary examination of a limited period of the social history of Belize—but, as such, it will of necessity re-evaluate the myth.

This article makes little mention of the Maya, many of whose magnificent artistic and architectural achievements remain to be seen, and discovered, in the area. This omission is made, not because the Maya had deserted the area, which they had not, but because there is little information about them in the period here under consideration. The Spaniards, who had such a devastating effect on the population and social organization of Mesoamerican societies, showed little interest in the area now known as Belize and never seem to have considered it suitable for settlement. Nevertheless, in a number of *entradas* during the 16th and 17th centuries they encountered Maya in various parts of what is now Belize. In the early 1530s Dávila, lieutenant of Francisco de Montejo, was sent to establish a base at Chetumal which, according to the archaeologist Thompson, was the capital of a Maya province "which stretched southward from the eastern shore of Lake Bakhalal (now Bacalar) to New River Lagoon, and possibly to the Belize River" and which was located "not far west of the present town of Corozal" (Thompson 1970: 59). The Spaniards were unable to hold Chetumal in the face of Maya counter-attacks so Dávila journeyed south along the swamps and lagoons of present-day Belize, raiding inland Maya villages for food (Chamberlain 1948: 120-4). In 1618 Father Bartolomé de Fuensalida travelled up the New River past many small villages until he reached Tipú, a Maya town comprising a hundred families near Negroman on the Eastern Branch of the Belize River (Bullard 1965: 9-10; Thompson 1970: 70-1). In 1677 a Dominican priest, Father Delgado, encountered many small Maya settlements when he crossed the south of Belize through what is now Toledo District (Stone 1932: 259-69).

The considerable Maya population inhabiting the area through that period may have been reduced by the ravages of European-borne diseases before the British arrived. Epidemics may have spread via Maya trade routes such as the Belize River, possibly introduced by Dávila's incursions or even by Cortés who, on his march from Mexico to the Golfo Dulce in 1524, passed through the Itza capital of Tayasal. The Manche Chol Maya who inhabited present-day Toledo District, after years of resistance to Spanish proselytism, were transported to the Guatemalan highlands at the end of the 17th century (Thompson 1938). At the same time, in 1697, the last major independent Maya centre, Tayasal, fell to the Spaniards near the western frontier of Belize.

The Maya who remained in Belize in the 18th century probably lived in small politically independent villages in the west of what are now Cayo and

Orange Walk Districts. Their experience of *los blancos* would not encourage them to make contact with the early British settlers on the coast and there is little mention of Maya in British records until an "attack of the Wild Indians"[2] is reported as having occurred on the New River in 1788. By this time the British woodcutters had exhausted the more accessible supplies of timber and moved further up the rivers and creeks, encroaching upon the Maya settlements and thus encountering resistance.

Owing to the paucity of material concerning the Maya of Belize in the 18th century, the recorded history of the Belize area in this period is substantially the history of the British settlers and their African slaves. This article is an examination and evaluation of the social relations and structure of the 18th century settlement which was created to export logwood.

The Settlement's Raison d'Etre: the Logwood and Mahogany Trades

The origins of the British settlement in the Bay of Honduras are obscure, some suggesting a settlement on the Cockscombe Coast in the south during the early 1630s (Winzerling 1946), others claiming it was founded about 1638 or 1640 by a Captain Wallace or Willis at the mouth of the Belize River (Calderón Quijano 1944: 34, 46-9). Whatever the details, which will probably remain doubtful because of the paucity of early records, the purpose of British settlement was to export logwood, a tree from which a valuable dye was extracted (Craig 1969). By the middle of the 17th century British buccaneers, who had previously plundered Spanish logwood ships, were engaged in cutting the tree themselves in various parts of the Yucatán Peninsula, particularly in Campeche in the Gulf of Mexico. The suppression of privateering that occurred after the Treaty of Madrid in 1667 encouraged the shift from buccaneering and raiding to logwood cutting and settlement. In 1670 Governor Modyford of Jamaica informed Lord Arlington that there were "about a dozen logwood vessels formerly privateers, selling the wood at £25 to £50 a ton and making a great profit; and that they go to places uninhabited or inhabited only by Indians". Modyford suggested that, "if encouraged, the whole logwood trade will be English and be very considerable to His Majesty, paying £5 per ton custom" (Burdon 1935: v. 1, 50). In 1672 Governor Lynch stated that England might become "the store house of the logwood for all Europe which may be worth £100,000 per annum to the trade and customs", but by 1682 Lynch was trying to stop the cutting of logwood in the Bays of Campeche and Honduras on the grounds that the country was Spanish. He sent Captain Coxen to the Bay of Honduras to remove the logwood cutters but the crews mutinied and Coxen himself joined the cutters. The trade continued, over twenty vessels being involved in it by 1687 (Burdon 1935: v. 1, 57).

By the early 18th century it was stated that for the previous twenty-five years the logwood cutters "have supplied a sufficient quantity of logwood (in exchange for British produce) for all the European markets"[3] and a report to the Council of Trade in 1705 mentioned "the River of Bullys, where the English for the most part now load their logwood."[4] A Board of Trade report in 1717, emphasizing the importance of the logwood trade, calculated that 15,000 tons of logwood had been imported in the previous four years which "tho' the Price is at present reduced from £40 to £16 the Tun" the value of which "cannot be computed at less than £60,000 per annum".[5] When the British were expelled from Campeche in 1717 the importance of the settlement in the Bay of Honduras in relation to the logwood trade became enhanced. By 1751 it was reported that: "There was cut last year in the Bay of Honduras above 8,000 Tun of Logwood Sold at an Average in England and elsewhere for at least £20 per Tun, £160,000 available Sum".[6] But at this time, the middle of the 18th century, the once profitable logwood trade began to encounter difficulties. There was only a limited demand for logwood in Europe, about 4,000 tons per year, so as production rose above the demand, the London merchants stocked up and reduced the price they paid to the cutters. Robert White, the London agent of the Bay settlers, stated the importance and difficulties of their trade in 1783:

> Logwood is chiefly used in dying Colours, Such as Blacks, Blues and Purples, Wherefore its Consumption is very great in all the Woollen, Linen, Cotton and Hatt Manufactories. From being possessed of this Commodity, We not only Supplied all our home Manufactories, but exported large quantities of it to Italy Portugal France Holland Germany and Russia.
>
> Prior to the Settlement of His Majesty's Subjects in the Bay of Honduras, the price of Log-wood in this Kingdom was from £50 to £60 per Ton. From that time the price continued decreasing until 1749, when it was reduced to £25 per Ton. From 1749 the quantity continued increasing, and the price of course diminishing untill 1756, when they exported from Honduras 18,000 Tons per Annum at £11 per Ton. Lastly from their Reestablishment in the Bay in 1763, their Exportations for this Article became immense, in so much that there were from 40 to 75 Sail of Ships loading continually in the Bay all the year round until about the year 1770; during which time the price continued lowering, till it came to about £6 and £5 per Ton. By the foregoing immense exportation of this Article from the Bay, and its importation into His Majesty's Dominions the Supplies so far exceeded the home Consumption and all the Demands from abroad, and the Dealers and Speculators were so Overstocked with it, that from 1770 to 1772 there were not above 5 or 6 Sail of Ships loaded at a time, and the whole exportation did not exceed from 5000 to 6000 Tons. For the Market Price here about 1772 became so low, as not to pay the freights and Expenses incurred in Sending it home.[7]

Table 1: Exports from the Bay of Honduras 1789-90, 1797-1802

Date	Logwood in tons	Mahogany in feet
1 Oct. 1787 - 1 Oct. 1788	1,766	5,271,275
1 Oct. 1788- 1 Oct. 1789	2,462	6,054,215
1 Oct. 1789 - 12 April 1790	940	1,897,000
1 Jan. - Dec. 1797	1,745	2,081,000
1 Jan. - 31 Dec. 1798	1,114	1,347,000
1 Jan. - 31 Dec. 1799	2,712	3,355,000
1 Jan. - 31 Dec. 1800	1,612	3,102,000
1 Jan. - 31 Dec. 1801	1,216	3,061,000
1 Jan. - 31 Dec. 1802	1,348	4,646,000

Source: Figures from "A Narrative of the Publick Transactions...", 8 March 1791, CO 123/10; "A Short Sketch of the present situation of the Settlement of Honduras..." by Supt. Barrow, 31 March 1803, CO 123/15.

The economic problems of the logwood trade were combined with frequent harassment by the Spaniards, but even when the Spanish attacks were successful they did not attempt any subsequent resettlement, so the British would return and resume operations after they had left. This occurred when the Bay was taken in 1754 but re-occupied by the British in 1755 "without any opposition, the Spaniards having entirely forsaken it".[8] The Anglo-Spanish Treaty of 1763 gave the British settlement some recognized status for the first time and Article 17 permitted the "Occupation of Cutting, Loading, and Carrying away Logwood".[9] Spanish sovereignty was asserted, however, and no British fortifications were to be allowed in the Bay of Honduras. Consequently, on 15 September 1779, soon after war had been declared, the Spaniards were easily able to capture St. George's Cay[10], the island on which many of the principal settlers resided, and the Bay was deserted until after the peace of 1783.

Despite the decline of the logwood trade by this time the British were eager to re-establish their tenuous Bay settlement which had acquired a new *raison d'être*. The 1763 Treaty had, for the first time, conceded the right of the British to cut logwood when logwood production was of marginal profitability. But already the settlers had begun to cut mahogany and, with the growth of the English luxury furniture industry, mahogany soon became the most important export of the Bay. It was reported in 1765 that between 25 March and 25 September there was loaded in the Bay "7,449 Tons of Logwood, and 401,231 feet of Mahogany which at £7.10 per Ton for Logwood and ten pence per foot for Mahogany, the Current prices those commoditys bear at present in London, amount to near Seventy three Thousand pounds Sterling".[11] These figures indicate that as early as 1765 mahogany accounted for about a quarter of the total value of exports and certainly by the 1770s it was much the more important export, though mahogany cutting was not officially permitted until the Convention of London in 1786. By 1783 Robert White stated that "the Mahogany consumed in Great Britain alone, is estimated at ten times the quantity of all the Log-wood consumed in Europe".[12] The following figures for the end of the 18th century demonstrate the importance of mahogany in the exports of that period (Table 1, see p. 21).

The Bay settlement, then, survived the economic crisis of the late 1760s and early 1770s when the price of logwood became so depressed. In the last quarter of the 18th century and, indeed, until quite recently, mahogany was the major export from Belize. The complete dominance of timber extraction in the economy has, in fact, retarded the agricultural development of the area, which for most of its history could be simply but not inaccurately described as a trading post attached to a timber reserve.

Social Relations: the Slaves

The process of timber extraction in the 17th and early 18th centuries must have been very simple: setting up temporary shelters for a camp, cutting the most easily available trees and rolling them down the river bank to be floated to the ships. The first settlers, known as Baymen, were ex-buccaneers and adventurers who lived a rough life, relieved only by the occasional visits of ships from Jamaica bringing rum for their carousing. Nathaniel Uring, who was shipwrecked near the Belize River in 1719 and spent some months among the Baymen, described them as "generally a rude, Drunken crew, some of which have been Pirates and most of them Sailors; their chief delight is in drinking ... they do most of the work when they have no strong drink, for while the Liquor is moving they don't care to leave it".[13]

The view that the woodcutters in the Bay preferred hard liquor to hard labour is supported by the fact that, as their business became more established and profitable early in the 18th century, they chose to find others to do their work for them. But before examining the relations of the African slaves with their British masters it is necessary to describe briefly the pattern of settlement and the operations of the woodcutting establishments as they developed through the 18th century.

Unlike the rest of the Caribbean, "cultivation forms no part of the leading pursuits of the British Settlers at Honduras. The cutting of mahogany and logwood is, therefore, almost their sole occupation" (Henderson 1809: 39). This meant that the plantation system, which is virtually synonymous with slavery from the Deep South of America to North East Brazil, was not characteristic of the Bay of Honduras, where the extraction of timber led to a less settled form of production unit. A settler could claim a limited area for exploitation, such a claim being known as a "location", but once the timber in that area was exhausted he would move on. Moreover, since the Bay was considered to be under Spanish sovereignty, the British had a right of usufruct but no system of freehold tenure. A resolution passed by a Public Meeting on 10 April, 1765, attempted to define the technique of "staking a claim":

> When a person finds a spot of logwood unoccupied and builds his hutt that spot shall be deemed his property; and no person shall presume to cutt or fall a tree or grub a stump within less than one thousand paces or yards of his Hutt to be continued on each side said hutt, with the course of the river or creek on both sides... no Inhabitant shall occupy two works at any one time in any one River... no inhabitant shall claim a double portion of logwood works, under pretence of a partner, except that partner is and deemed to be an inhabitant of the Bay... [14]

This attempt to bring some order and regulation to what must have been a greedy scrambling for the natural resources was extended by another resolution the following year:

> ...t he method of measuring logwood work shall be a straight line of two thousand yards or paces, to be begun and ended at the rivers side, and that the division line be run parallel to the general course of the River; and that no logwood work shall be deemed to be evacuated, as long as the owner lives in the Bay, except he occupy some other work in the same river. [15]

The rivers, creeks, and lagoons of the Bay from the Rio Hondo south to the River Sibun were dotted with small timber works, therefore, some occupied and some unoccupied, the intervening country remaining untouched bush.

The most complete description of wood-cutting is by Captain Henderson who was stationed in the Bay with the 5th West India Regiment at the beginning of the 19th century. The features he describes would not have differed appreciably from those characteristic of the 18th century. According to Henderson's account there were "two seasons in the year for the cutting of mahogany: the first commencing shortly after Christmas, or at the conclusion of what is termed the wet season, the other about the middle of the year. At such periods all is activity, and the falling of trees, or the trucking out those that have been falled, form the chief employments" (Henderson 1809: 46). The extraction of the timber was executed by small gangs of slaves who did not appear to experience the hierarchy of control which characterized the plantation system.

Once the trees had been found and felled they would be brought, with much difficulty and the use of cattle, to the riverside where they were floated to a boom and formed into rafts to be sent to the river mouth and prepared for export. (Transport in the settlement until the 20th century has been primarily by water, the slaves acquiring great proficiency in handling small craft: "There are no roads ... in Honduras but rivers creeks and lagoons and consequently no travelling without canoes and Negroes to paddle them ... ").[16] The organization required for timber extraction, therefore, meant that the slaves were distributed in small groups, with little supervision but great knowledge of the terrain, throughout hundreds of miles of uncultivated and essentially uninhabited bush.

The African slaves who were imported to cut logwood were brought through the West Indies. One early 19th century account stated that "these have mostly been imported from Africa by the intercourse with Jamaica, no direct importation having ever taken place" (Henderson 1809: 59), but later it was stated that "the Blacks ... have been ... imported from Africa, either direct or through the West India Islands" (*Honduras Almanack* 1830: 6). Though many of the slaves brought to the Bay had probably been "seasoned" in the West Indies and some born there, yet others must have been brought from Africa via the Jamaican slave markets. In 1769 a complaint that the Spaniards granted escaping slaves an asylum in Yucatán on the grounds of their supposed conversion to Catholicism informs us that "many of them are New Negroes, that can't speak a single word of any European Language, and Consequently not very solicitous about any religion".[17] Clearly many of the slaves brought their African culture to the Bay but the 18th century records are unfortunately too slight to provide any idea of the proportions of the imported slaves who were newly arrived Africans or were "creolized" in the West Indies.

The presence of African slaves in the Bay has been suggested as beginning in 1722 or 1724 (Waddell 1961: 14). A report of a Spanish attack up New River in a Guatemala gazette dated 1730 stated that "they made prisoners sixteen Englishmen and an Englishwoman with her daughter, sixteen negroes and four negresses" (Gibbs 1883: 34). In 1745 the Bay settlers, appealing for military assistance in the face of Spanish threats, wrote:

> We the Inhabitants of this Place shou'd be Assisted, and being now driven to the Highest distress that can be and reduced to a small quantity of People, not exceeding above Fifty white Men, and about a hundred and twenty Negroes, which Number of the latter we cannot tell how many may prove true in the time of Engagement ... we are obliged to Fortifie ourselves on shore with our slaves to hold our Liberties ... [18]

This shows, not only that the slaves already outnumbered their masters, but also that the latter were concerned about the slaves' loyalties. It has been so frequently claimed that slaves in the Bay were well treated and loyal to their masters that the evidence has hardly been examined. The 19th century assertion of "the devotion and zeal of the Negroes in the Defence of their Masters' lives and properties"[19] during the Spanish attack on St. George's Cay in 1798 was repeated in the 20th century by a celebration of the same battle, "Shoulder to Shoulder" (Metzgen 1928). Again, the 19th century assertion of "the good treatment, the extraordinary good Provision, & the attachment the Slaves shew to their Owners"[20] is echoed by a colonial apologist in the 20th century who wrote of the "humanity" and "egalitarianism" of the masters and of an "attitude of mutual esteem, loyalty, and even affection" (Caiger 1951: 26, 125).

Though one would expect *a priori* that the conditions of slavery on a woodcutting establishment would differ from those on plantations prevalent elsewhere in the Caribbean, the evidence of the 18th century records does not support the view that the slaves were content to be dominated or that they felt "devotion" towards their masters. The feelings of the slaves should be deduced, not from the ideological statements of their masters, but from reports of the actions of the slaves themselves.

During the economic crisis of the 1760s and early 1770s, despite the attempt of Admiral Burnaby to regulate the settlers' behaviour with his Code in 1765,[21] the Bayman's behaviour reflected the tensions engendered by their tenuous position. The Lords of the Admiralty received a letter from Rear Admiral Parry informing them that in 1768 "the Bay-men at Honduras have shook off all subjection to the Magistrates, have resisted their power, and that all is riot and confusion in these parts", and later in the same year Parry reported that they "seem'd to encrease in their dissensions and anarchy". He described the settlers as "a most notorious lawless set of Miscreants [who] pursue their licentious conduct with impunity".[22] In 1771 a petition from "the principal subjects" of the Bay was sent to Admiral Rodney complaining that they

> now are and for some time past have been in a State of the utmost disorder and Confusion. The Annual Election of Magistrates has been stopped by the Proceeding of a Mob, and an Election carried by force wherein some persons are invested with a power to Administer justice who have on many Occasions done their utmost to subvert it; the Houses of some have been threatened with fire and one in particular broke open and Effects destroyed; peaceable and orderly men have been knocked down in the Street, insulted and abused when attending their necessary business . . . [23]

Although ships of war occasionally visited the Bay from Jamaica, the lack of any permanent police meant that Burnaby's Code was unenforceable. But it also meant that the settlers had little ability to control the slaves, who, undoubtedly forced to bear a good deal of the hardship engendered by the economic crisis, rebelled at least three times between 1765 and 1773. The situation is clearly described, and the settlers' fears intimated, in a letter from Joseph Maud to Governor Lyttleton in 1765:

> ...if His Majesty would be graciously pleased to appoint us some form of Government ... some power to punish evil doers amongst ourselves, for as to the Spaniards they seem at present very quiet, and (excepting the circumstance of granting an asylum of our runaway Negroes) not bad neighbours. The want of power we lately very severely experienced in a very dangerous case viz the Negroes belonging to one Mr. Thomas Cooke late of Jamaica, rebelled, killed their Master and a Carpenter robbed the house of every thing that was valuable, and fled to the woods; a few days after they murdered three Men in a small Schooner of mine, that went into the New River to load Logwood, and the poor people unhappily falling into the hands of those inhuman wretches fell a sacrifice, and they sunk the vessell; For want of power to compel people to take arms against them we have not been able to raise a party, and they still continue in Rebellion and have entirely stopped the communication of the New River, altho there are not above ten or twelve men able to carry arms amongst them all, and if they do not destroy one another by their own Cabals (as we have some hopes they will do, two or three being killed by the others) we do not know when it will end.
>
> Many people tired of living in a state of anarchy are withdrawing their Negroes and effects, so that it appears as if this settlement would dwindle away...[24]

There was another slave revolt in 1768, similarly exposing the helplessness of the disorganized settlers:

> Matters are come to this miserable pass, that [by 8 March 1768] Twenty three British Negroes, Armed, had gone off from the New River to the Spaniards, and many more were expected to follow them; so that business of every kind was at a dead Stand, All his Majesty's Subjects there being reduced to the last necessity, of protecting their Houses from being plundered, and themselves from being slain- being thus unprotected in their property & unredressed for the Injuries and Losses they have suffered, some of the Baymen have already quitted the Country, more of them are preparing to follow...[25]

A petition from the Bay settlers to Governor Trelawny in 1771 complaining of their indebtedness to the merchants of England and His Majesty's Plantations, estimates that there were then over two thousand slaves in the country, which they valued at £50 each.[26] As the indebted settlers struggled to survive their economic crisis they must have had difficulty in securing provisions and their two thousand or more slaves were certainly the first to be required to tighten their belts. The outcome was the biggest slave revolt of all, in 1773, which lasted about five months and was only repressed with the help of a naval force from Jamaica.

The rising began in May 1773, on the Belize River and on 23 May, Captain Davey arrived at St. George's Cay and sent an officer and some sailors to quell the revolt. The following is from his report to Admiral Rodney on 21 June:

> The Negroes before our People came up with them had taken five settlements and murdered six White Men and were join'd by several others the whole about fifty armed with sixteen Musquets Cutlasses, etc. Our People attacked them on the 7th inst. but the Rebels after discharging their Pieces retired into the woods and it being late in the afternoon we could not pursue them.

Shortly after, fourteen slaves surrendered but Davey was finding difficulty in taking the rest, although he was organizing a militia in three parties of forty each "to endeavour to surround and destroy them, which if they do not effect they must give up the Trade, as they will be continually exposed to their incursions and there will be an Asylum for all the Negroes who choose to run away from their masters". Davey reported that, apart from two settlements, trade in the Bay area was at a standstill and that settlers in other rivers were apprehensive, particularly as he had to leave for Jamaica on 10 July, according to his orders. Davey's report continued:

> The Inhabitants are in a very bad situation: they have neither Arms or Ammunition and those that are here are obliged to keep Guard for fear of the Negroes on the Kay, and what is much worse their fears will not make them unite and there is not the least subordination—they are continually quarrelling and fighting.

The revolt continuing, on 8 August Admiral Rodney instructed Captain W. Judd, Commander of *HMS Garland*, to proceed direct to the Bay.[27] In October a Committee of Baymen informed Admiral Rodney that nineteen of the surviving rebels were trying to reach the Spaniards and that Captain Judd had sent fifteen marines to cut them off. Nevertheless, eleven rebels were reported as having reached the Spanish post on the Rio Hondo, where the Commandant of Bacalar refused to give them up. These rebels had traversed probably a hundred miles of bush in the five months since the initial insurrection. Not until November 1773, did Captain Judd arrive in Jamaica with the news that the revolt was over.[28]

Apart from these revolts the other major evidence of slave discontent is the complaints from the settlers that the Spaniards north of the Rio Hondo in Yucatán gave asylum to runaway slaves. These complaints are a continual refrain running through the records of the 18th century and up to 1838. The Spaniards were certainly not being altruistic in promising freedom to runaway slaves but were adopting their policy in the hope of undermining the settlement by enticing away its labour force. The fact remains, however, that large numbers of slaves in the Bay preferred the hope of freedom amongst the Spaniards in Yucatán to the certainty of enslavement to the Baymen.

The organization of wood-cutting, as previously stated, left small groups of slaves, much less supervised than were slaves in plantations, in remote parts of the sparsely-populated country. This form of organization and settlement, coupled with the expertise possessed by many slaves with respect to traversing the bush, provided many opportunities and facilities for their escape, whenever the promise of asylum was extended to them by the Spaniards. In the words of Superintendent Hunter in 1790: "Slaves, in this Settlement, being so by choice only; for the Vicinage of the Spanish Out Posts and the encouragement held out to seek freedom, by embracing the Roman Catholic Religion, afford them temptations to elope from their Owners. Many of the Settlers of this Country have been entirely ruined by these circumstances, and all experience frequent and heavy losses".[29]

The Africans were, of course, slaves by compulsion rather than "by choice", but that so many slaves chose to seek freedom is further testimony to the fact that they were dissatisfied with the conditions of slavery in the Bay. Two examples of the dozens of settlers' complaints are here given:

> ...there is one circumstance which...serves to discourage our Industry & even threaten the total ruin of the Trade of this Settlement, & that is the Desertion of our Negroes to the Spaniards which increases daily & that of late to such an alarming degree, that no one Man however well disposed he may consider his Negroes, can think his property safe for a single Night. It is but a Week ago since a whole Gang about twelve in Number ... Deserted in a Body to the Spaniards, got safe in to the Look out & were as usual joyfully received, this last Desertion has caused a general dread & apprehension amongst the inhabitants of this Settlement, who perceive nothing less than the total ruin of their Property, should a speedy Stop not be put to a practice so disgraceful to Society & so repugnant to justice...[30]
>
> That your Memorialists have very recently experienced an additional loss by having 24 of their Negroes revolted who have been enticed by the Spaniards (under a pretence of granting their Freedom) to Bacalar...
>
> That unless some means is speedily devised to render their conditions more safe, and to prevent the Desertion of the Negroes in future the Settlement at Honduras must be inevitably ruin'd.[31]

Some of the slaves who rebelled and escaped to the Spaniards helped the latter in attacking the English settlers. For example, when St. George's Cay was taken in 1779 it was observed that among the Spaniards "there were several negroes in arms, who had formerly run away from the inhabitants of the Bay; particularly a negroe man named Dover, formerly the property of Mr. John Tucker, who had, a few days before the Spaniards landed, killed a white man, Lawrence Rawson, in the New River".[32]

By these two means, then, revolt and escape, the slaves demonstrated their hatred of slavery and, by their actions, frequently threatened the very existence of the Bay settlement. The geographical conditions in the Bay of Honduras certainly favoured the slaves should they have chosen to engage in protracted guerrilla warfare to destroy the whites or to establish independent communities within the settlement area.[33] Yet, with the exception of 1773 when they did for some months become guerrillas intent upon destroying white domination, these paths of action were not generally followed. As responses to slavery they were not such pressing alternatives when the Spaniards were offering freedom on the border of the settlement.

Towards the end of the 18th century a militia was organized in the settlement and regular troops of the West India Regiments were generally stationed at Belize. The presence of such military force (coupled with the experience of the slaves, most of whom were from the Mosquito Shore where a major revolt had been crushed by force in 1780)[34] may have inhibited revolt, though escapes continued on a large scale. Though there are no recorded revolts late in the 18th century the settlers continued to be afraid of the possibility.[35]

In 1791 the uneasy settlers legislated against "any free person of Colour or Slave" associated with the practice of Obeah which in the Bay settlement, as elsewhere in the Caribbean, was associated with revolt. Obeah men could henceforth be punished with death, the severity of the punishment indicating the white settlers' fear of what must have been a widespread influence upon the slaves, African customs being utilized to support revolts and escapes.[36]

Undoubtedly a number of acts by individual slaves against the masters occurred without being recorded, but the following illustrates the way in which such acts were savagely punished as a deterrent to other slaves:

> A Negroe man named Joe the property of Mr. Henry Jones was yesterday tried for the murder of a white man & found guilty.... He was therefore according to the former usage & Custom of Honduras condemned to be hanged this day & his body afterwards to be hung up in Chains. Necessity & Custom can only justify these proceedings.... Example is certainly wanting among the Negroes, who had of late acted as if they thought it impossible for this Country to punish them.[37]

Superintendent Despard described the savagery with which rebellious slaves were tortured and killed, though it is not clear to which rebellion he is referring. He stated that a number of slaves were sent to the Bay after the 1762 revolt in Jamaica, and "these negroes some years afterwards so far shewed a continuance of their dispositions as to create a rebellion in the Bay, and murder a considerable number of the Inhabitants (sixteen to the best of my recollection),[38] when it was found necessary to put several of the ringleaders to death, by burning, gibbeting & other methods of torture at St George's Key".[39]

Apart from such instances of brutality the settlers' treatment of their slaves may have improved towards the end of the century,[40] but if this was the case, and there is nothing but the claims of settlers themselves to indicate it, it was surely through their fear of the settlement being ruined by fresh insurrections or mass desertions rather than through any spirit of "egalitarianism".[41] Though the conditions of slavery in the Bay differed somewhat from those on the Caribbean plantations, the slaves in the Bay, like other slaves, rejected and rebelled against their conditions, some of them struggling for a freedom which they may never have experienced but for which they were willing to risk all.

Social Relations: the Free

"The legal and constitutional position of the British settlers in the Bay of Honduras", wrote diplomatic historian Humphreys, "had been highly anomalous" (Humphreys 1961: 6). Not until 1763 was the settlement: given any recognized status and then the treaty only gave the right to cut logwood in a limited and ill-defined area. The logwood-cutting operations were frequently extended outside the official limits but the actual area of the settlement, which from the Rio Hondo in the north did not reach as far south as latitude 17°, nor west of Roaring Creek, was about a third of the present size of the country. Most of this settlement, however, consisted of more or less temporary logwood works and small provision grounds. The character of the Bay settlement was described in the following terms in 1779, when the author did not yet know that war had been declared:

> The English Settlers with their Wives Children and Domesticks, live on St. George's Key, where there is an exceeding good Harbour, at present defenceless... although this Key is the general place of residence of the Settlers, yet they have Plantations which they visit occasionally, where they employ their Slaves in raising Provisions and cutting Logwood—these Plantations extend along the banks of several Rivers, such as Rio-Honde, New River, Rowley's Bight, Northern River, Belize-River, Chaboon River and Manatee Lagoon, for 100 Miles and upwards;—the Banks of the Belize in particular are settled above 200 miles. The number of English on the Bay may amount to five hundred, 200 of which are able to bear arms; their Slaves of different Ages and Sexes to three thousand, of these there may be 500 to be depended on. The Indians who live near the English are so inconsiderable that it is unnecessary to take any notice of them...[42]

The principal place of the settlement was St. George's Cay, a small island a few miles off the Belize River mouth, which was preferred to the mainland for

Table 2: People from the Mosquito Shore who were Evacuated to the Bay of Honduras in 1787.

	White and Free	Slaves	Total
Men	267	772	1,039
Women	155	521	676
Children	115	384	499
	537	1,677	2,214

Source: Col. Lawrie to Napean, 26 Jan. 1788, CO 123/6

its healthier prospects. "There were 101 White people on the Key, when it was taken & 40 of mixed Colour…about 200 or 250 negroes, men, women, and children mostly House-negroes…the principal part that carry on the Logwood & Mahogany cutting business were then up the River".[43] When St. George's Cay was taken by the Spaniards on 15 September 1779 the captured settlers and their domestic slaves were marched to Mérida and some sent on to Cuba,[44] but it is not clear what happened on the mainland, though the rivers were probably also taken. It was reported to Governor Dalling of Jamaica that 50 white men and 250 slaves from the Bay arrived at the islands of Ruatan and Bonacca early in October,[45] these coming presumably from amongst the men who had been up the various rivers at the time the Cay was captured. But this leaves unaccounted for some 2,500 other slaves who may well have taken the opportunity to flee, which, if they did, constituted the most massive escape in the history of slavery in the Bay. Certainly after the peace treaty of 1783 not more than five or seven hundred people settled in the Bay,[46] so it appears most likely that the majority of the slaves who had been up the rivers in September 1779 fled the settlement.

In the Treaty of Versailles, 3 September 1783, the logwood concessions were defined more precisely than they had been twenty years before but the permitted area was confined to that between the rivers Hondo and Belize. As this area had already been exploited for some time it contained little accessible timber, but in 1786 an extension of the treaty, the Convention of London, recognized the *de facto* situation prior to 1779, permitting the extraction of both logwood and mahogany as far south as the Sibun River, the area between the Belize and Sibun rivers being referred to as the New Limits. But this same agreement expressly forbade any fortifications, formal government, and agricultural or other productive economic activities apart from wood-cutting. The Convention preserved Spanish sovereignty and made the provision that Spanish Commissioners were to be admitted twice a year to examine the settlement. It also agreed that all other British settlements in the area, notably the Mosquito

Shore and Ruatan, should be given up. The evacuation of the Mosquito Shore settlers and their slaves to Belize was to prove the most important event in the social history of the Bay settlement in the late 18th century.

When the Mosquito Shore was evacuated in 1787, 2,214 of the 2,650 who were removed went to the Bay of Honduras, the remainder going to Jamaica, the Bahamas, the Caymans and other places and 46 slaves were reported as having deserted during the evacuation. The 2,214 who were sent to the Bay were as shown in Table 2.

This relatively large influx of immigrants from the Mosquito Shore (they were said to outnumber the people of the Bay by five to one)[47] created grave difficulties in the Bay settlement, despite the recent extension of the area of concession.

In August 1787 a list was made of 1,420 people from the Mosquito Shore who required a supply of provisions.[48] 903 of these people were slaves [49] and 517 were free, 215 of the latter being described as "Heads of Families". Over half of these heads of families (112) possessed no slaves at all and another 42 of them possessed only 102 between them. On the other hand almost half of all the slaves (445) were in the possession of just nineteen heads of families, a mere eight of the latter owning 259 slaves. That it was the poorest of the Mosquito Shore settlers who required provisions is clear when it is calculated that the remaining twenty free people not accounted for in that list possessed between them the remaining 774 slaves (and not all these twenty free people were likely to be heads of households). It is clear, then, that while most of the Mosquito Shore settlers owned no slaves or very few, some of them owned large numbers.[50] From this estimation, there were fewer than forty "large" settlers from the Mosquito Shore, but they were bringing to the Bay over 1,200 slaves, or almost three-quarters of the total. These, as well as the less "propertied" settlers, were in potential competition with the recently resettled old Baymen over wood-cutting claims or "locations".

In 1784 an Irish Colonel, Edward Marcus Despard, had been appointed Superintendent of the Bay settlement at Belize, and soon after his arrival in 1786 Despard found himself embroiled in the difficulties of resettling the people from the Mosquito Shore. While his chief responsibility was to enforce the terms of the Convention of London, Lord Sydney had instructed Despard to give priority to accommodating the recently-dispossessed Mosquito Shore settlers when distributing the newly-conceded land between the Belize and Sibun rivers.[51] However, this instruction, which Despard tried faithfully to execute, did not take account of the fact that the Baymen had been illegally working those lands for years. These old settlers soon informed Despard, at a time when barely five hundred people had arrived from the Shore, that "every logwood and Mahogany tree therein are private property". Despard mentioned some thirty settlers who "have divided the whole of the old District among them and will suffer no interlopers there....Until the late Convention, the Cutting Mahogany, was always held even by the Old Baymen to be contraband, and, therefore, they cut it where ever they could find it; and they now claim all the wood which they can find in or near the Places which they formerly held in this illegal manner...Messrs Hoare, O'Brien, McAuley, Bartlet, Potts, Meighan, Armstrong, Davis, Tucker, and Sullivan and Garbutt, who alone possess at least nine Parts in twelve of the present augmented Districts."[52] (Some of the people coming from the Mosquito Shore must have been in the Bay previously as they already held "extensive possessions" in the Old Limits but went on to claim parts of the New Limits because they were evacuees from the Shore. Among these people were "Messrs McAuley, O'Briens, Bartlet, Tucker, Meighan and Davis".)[53]

By 4 August 1787, as the last of the evacuees was arriving, a resolution was passed at a meeting of the Bay settlers at the Court House on Belize Point:

> Resolved that no person who is not actually possessed of four able Negro men Slaves shall be entitled to a mahogany work in any of the rivers without leave first had and obtained of a majority of the Magistrates.... Provided always that nothing herein shall in any wise affect persons who formerly resided or now possess or occupy works in Honduras, and that every Freeholder agreeable to the usage of Honduras be entitled to a Logwood work.[54]

When it is observed that the magistrates who had been elected in 1786 were Messrs Hoare, Armstrong, Sullivan, Bartlet and Potts, it is apparent that the rich settlers were legislating through the Public Meeting to protect their claims against the poorer of the newcomers. This interpretation was adopted by Superintendent Despard who, on 17 August, wrote to Lord Sydney concerning this resolution:

> How hard it would be upon many of the Inhabitants who have arrived from the Mosquito Shore, numbers of whom are very poor, but who with one or two Negroes, together with their own labour might support themselves and their families, with some degree of comfort, by cutting Mahogany. Besides the partiality of this law to rich people, I must observe that whatever it may have been formerly, the cutting of Logwood is at present very far from being anywise profitable; and that several very opulent Inhabitants, both of this Country and the musquito Shore, began cutting Mahogany with a single Negro, some without one ... the resolution respecting the distribution of Mahogany grounds ... would most effectively exclude the new settlers from any participation of the advantage arising from Mahogany cuttings.[55]

By our estimation the resolution deprived at least two-thirds of the heads of families so recently arrived from the Mosquito Shore of engaging in the territory's principal form of economic activity. But the situation was complicated by the fact that agriculture had been specifically forbidden by the 1786 Convention. Despard, though he seemed sympathetic to the problems of the poorer evacuees, and at first tried to find provision grounds for them,[56] later carried out the terms of the Convention to the letter, even using Spanish troops to enforce his orders.[57] This proved highly unpopular.

Despard was left with the problem of settling the poorer evacuees within the terms of the Convention and of his instructions, both of which he was interpreting very strictly. He planned a new settlement, called Convention Town, to be built on the south point of the Belize River in lots of fifty feet front and a hundred feet depth. These lots and small mahogany works, at 40 yards of river course each, were to be drawn for in a lottery. This plan of Despard's angered the magistrates and other well-established settlers. In the first place it was emphasizing the priority of the claims of the evacuees within the New Limits south of the Belize River. And secondly the lottery method for distributing land gave no advantages to those in the community with wealth, prestige, and privilege. A letter from a Committee of Honduras Settlers, signed by Bartlet, O'Brien, Teeling, Davis, Hoare, Young, and Potts, complained of Despard's method of

> dividing the newly ceded district...after the manner of a Lottery, without preference to those who had formerly clear'd ground or built houses, or without any distinction of Age, Sex, Character, Respectability, Property, or *Colour*, the lowest Mulatto or free Negro, had an equal chance with the Honble Col. James Lawrie, lately His Majestys Superintendent & President of His Council on the Mosquito Shore and the Honourable the Members of that same Council, with the Chief Judge of the Colony, were reduc'd in one instant to the same footing with Negroes and indented Servants & in fact Col. Despard has said & continues to say that they are on an equal footing & that he cannot & will not know any distinction between these very different classes of Men.[58]

Of course, it was not true that the rich and privileged were being reduced to an equal footing with the poor and deprived. The former would keep their riches and privileges while the poor were merely being given a chance "to get the means of subsistence by their labour and industry."[59] The magistrates attempted to use the power of their resolutions not only to discriminate against the poor, through the ruling excluding those not possessing at least four male slaves from participating in mahogany cutting, but also against the "free coloured", some of whom were quite wealthy. Thus the magistrates legislated that the "free coloured" were excluded from any logwood or mahogany works unless they were "naturalized" by the unanimous consent of all the magistrates. The magistrates also threatened to withdraw whatever privileges and rights the "free coloured" might have unless they publicly supported the magistrates' legislation.[60]

A number of groups can be identified in the social structure of the settlement at this time. First, there are the slaves who constituted about three-quarters of the population, most of whom had been brought from the Mosquito Shore as the property of a few rich settlers. Secondly, there are a few hundred free blacks or "coloured" and their dependents, most of whom possessed little property and few slaves. The same can be said for many of the third group, the poorer white settlers; most of the people in these two groups had just arrived from the Mosquito Shore in 1787 and were consequently seeking their means of livelihood within the Bay settlement. The richest of the white evacuees, some of whom had previous connections in the Belize area, soon joined the established Baymen who, with their large numbers of slaves, extensive locations, and their control of the magistracy, can be distinguished as the fourth group. Finally, there was the superintendent and his immediate associates, such as David Lamb the surveyor, who constituted a distinct, though not the sole, centre of authority. Some of the tensions which existed between these groups, particularly between the "free coloured" and the rich white settlers, and between the magistrates and the Superintendent, came to a head on the weekend of 18 and 19 August, 1787.

On 18 August Aaron Young, a magistrate, complained to his fellow magistrates that Joshua Jones, "a free man of Colour", had knocked down Young's cookhouse which was built apart from his dwelling on the South Point of the Belize River. Having obtained a warrant, Young secured Jones's arrest that evening and the prisoner was held in the Court House. During the night the magistrates and their friends seem to have been apprehensive that the "free coloured" would attempt to release Jones and they mounted an armed guard. The "Principal Inhabitants and Merchants", either through panic or a decision to make a show of force, armed themselves and assembled at the Court House the following morning. They claimed that "a Scene of the most alarming nature appear'd, a few white people of the very lowest class, a number of Mustees, Mulattoes, and free Negroes running about the Streets and assembling under Arms to the infinite terror of the more respectable & peaceable part of the Community."[61] The "principal inhabitants" seem to have exaggerated the activities of their opponents but their description exposes their fears of the "Commotions rais'd by the People of mix'd Colour and Negroes, who they asserted would soon rule them with a Rod of Iron if not immediately disarmed."[62] It was also reported that "the magistrates and people of property were much alarmed and even terrified; a few went up the river Belize, to be out of the way of the impending evils, others flew to the court-house with what arms, time or chance put in their way".[63]

The situation certainly appears to have polarized, the "principal inhabitants" collecting at the Court House and the "free people of colour" assembling at the store of Mr Bogle, Commissary of provisions. When Despard arrived at Bogle's store "the people then assembled told him that if he thought it proper they

35

would rescue Jones by force, which they were confident they were very able to do."[64] Despard persuaded them to be peaceable, however, before going to the Court House. When Despard entered the Court House he demanded to know why Jones was held a prisoner and, on being informed, he replied that Jones had acted on his authority and by his order in pulling down Young's kitchen. There followed a lengthy discussion concerning the extent, limitations, and source of the Superintendents authority in relation to Burnaby's Code, the "principal inhabitants" stating that they "could not in their humble opinion justify the steps which he had taken & said he would take to settle & accommodate a set of men of Colour calling themselves the People of the Mosquito Shore, and who they contended were not so, almost every person of property particularly the WoodCutters of that Country being then present & fully satisfied with the Provision made for them by their representatives in joint Committee with the old Settlers of Honduras."[65] Despard then attempted to release the prisoner, declaring him free, but the magistrates laying hold of him, Despard was forced to leave him in their power.

On the following day, 20 August, Despard met with a deputation consisting of Messrs Hoare, O'Brien, Young, Usher and Bartlet. Despard represented the views and forwarded the complaints of the "new Settlers, particularly the people of colour"[66] while the deputation expressed their concern over the assembling of these people the previous morning. The meeting's outcome was inconclusive and the sources of tension in the Bay settlement remained.

Two major sources of tension and conflict can be identified. The first of these, the socially ambiguous position of the "free coloured", who were not slaves yet were not accepted as the equals of the white masters, will be examined later in terms of their position in the whole social structure. The other, the problem of the location of executive authority, will now be examined in relation to the settlement's primitive legislative and judicial institutions.

By agreement with Spain, Britain was not allowed to create any formal government in the Bay. From quite early in the 18th century the settlers were in the habit of holding meetings to conduct and comment upon affairs of common interest and to elect magistrates from among themselves whose business it was to administer and enforce the simple rules of conduct which became known as the "Customs of the Bay". At the time of Burnaby's visit in 1765 the magistrates were accorded some rather vague official recognition without their authority being clearly defined.[67] With the appointment of a Superintendent in 1784 the location of executive authority was more doubtful than ever. The Superintendent's chief responsibility being to enforce the terms of the Convention, Despard soon found himself cooperating with the Spaniards, in the person of their visiting commissioners, in restricting the settlers to the treaty limits and in destroying the provision grounds. The settlers, who had been accustomed to ignoring the terms of treaties with Spain, opposed the Superintendent and Despard was obliged to assert his authority which, Lord Sydney wrote, overrode that of the settlers and their regulations.[68]

The Public Meetings of the Bay settlers, which have been characterized as "popular democracy" and likened to the New England model (Lewis 1968: 289-90) were far from that.[69] They were occasional crude gatherings of the upper caste which were dominated by ten or twenty of the richest inhabitants. The slaves, who comprised more than three-quarters of the population, were not, of course, involved at all in the Public Meetings. A property qualification of £65 (Jamaican currency) in 1789[70] was raised the following year when it was reported that "any person entitled to vote at elections for Magistrates for this Settlement...must be possessed of a fixed Habitation or a Negro Slave or a Mahogany or Logwood work or visible property to the amount of Eighty Pounds Current money of Jamaica and that no person of colour was allowed to vote..."[71] Elections were the privilege of a mere handful of white settlers: in June 1784 five magistrates were elected at a meeting with seven electors, and on 27 June 1786 five magistrates were elected by sixteen persons, no poll being opened on either occasion. In 1787, although a poll was opened for a month and there were many persons recently arrived from the Mosquito Shore in addition to former electors, there were only thirty-nine voters; in 1788 and 1789, under the same conditions, the number of voters was twenty and forty respectively.[72] This little oligarchy struggled to protect and expand its power and privileges at the expense of the office of the Superintendent, of the poor white settlers, and of the "free coloured".

Having at last succeeded in getting Colonel Despard suspended in November 1789 a new election was held on 3 May 1790, after Colonel Hunter had arrived as successor. Despard offered himself as a candidate and topped the poll with an unprecedented 203 votes, 250 people having voted.[73] Four of the defeated magistrates complained about Despard's canvassing techniques, the number of ineligible voters and the breadth of the franchise. They grumbled about "ignorant turtlers...men of colour, possessing no species of property or any fixed residence" voting for ex-Superintendent Despard. "There are not above 76 wood cutters of all descriptions in the Bay of Honduras, of whom, at least, Twenty hardly deserved that name, and about 40 White housekeepers, being traders and tradesmen, so that, in our opinion, there cannot be above 110 good voters in the Settlement; and on this principle...few of Colonel Despard's friends, or even himself, would have been returned as Magistrate".[74] It is equally clear that few, if any, of the people usually returned as magistrates would have been elected if so many people had voted before, but, by their own admission, these men wanted to keep the electorate to a mere 5 per cent of the total adult population or about 20 per cent of the free adults. It was, however, an empty victory for Despard, who shortly after sailed for England where he was disgraced, arrested in March 1798, and finally was hanged in 1803 for trying to liberate his native Ireland.[75]

It has been charged that Despard was attempting to replace the magistracy and the Public Meeting "by direct administration by himself and his nominees" (Waddell 1961: 12). Though it would be hard to substantiate such a charge, Despard certainly had no liking for the magistrates who, with their associates, he described as "a very arbitrary aristocracy" who attempted to monopolize the mahogany business.[76] Despard described the magistrates as "almost our sole importers, exporters, and retailers, too; and they had the equity to import, just what served themselves; and their private purposes of keeping the people poor and totally dependent upon them; for they not only set their own price upon their goods, but also upon the logwood and mahogany which they received in payment of them."[77] The control of taxation was also in the hands of the magistrates. In the face of these monopolists who were determined to keep power to themselves by indebting and disenfranchising the poor, Despard had great difficulties in carrying out his instructions with regard to the resettlement of the poorer Mosquito Shore evacuees, for whom he seemed to have considerable sympathy. Despard wrote to Lord Sydney that

> The Magistrates have been at great pains to give out that the people who wish to support my authority, are people of the lowest rank, and most infamous Characters. This Charge, I must say, is by no means founded upon fact, but that the Contrary they are a remarkably quiet and inoffensive sett of people, well attached to his Majesty's Government.... Many of them, it is true, are poor, but on the other hand there are numbers of them possessed of very considerable properties in Slaves, who at present are rather a Burden upon them than any advantage, from the total monopoly exercised by the old Inhabitants.[78]

But the "principal inhabitants" argued that Despard's approach would have repercussions which would undermine the social fabric they were so eager to preserve. Thus their London agent argued their case against Despard's lottery plan:

> it breaks in pieces all the Links of Society, and destroys all Order Rank and Government. The Mulattoes and Free Negroes make good Servants: that they are happy, and well taken Care of in that Station; and rise in Circumstances, according to their Industry Frugality and Ability, preserving still their proper Rank & Station in the Community. But upon this wild and Levelling principle of Universal Equality, they would become entitled not only to elect Magistrates, but themselves to be elected; and what kind of Government must thence ensue, is submitted to Your Lordship. But this is not all. For the Negroes in Servitude, observing the Now exalted Station of their Brethren of Yesterday, would be thence induced to revolt, or to desert to the Spaniards; unless they themselves

were likewise made Free. Whichever of these Events took place, the Settlement must be ruined; especially if of good slaves & Servants, they should become Turbulent Seditious & Bad Citizens.[79]

This emotional exaggeration of Despard's very limited "egalitarianism", appealing to motives of conservatism, law and order, and racism is typical of the approach of the "principal inhabitants" which won the debate over Despard's request that the poor and the "free coloured" be given a chance in their new surroundings. Consequently Lord Sydney's instructions to Despard in 1788 made it clear that the "people of Colour, or Free Negroes" should be kept in a position dependent upon and subservient to the white settlers:

> I will do you the justice to believe that in the distribution of those Lands you were actuated by the best motives, though at the same time it could have been wished that you had made some Distinction in the Extent of Lots so to be disposed of, between affluent Settlers and Persons of a different description, particularly people of Colour, or Free Negroes, who, from the natural Prejudices of the Inhabitants of the Colonies, are not, however valuable in point of character, considered upon an equal footing with People of a different Complexion...some measures should be taken to find Employment for the people who have lately arrived in the District, particularly those of small property, and people of Colour, to prevent their becoming a Public Burden....I would recommend your calling to your assistance some of the most respectable of the Inhabitants, and having the benefit of their advice, endeavour to fix the people above mentioned in some employment, from whence they may be likely to obtain subsistence.[80]

Not even the immediate problem of the resettlement of the Mosquito Shore evacuees was resolved to everyone's satisfaction as can be seen from the fact that fourteen of them petitioned in 1793 that they, together with their families and slaves, should be permitted to return to the Shore. They stated that they were unable to support themselves by cutting wood or growing provisions and "we do not wish to be half British Subjects as we are at present".[81]

The sources of the conflicts that existed among the free population of the Bay settlement were to persist well into the 19th century. When Superintendent Hunter arrived in 1790 he declared the "Ancient System of Regulations to be restored" (Burdon 1935: v. 1, 184) and from the following year, when he left, the settlers managed themselves. When war broke out again in 1796 Lt-Col. Barrow was appointed Superintendent largely for military reasons, but subsequent superintendents found themselves in conflict with the magistrates over the question of the location of authority. Thus Superintendent Hamilton wrote in 1807 that "the powers of His Majesty's Superintendent are not defined and the Magistrates would wish to insist that he has no Civil power over them

Table 3: Population of the Bay of Honduras by Legal Status and Sex, 1790 and 1803

	Free								Slaves				
	White				"Coloured" or Black								
Date	Men	Wom.	Ch.	Total	Men	Wom.	Ch.	Total	Men	Wom.	Ch.	Total	Total
Oct. 1790	174	46	41	261	102	132	119	371	1,091	515	418	2,204	2,656
March 1803	120	50	55	225	180	275	320	775	1,700	675	584	2,959	3,959

Source: CO 123/9 and CO 123/15.

whatsoever. This is a point I will not give up. I consider myself as Chief Magistrate..."[82] Hamilton's successor, Lt-Col. Smyth, was told by the magistrates that they "did not know how far they were amenable to the Laws of Great Britain," which Smyth protested was "an extraordinary assertion" from Magistrates of a British settlement.[83] Superintendent George Arthur summed up the problems of his position by saying that "The Office is, and ever has been, so very undefined as to deprive the Representative of the Crown of the Authority necessary for the administration of Public Business"[84] Whenever a Super-intendent acted, it seems, he offended some vested interest or other and, although the Superintendent's powers were slowly extended, he was not given clear control over the magistrates and the Public Meeting which represented those vested interests and which continued to raise taxes and make and execute laws. Until 1854 the anomalies of the Bay settlement's "constitution" remained unresolved, the Colonial Office avoiding the problem because the settlement was not recognized as British territory.

The Social Structure in the Late 18th Century

The social structure of the Bay settlement can be more closely ascertained through the study of two documents: "General Return of the Inhabitants in the Bay of Honduras, Free People of every description and Slaves, returned 22nd October, 1790",[85] and "List of the Inhabitants of Honduras, taken by His Majesty's Superintendent, in January and February 1790, in consequence of His Catholic Majesty's Concession of 30th May 1789, permitting them to cultivate gardens".[86] The former census lists inhabitants by name, distinguishing between men, women and children, "White", "Free", and "Slave", while the latter names

Table 4: Population of the Bay of Honduras by Area, 1790

	No	%
River Sibun and its branches	239	8
River Belize, its branches and creeks	1,687	58
Salt Creek, Northern River, Rowley's Bight and New River	989	34
Total	2,915	100

Source: CO 123/11.

"heads of families" (in three districts, Sibun, Belize, and the north) and enumerates the men, women and children, both free and slave, in each household. From these two documents a fairly clear picture of the social structure can be ascertained, though the figures are not, of course, wholly reliable.

The population of the settlement increased towards the end of the century, from almost 3,000 in 1790, to an estimated 3,500 in 1796[87] and about 4,000 in 1803.[88]

The increase may be chiefly accounted for by an increase in the number of slaves from about 2,100 in 1790 to about 3,000 in 1803, particularly men who increased by about 550 in that period. The "free coloured" more than doubled their numbers but, in this case, it was particularly the women and children who increased. These figures indicate that slaves continued to be brought into the settlement and that the number of manumissions of women and children increased in the last years of the century. There was an absolute decline in the number of white men, white people as a whole dropping from about 10 per cent of the population in 1790 to less than 6 per cent in 1803. The "free coloured" rose from about 14 per cent to about 20 per cent, while the slaves remained about three-quarters of the population (Table 3).

When Superintendent Despard enumerated the population in January and February 1790 the total was 2,915 (more than were counted in October 1790) though he said there were "besides fifty or sixty more (mostly persons employed in fishing and piloting) who did not give in their names for garden grounds".[89] This "census" did not attempt to enumerate the Maya who were outside the British settlement, which at that time did not extend west of a line from New River Lagoon to Roaring Creek. The "census" divided the territory into three areas, the proportion of the total population in each being shown in Table 4.

Though these figures would fluctuate with the seasonal nature of employment, by 1790 most of the people were reported to be living in the

Belize River valley and the hundreds of smaller rivers, creeks and lagoons to the north. This census distinguished those people who were living in Convention Town, the settlement created by Despard on the south point of the Belize River mouth for the poorer evacuees from the Mosquito Shore. In 1790 this town held 470 people, or about 16 per cent of the total population. The town that was developing on both banks of the Belize River mouth at the end of the 18th century had replaced St. George's Cay as the centre of the settlement. By the beginning of the 19th century Henderson referred to "Belize" as "the only regular establishment which the English settlers have formed in this country" (1809: 11). He described the town as consisting then of about two hundred houses, many of which, particularly those owned by the "opulent merchants, are spacious, commodious, and well finished" (1809: 13), though all the houses until a few years before, when shingles were introduced, were still thatched with the palmetto leaves Dampier had described in Campeche more than a century previously (Dampier 1699: v. 2, 54, 79-80). If even the best houses were thatched in the 18th century, the elite of the settlement, though relatively rich in terms of the Bay, were certainly not living in the ostentatious splendour some of the West Indian planter class exhibited with its Great Houses.

The "estates"[90] of the Bay were indeed small compared to those of, say Jamaica (Patterson 1967: 53; Brathwaite 1971: 121), having only one with over one hundred slaves, but the twenty estates which had at least thirty slaves possessed between them 1,085 slaves or half of all the slaves in the country. At the other end of the spectrum thirty-five of the 159 listed free "Heads of Families" possessed no slaves at all, and another eighteen owned only one, two, or three slaves, that is, less than the minimum of four slaves required by the regulation of 1787 for a new settler to be allowed to cut mahogany. At least a third of these listed free heads of families were deprived, therefore, of engaging in the principal economic activity of the country, which was dominated by a few large estate owners.

The list of inhabitants taken in January and February 1790 describes one James Pitt Lawrie as the head of a family with 126 slaves and a "List of Free people of Colour in Honduras employed in or contributing to the defence of the settlement" names James Pitt Lawrie as the Commander of the Right Wing of the 1st South Side Battalion. James Pitt Lawrie, a "Free man of Colour", was the largest owner of slaves in the Bay settlement at the end of the 18th century. Most of the other large owners (including Richard O'Brien, Henry and Edward Jones, William Tucker, Lawrence Meighan, Richard Hoare, Charles Alder, Thomas Potts, and the partnership of McAuley and Bartlet) were white men, but not exclusively so. Jonathan Card and Stephen Winter, both described as "coloured men", possessed over thirty slaves each, and were thus in the top twenty. John Neal and George Crawford, described by Despard as "people of colour, very intelligent...and both possessed of very considerable properties in slaves",[91] owned twenty-three and fifteen slaves respectively. James Hewm, another "coloured man" who, like Jonathan Card, was to command a division of troops in the settlement, possessed twenty-two slaves, and Joshua Jones, the "free man of Colour" who was arrested on 18 August 1787, owned seventeen slaves.

The "free coloured" group, though denied at this time the political privileges, was, in its possession of slaves and its participation in the military, demonstrably trying to "join the system" which was created and dominated by the white settlers. The majority of the free blacks or "coloured", however, did not acquire economic wealth any more than political power, but became the employees of the rich cutters and tradesmen or drifted away from the settlements dominant economic mode to become subsistence fishermen or farmers. Much the same is true of the poorer whites, who were small tradesmen, turtlers or fishermen, or were the employees of wood-cutters and others. These "poor whites" would have amounted to fewer than one hundred and fifty people, with few slaves and little influence in the settlement. It is of interest, here, to quote in full a contemporary attempt to classify the population of the Bay settlement (See Table 5, page 44).

It would appear that while the Bay settlement was dominated by a small group of about fifteen white men who (through their extensive locations, their possession of about half the slaves, and their control of commerce and of the Public Meetings and the magistracy) managed to withhold privileges and rights from the less fortunate settlers, the ownership of slaves and participation in the economy was not an exclusive prerogative of white men. The social structure was not simply one of white masters and black slaves, though this was the fundamental distinction which affected the social position of the more ambiguously placed people—poor white men and richer slave-owning black men. Between the tiny elite and the masses of slaves there were several hundred people who were either employees, dependent upon the elite, or were self-employed at a subsistence level, gardening and fishing for their livelihood. This intermediate social stratum did not constitute an integrated "middle class", however, as caste-like factors intervened to divide it. It is clear that the "natural Prejudices" mentioned by Lord Sydney continually operated, as they did during the resettlement of the Mosquito Shore evacuees in 1787, in favour of the white group and to the disadvantage of the black group within this stratum.

Yet the "free coloured", many of whom may once have been slaves themselves, were not concerned with eliminating the fundamental social distinction of the society, but were eager rather to increase their own rights and privileges within the existing social order. The "free coloured" group had no means with which to ease concessions from the oligarchy, power in the settlement being exercised by the white settlers who had economic and military forces at their disposal, and resting, latently, among the slaves. Had the "free coloured", many of them slave owners themselves, appealed to and roused the

Table 5

His Majesty's Subjects who occupy the district allotted for cutting wood in the Bay of Honduras by the Definitive Treaty of 1783 and the Convention of 1786, may be classed in the following manner:

Description	Number
1. Cutters and Exporters of wood possessed of considerable property	13
2. Cutters of wood possessed of less property	34
3. Cutters of wood possessed of small property	24
4. Traders and Housekeepers	24
5. Tradesmen and Housekeepers	18
6. People of small property in the service of Wood Cutters, and employed as Clerks, Overseers, and Masters of Droggers	12
7. People of no property, and employed by Wood Cutters and others as Clerks, Masters of Droggers, Tradesmen, and Labourers	37
8. Housekeepers of very little property, principally Refugees from America, who support themselves and Families by raising Vegetables, hunting and fishing	14
9. Turtlers residing in the district, possessed of Boats and Nets fit for carrying on the business, and who employ Servants	8
10. Turtlers of no property, of no fixed place of Residence and employed by the Master Turtlers among the Keys and Reefs along the Coast	63
11. People of mixed Colour possessed of property, and of whom, about one third are Wood Cutters of the 2nd class, but not enumerated there	16
12. People of mixed Colour, possessed of no property, and employed by Wood Cutters and others, as Tradesmen, Fishermen and Labourers	24
Total	287

"It is believed there may be about Fifty British Subjects in Honduras not enumerated in the above Statement, consisting of Turtlers, Fishermen and free Negroes, many of whom have no place of fixed Residence and are possessed of no property."

"The number of Slaves in Honduras, may be estimated at Two Thousand, and are principally in the possession of the 1st, 2nd, 3rd, 4th and 11th Classes and are indeed their most valuable property."

Source: CO 123/9 and CO 123/14.

slaves, the distinctiveness of their own position vis-a-vis the slaves, which was what they wanted to preserve and extend, may well have been swept away in a tide of social change. Thus, in the incident in August 1787, described above, the "free coloured" chose not to involve the slaves on their behalf but to rely upon the representation of the Superintendent. Unwilling to risk their existing status, the "free coloured" remained in an ambiguous social position, denying their affinity to the slaves, yet being themselves denied identity with the whites. The social structure remained essentially unchanged, then, while the white settlers and merchants became even more entrenched in their economic and political power.

While the white oligarchy maintained its power, it remained uneasy. Though the threat from the Spaniards had been checked in 1798 the legal and constitutional status of the territory at the end of the 18th century provided little security for the settlers. But more importantly, because it could not be settled by periodic peace treaties, was the continual and pervasive apprehension about the possibility of further slave revolts. On 18 August 1800, for example, a Public Meeting discussed their "apprehension of internal convulsion and the horrors of St. Domingo" (Burdon 1935: v. 1, 282). If the masters were at all inhibited in their treatment of slaves it must have been through fear of the by then frequently demonstrated ability of the slaves to act against them. The slaves were armed and had had some experience of military action—the slaves, therefore, had something of the means which command respect.

Notes

01. Belize is the name used in this article, in preference to the colonial name of British Honduras, to refer to the whole territory within the present-day boundaries established in the mid-19th century. The term "Settlement in the Bay of Honduras" was used in the 18th century and is retained here to refer to that settlement whose boundaries were within but not the same as those of modern Belize. The only general history of Belize to date (2003) that is written from the perspective of a Belizean is Assad Shoman's *13 Chapters of aHistory of Belize,* Belize City: The Angelus Press, 1994.

02. Thomas Graham's "Journal of my Visitation of Part of the District granted by His Catholic Majesty for the occupation of British settlers...", 27 Oct. 1790, CO 123/9, and "A Narrative of the Publick Transactions in the Bay of Honduras from 1784 to 1790" by Edward Marcus Despard, 8 March 1791, CO 123/10.

03. Anonymous and undated paper, CO 137/48.

04. CO 137/5.

05. Board of Trade Report to George 1, 25 Sept. 1717, CO 123/3.

06. Letter from Robert Hodgson, 10 April 1751, CO 137/59.

07. "The Memorial of His Majesty's Subjects driven from the Bay of Honduras in September 1779..." from Robert White to Thomas Townshend, 10 Feb. 1783, CO 123/2.

08. Gov. Knowles to Sir Thomas Robinson, 13 April 1755, CO 137/60.

09. "The Definitive Treaty of Peace", 1763, CO 123/1.

10. See "An Account of the Spaniards landing at and taking of St. George's Key, by the subscriber, who was then on the place, and an Inhabitant", by Edward Felix Hill, 1 Oct. 1779, CO 137/76.

11. Joseph Maud to Gov. Lyttleton, 7 Oct. 1765, CO 137/62.

12. White to Townshend, 10 Feb. 1783, CO 123/2.

13. *A History of the Voyages and Travels of Capt. Nathaniel Uring*, 1726, quoted in Leon 1958.

14. CO 123/5.

15. Ibid.

16. Despard to Lord Sydney, 6 June 1788, CO 123/6.

17. "The Memorial of the Magistrates & Principal Inhabitants settled at the Bay of Honduras" to Lord Hillsborough, 1769, CO 137/65.

18. The Inhabitants of the Bay of Honduras to Major Caulfield, 8 June 1745, CO 137/48.

19. "An Account of the Descent of the Spaniards on the Settlement in the Year 1798" in *Defense of the Settlers of Honduras . . . 1824*, 93.

20. Br. Gen. H. T. Montresor to Gov. Sir Eyre Cootes, 22 Oct. 1806, CO 123/17.

21. CO 123/5.

22. Lords of the Admiralty to Hillsborough, 27 July and 23 Aug. 1768, CO 137/63, and Admiral Parry to Secretary Stephens, 12 Dec. 1768, Adm. 1/238 in Burdon 1935: v. 1, 116.

23. Petition from the principal subjects of the Bay of Honduras to Admiral Rodney, 12 Sept. 1771, CO 137/67.

24. Maud to Lyttleton, 7 Oct. 1765, CO 137/62.

25. "The Memorial of Allan Auld of London Merchant, & Trading to the Bay of Honduras" to Hillsborough, July 1768, CO 137/63.

26. Petition from the Bay Settlers to Gov. Trelawny, 19 Feb. 1771, CO 137/66.

27. These instructions include mention of three fugitive slaves who killed someone called McDougal on the Rio Hondo, an incident which appears distinct from, but may or may not have been connected to, the Belize River revolt.

28. See the various reports from Adm. 1/239 in Burdon 1935, v. 1, 121-4.

29. "Plan of Police proposed . . . " by Supt. Hunter, 18 May 1790, CO 123/9.

30. Letter from Thomas Potts, 28 May 1792, CO 123/13.

31. "The Memorial of Benjamin Garnett and Charles Armstrong late of Honduras Bay" to Henry Dundas, 11 June 1793, CO 123/13.

32. "An Account of the Spaniards landing . . . St. George's Key . . . " CO 137/76.

33. As did the "Bush Negroes" of French Guiana and Surinam, the Maroons of Jamaica, and the escaped slaves of Palmares in Brazil, 1630-97. Some runaways did establish independent communities in the Belize area early in the 19th century, reference being made to one "near Sheboon River, very difficult to discover, and guarded by poisonous Stakes" in 1816 (Burdon 1935: v. 2, 184). This may explain the name, Runaway Creek, of a tributary of the Sibun River. In 1817 Supt. Arthur reported that "a considerable body of runaway Slaves are formed in the interior". Arthur to Major Fraser, 12 June 1817, CO 123/26.

34. See Affidavit of Joseph Everett, 3 June 1780, CO 137/78.

35. For example, when the slaves' provision grounds were destroyed by the Spanish Commissioners: see Hoare to White, 25 Aug. 1788, and letters from George Dyer and White to the Duke of Leeds, 28 July and 31 July 1789, CO 123/7.

36. "Regulation respecting Obeah", 11 Oct. 1791, Burdon 1935: v. 1, 195-6.

37. James Bartlet to Despard, enclosed in Despard's despatch to Evan Napean, 21 Oct. 1787, CO 123/5; see also Burdon 1935: v. 1, 210, for the court report of a slave who was hanged for chopping his owner with a machete, the owner receiving £60 Jamaican currency as compensation, in 1794.

38. Though Despard did not arrive in the Bay until 1786 he may have been referring to an earlier time.

39. "A Narrative of the Publick Transactions...", CO 123/10.

40. Legal action may also have inhibited some of the settlers. In 1791 a man was fined £100 and banished from the Settlement for flogging a slave to death, though one month later a magistrate was fined only £10 for mutilating one of his slaves (see Burdon 1935: v. 1, 194-5).

41. Fifteen slaves who escaped "from their master, Mr. Paslo, an Englishman, because of ill-treatment and starvation" reached the Spaniards north of the Hondo in 1813. (Manuel Melendex to Manuel Artazo, 15 March 1813), "An Inventory of the Manuscript Collections of the Middle American Research Institute", New Orleans, Tulane University of Louisiana, Oct. 1939 (mimeo.), pp.120-221. Thomas Paslow was one of the Baymen whose slaves were supposed to have fought by his side with "devotion and zeal" fifteen years before at the Battle of St. George's Cay.

42. Unsigned letter of Gov. Dalling, 3 Sept. 1779, CO 137/75.

43. "An Account of the Spaniards landing at... St. George's Key...", CO 137/76.

44. See the memorandum relating to Mr. Ogilvie sent by White to Lord Shelburne, 2 July 1782, and the Memorial from White to Lord North, 8 April and 11 Dec. 1783, CO 123/2.

45. Bartlet to Dalling, undated, CO 137/76.

46. This figure would include "several loyalists from the American States" who came to the Bay at this time; see the Memorial from White to Sydney, 28 May 1787, CO 123/5 and CO 123/14.

47. Letter from Despard, 23 Feb. 1787, CO 123/5.

48. "Return of such of the Inhabitants from the Mosquito Shore as His Majesty's Superintendent has found it necessary to issue a further supply of provisions to," 24 August and 20 Oct. 1787, CO 123/5.

49. A small number of these slaves were Mosquito Indians, the majority being African; see *Defense of the Settlers of Honduras...*, 1824: 45-6.

50. This view is supported by a letter from the Mosquito Shore some years earlier, stating that one William Pitt was on his deathbed and that "his Possessions are much the largest of any here among them are about four hundred high spirited Negroes from whom an immediate danger more than threatens...", Hodgson to Trelawny, 14 April 1771, CO 137/6.

51. Sydney to Despard, 31 July 1786, CO 137/86.

52. Letters from Despard, 23 Feb. and 31 Oct. 1787, CO 123/5 and CO 123/6.

53. Letter from Despard, 23 Feb. 1787, CO 123/5.

54. CO 123/5.

55. Despard to Sydney, 17 Aug. 1787, CO 123/5.

56. Despard to Sydney, 23 Feb. 1787; and on 14 Aug. 1787 Despard wrote to the Spanish Commissioner, Col. Grimarist, pleading for permission for "the poorer sort of people to maintain themselves... [by planting] a small quantity of Land from two to four acres for each family with Cabbage, Beans, Peas, Potatoes, Yams Plantions and Pumpkins which is indispensably necessary for their maintenance", CO 123/5.

57. Settlers to London merchants, 26 Aug. 1787, CO 123/5.

58. 27 Aug. 1787, CO 123/5, emphasis in original.

59. Despard to Sydney, 17 Aug. 1787, CO 123/5.

60. See the undated petition "To the Honble Colonel Edwd. Marcus Despard & the Honble Col. Gamarazett Greeting", signed by eight of the Settlements free coloured: "It will be really impossible for us to procure a lively hood in this country, particularly as we are not allowed the privaleges of British subject, and as colour'd persons treated with the utmost disrespect. Evenly threatened of being deprived of the Laws and privileges of this Country in case we do not sign and agree to a certain resolution made by a Committy…", CO 123/5.

61. "Letter from the Committee of the Honduras Settlers, to the Merchants in London", 27 Aug. 1787, CO 123/5.

62. Ibid.

63. An account of 18 Aug. 1787 by Bartlet, Douglas, Pitts and O'Brien, 12 March 1791, CO 123/13.

64. "A Narrative of the Publick Transactions…", CO 123/10.

65. "Letter from the Committee of the Honduras Settlers…", CO 123/5.

66. Despard to Sydney, 24 Aug. 1787, CO 123/5.

67. The importance of Burnaby's Code has been greatly exaggerated. It hardly established a constitution, except in a most elementary fashion and it is certainly untrue that "the close of the 18th Century saw the confirmation of this native born constitution by Royal Authority" (Burdon 135: v. 1, 1). James Stephen, a senior Colonial Office Official, though he described the "constitution" in 1838 as "the most pure and perfect democracy" (CO 123/54), emphatically stated that the institutions of the Bay "have never been acknowledged by the Government here as lawful" (17 Dec. 1839, CO 123/55). The chief concern of Burnaby's Code was the maintenance of law and order; but that his rudimentary constitution was not sufficient to ensure this is demonstrated by his proviso that the Commanding Officer of any ship of war "shall have full power… to enforce and put in execution all such Laws and Regulations…" (Burdon 1935: v, 1, 104).

68. Sydney to Despard, 6 Feb. 1788, CO 123/6.

69. A description of the Public Meetings as "the nearest approach to true democracy since the days of the Greek city state" (Jones 1953, 136), is a more accurate comparison —Greek democracy being the privilege of a free minority in a society divided between the free and the enslaved.

70. "Regulations framed by the Committee chosen by the British Inhabitants of the District", 10 June 1789, CO 123/12.

71. "Minutes of a meeting of the Magistrates…", 23 April 1790, CO 123/12.

72. "A Narrative of the Publick Transactions…", 123/10.

73. CO 123/9.

74. The Account by Bartlet, Douglas, Pitts and O'Brien, CO 123/13.

75. Letter from Despard from the county jail, Shrewsbury, 26 Dec. 1800, CO 123/4; see also Oman 1922: 1-21; Thompson, E.P. 1963: 478-84.

76. "A Narrative of the Publick Transactions…", CO 123/10.

77. Letter from Despard, 11 Jan. 1788, CO 123/6; see the resolution establishing the price of logwood and mahogany on 12 June 1784, CO 123/5.

78. Despard to Sydney, 24 Aug. 1787, CO 123/5.

79. "The Memorial of his Majesty's Subjects settled on the Coast of Yucatán in the Bay of Honduras", from White to Sydney, 21 Feb. 1788, CO 123/6.

80. Sydney to Despard, 6 Feb. 1788, CO 123/6.

81. Petition to William Pitt, 13 Aug. 1793, CO 137/92.

82. Supt. Hamilton to Cootes, 26 Nov. 1807, CO 123/17.

83. Supt. Smyth to Lord Liverpool, 31 Aug. 1810, CO 123/19.

84. Supt. Arthur to Lord Bathurst, 31 July 1819, CO 123/28.

85. CO 123/9.

86. CO 123/11.

87. Magistrates to Gov. Balcarres, 18 July 1795, CO 137/98.

88. "A Short Sketch of the present situation of the Settlement...", CO 123/15.

89. "A Narrative of the Publick Transactions...," CO 123/ 10. Note that some of Despards' sub-totals are incorrect; the figures used in this article are obtained from the original enumeration in CO 123/11.

90. The term "estate" is used here to refer, not to a fixed and defined area of land like a plantation, but to the economic units in the Bay settlement, consisting chiefly of claims to woodcutting areas, the locations, and property in slaves. Since there was no regular system of freehold tenure and the registration of land ownership was not instituted until 1858, the measure of the size of an "estate" and the wealth of a settler is the number of slaves he possessed.

91. "A Narrative of the Publick Transactions...", CO 123/10.

2. Slavery in Belize

Introduction

The Purpose of the Article

Throughout the Caribbean and in most of the so-called New World slavery has been associated with the plantation production of crops such as sugar and cotton. Consequently, studies of the organization of slavery in the New World have been primarily of plantation production systems, to the point where slavery and plantation organization have been virtually synonymous. In Belize, however, slavery was organized for the extraction of timber, first logwood and then mahogany. A question therefore arises concerning the differences in the organization, conditions, and treatment of slaves associated with this different economic function. Underlying this question there is the continuing debate in the literature on comparative slavery concerning the relative importance of economic and cultural factors in determining the nature of slave systems.[1]

The assumption that slavery is primarily a legal institution supports the notion that a slave system will reflect particular national cultural traditions and that differences between slave systems may be explained in terms of variations in the predominant legal/cultural heritages. The classic statement of this view is by Frank Tannenbaum (1946) and it has been used more recently by Herbert Klein (1967); both authors stress the differences between Iberian and British slave societies. A contrasting view examines slavery primarily as an economic institution and explains changes and variations in the nature of slave systems in terms of changes in the prevailing economic order. The classic statement of this conception is that by Eric Williams (1944) who argued that even the success of the abolitionist movement was more a result of changed economic conditions than of humanitarianism. More recently, Franklin W. Knight (1970) has demonstrated that the nature of slavery in Cuba changed from the 18th to the

50

19th centuries as a result of the transformation of the economy into a plantation system. It is claimed that when slavery is compared in Iberian and British societies based upon plantation agriculture the differences are less significant than the similarities and, hence, that economic factors are paramount over legal or cultural traditions.

First, in the context of this debate, this paper indicates that, although Belize shared a common legal and cultural tradition with other British colonies, there were significant differences in the organization of slavery resulting from its different economic function. Second, this paper shows that, though the masters sought to treat their slaves as so much capital equipment and labour power, the slaves frequently sought to change their situation, sometimes by adjustment and sometimes by rejection. Studies of slavery which emphasize the analysis of the formal legal structures often overlook the importance of informal customary behaviour. Such studies tend to overemphasize the stability of the slave systems and detract from the slaves' ability to respond and, through their responses, to modify the institution within which the masters sought to define them.

On the one hand, slavery is, by its very nature, oppressive and it would be hard to exaggerate this oppression.[2] On the other hand, it is possible to overestimate the disorganization and demoralization which is a consequence of slavery. Recent works by Blassingame (1972) and Gutman (1976) have shown the strength and persistence of the communal and family life of slaves in the U.S.A. The second purpose of this paper, therefore, is to show that the actions of the slaves in Belize succeeded to some extent in affecting the masters' treatment of them and that the slaves maintained a degree of control over their family and community life, thereby contributing significantly to the emergence of a Creole culture and identity. The slaves' resilience was such that they made this important contribution to Belizean culture despite the oppressive nature of the system of slavery.

The Settlement's Political Economy and the Demand for Slaves

The initial *raison d'être* of British settlement in the Bay of Honduras in the 17th century was the exportation of logwood, a tree from which a dye valuable in the woollen industry was extracted. In 1763 the Treaty of Paris conceded the right of the British to cut logwood but it was a time when logwood production was actually of marginal profitability. By 1770, when the depression in the logwood trade was acute, the settlers were exporting mahogany, an enterprise which was legalized by the Convention of London in 1786 and which was to remain the major export of Belize until the middle of the 20th century.

51

The shift from the preeminence of logwood to the preeminence of mahogany in the settlements economy encouraged the tendency for control of the economy to concentrate in the hands of a few settlers, because the extraction of mahogany was a much larger-scale operation, requiring more land, labour, and capital, than that of logwood. In 1787, just twelve of the settlers claimed possession of four-fifths of all the land permitted by the Convention between the Rio Hondo and the Sibun River, or about two thousand square miles. Because Britain recognized Spanish sovereignty over the area the Crown did not assume the authority to allocate land until 1817, with the result that the richer settlers controlled the distribution of land themselves.

Until the middle of the 19th century the leading settlers controlled not only the land, labour, and commerce of the settlement, but also the instruments of its Government and the agencies of its administration. The first Superintendent, Colonel Despard, arrived in 1786 and soon came into conflict with the Magistrates, a group of settlers who functioned in an executive as well as a judicial capacity. Despard lost that conflict and the settler elite maintained their oligarchic control. The Superintendent was placed in a weak and anomalous position when opposed by a united settler elite and as late as 1838 it was stated that "The Crown is represented by a Superintendent who is not much more than a Looker-on".[3]

Throughout the period of slavery, therefore, Belize was a colony without colonial status, a settlement in which the settlers reigned supreme. Britain, unwilling to assert its sovereignty, was unable to impose its authority and, consequently, left control of the settlement in the hands of the settler oligarchy. The slave-owners of Belize had little to inhibit them, therefore, but their slaves.

When the British were expelled from Campeche in 1717 their settlement in the Bay of Honduras became more important and the settlers strove to expand their lucrative logwood trade. There was no shortage of land there were plentiful supplies of accessible logwood. The problem for those settlers who wished to expand their enterprises was to secure adequate supplies of labour. The British settlers of Belize, unable to enslave the Maya who had withdrawn into the interior, relied, like their planter counterparts in the Caribbean islands, upon slave labour from Africa. The earliest reference to the presence of black slaves in the Bay of Honduras is provided by a Spanish missionary who reported in 1724 that the British settlement consisted of "about three hundred English, besides Mosquito Indians and negro slaves, these latter having been introduced but a short time before from Jamaica and Bermuda." (Bancroft 1883-87: v. 2, 626).

The Slave Population

Origins

The slaves who were brought to the Bay of Honduras were imported through the West Indian Islands. One early 19th century account stated that "these have been mostly imported from Africa by the intercourse with Jamaica, no direct importation having ever taken place; but many of these people are Creoles of the different West Indian Islands, and several have been brought into the Settlement, by their owners, from the United States." (Henderson 1809: 59) Later it was stated that they were "imported from Africa, either direct or through the West India Islands." (*Honduras Almanack* 1830: 6). Though there is no indication from the 18th century records of the proportion of the slaves who were of African as opposed to West Indian birth, in 1823 it was estimated that there were in Belize "near 1500 Africans" in a slave population of about 2,300, "the remainder being Creoles and descendants of Indians,"[4] the latter from the Mosquito Shore. If it is correct that about three-fifths of the slaves were African-born in 1823 it can safely be assumed that the Creoles were always a minority of the slaves.

Additional to the distinction between African-born and Creole slaves was the difference in the tribal origins of the African-born slaves. Because these slaves were brought through island slave markets there are no shipping records to indicate their tribal identity but the names of many of the slaves recorded in a 1790 census[5] indicate a variety of national origins, for example, such names as Congo Will, Angola Will, Guinea Sam, Eboe Jack, Mundingo Pope, and Corromontee Tom. Most of the slaves were brought to the Bay settlement in the second half of the 18th century, at which time the principal sources of British slaves were the Niger and Cross deltas in the Bight of Benin (from 1730 to 1790) and southwestern Africa, particularly the Congo and Angola (from 1790 to 1807).

The Eboes or Ibos appear to have been particularly numerous in Belize. One section of Belize Town was known throughout the first half of the 19th century as Eboe Town and in 1850 it was stated that there were in Belize "Congoes, Nangoes, Mongolas, Ashantees, Eboes, and other African tribes" (Crowe 1850: 33, 50), indicating that tribal distinctions and identifications persisted well after emancipation.

Demographic Features

One of the major factors affecting master/slave relations in Belize was the overwhelming numerical preponderance of the blacks, more similar to Jamaica and Barbados than to the North American colonies. Before the middle of the 18th century the slaves were the majority of the population and at the time the

Table 1: Slave Population of Belize, 1745-1832

Date	Number of Slaves			Total	Slaves as Percentage of Total Population
	Male	Female	Children		
1745	....	....	....	120	71
1779	....	....	....	3,000	86
1790a	1,216	550	411	2,177	75
1790b	1,091	515	418	2,024	76
1803	1,700	675	584	2,959	75
1806	1,489	588	450	2,527	72
1809	....	....	....	3,000	73
1816	....	....	....	2,742	72
1820	1,537	600	426	2,563	....
1823	1,440	628	400	2,468	60
1826	1,373	577	460	2,410	46
1829	1,113	486	428	2,027	52
1832	895	435	453	1,783	42

Sources: 1745, Inhabitants of the Bay of Honduras to Major Caulfield, 8 June 1745, CO 137/48; 1779, unsigned letter to Gov. Dalling, 3 September 1779, CO 137/75; 1790a, "List of the Inhabitants of Honduras...January and February 1790." CO 123/11; 1790b, "General Return of the Inhabitants in the Bay of Honduras...22nd October, 1790;" CO 123/9; 1803, "A Short Sketch of the present situation of the Settlement of Honduras..." from Supt. Thomas Barrow, 31 March 1803, CO 123/15; 1806, Br. Gen. H. T. Montresor to Gov. Sir Eyre Coote, 22 Oct. 1806, CO 123/17; 1809, "Remarks upon the Situation Trade etc..." by Barrow, I May 1809, CO 123/18; 1816, Census of the Population, GRB; 1820, Census of the Slave Population, 31 Dec. 1820, GRB; 1823, 1826, 1829, 1832, Censuses of the Population, GRB.

Spaniards captured the settlement in 1779 there were an estimated three thousands slaves in the Bay[6], or about 86 per cent of the total population. After the resettlement following the peace of 1783 about 75 per cent of the population was slaves, 14 per cent was free blacks and "coloured", and about 10 per cent was white.[7] With the development of the demand for mahogany the settlement expanded again and hundreds more slaves were imported prior to the abolition of the slave trade in 1807. Following the abolition of the trade, the number of slaves in the settlement decreased from about three thousand to under two thousand at the time of emancipation. During this quarter century the proportion of the slaves also declined dramatically from about three-quarters to less than half of the population, while the free black and coloured increased from about one-quarter to almost a half and whites remained about one-tenth of the population (Table 1).

The slaves in Belize were unable to reproduce themselves. There was probably a high rate of mortality resulting from such factors as disease, malnutrition, ill-treatment, and overwork, and the slaves sometimes killed themselves.[8] Moreover, the rate of reproduction was very low, partly because of a severe imbalance of the sexes (generally two or three men to every woman) and because of the practice of abortion, said to be "extremely common" and having "its avowed professors" among the slave women (Henderson 1809: 75). The slave population was also a relatively old population, the proportion of the slaves who were under ten years of age generally being about 17 per cent in the 1820s while the proportion of the slaves who were forty years old or more increased from about one-fifth in 1820 to about one-third in 1834. However, the fact that, at this latter date, men outnumbered women by only seven to six under the age of forty, compared to ten to three at age forty years or more, suggests at least a potential for greater demographic stability in the slave population shortly before emancipation.

So long as slaves could be imported to Belize their number increased, but with the abolition of the slave trade the number of slaves, and their proportion to the rest of the population, declined dramatically. This decline was due, in part, to high mortality rates but also to a variety of factors which kept birth rates low. In addition, one must consider the relatively high incidence of manumission and the large number of slaves who escaped from the settlement. However, even when it is taken into account that about six hundred slaves were manumitted and about two hundred escaped between 1807 and 1834, it is apparent that the slave population was not able to reproduce itself. Even if these eight hundred people had remained in slavery, there would have been fewer slaves in 1834 than there were in 1807 because of a natural decrease in population.

The fact that in 1834, 26 per cent of the slaves were men aged forty years or more reflects the great importation of young male slaves in the years immediately preceding the abolition of the slave trade. This emphasis on young men in turn reflected the nature of the labour demands in an economy that was devoted almost exclusively to the arduous tasks of mahogany extraction.

The Organization of Work

Timber Extraction

The organizational requirements of timber extraction in Belize differed from those of plantation production, with consequent differences in the experiences of the slaves. First, the extraction of timber entailed the continual shifting of the production units from one location to another as the timber resources became exhausted in a particular area and the settlers laid claims to new areas of exploitation. The nature of timber extraction led to the existence of a large number of small timber works, some occupied and some unoccupied, dotted along the rivers, creeks, and lagoons of Belize, while the vast intervening space remained untouched bush. The slaves worked, therefore, in small, more or less temporary and isolated camps in the middle of an uncultivated and essentially uninhabited area.

The second difference between the experience of slaves in Belize and those on plantations resulted from the actual process of cutting and extracting the timber. The extraction of logwood was a very small scale operation, so that it was possible initially for the white settlers to undertake it themselves "with a single negro, some without one."[9] With the shift towards mahogany extraction in the second half of the 18th century, however, there was an increase in the amounts of capital, land, and labour required because the mahogany tree was larger, grew further inland, and in a more scattered manner, than logwood. The chief occupation for most slaves in Belize after about 1770 was the extraction of mahogany.

The extraction of mahogany was a seasonal occupation, each season of cutting and trucking requiring the labourers to spend long periods of time, likened to "a long confinement on shipboard," (Henderson 1809: 75) in the isolation of the camps. The mahogany trees, once found, cut and trimmed, were trucked through temporary paths in the bush to the nearest riverside, at the place called the "Barquadier", from whence the gangs fanned out to cut the mahogany, bringing the trees to the river to be formed into rafts. From the various barquadiers the rafts would float down river, usually in the rainy season, to a boom, before the trip to the river's mouth where the logs were finally squared ready for shipment.

A number of distinct occupations were required by the process of mahogany extraction. First, there were the huntsmen whose job it was to search and survey the forest to discover and locate the mahogany trees. This task, generally carried out in the fall when the tinge of the leaves distinguished the mahogany trees, was solitary and highly skilled and, like that of the boilermen on the sugar plantation, was one upon which rested the success of the entire enterprise. It was quite possible, and not unknown, for a successful huntsman to trick his owner, and granted the irregular and unsystematic nature of land tenure, to bargain with other masters when he found a considerable stand of timber. The master depended not only on his huntsman's skills in finding the mahogany but also on his sense of duty in reporting his discovery. The nature of his work and the master's reliance upon him gave the huntsman considerable independence and made him the most valued slave of all. The occupation of huntsman must have had considerable prestige and status among the slaves and must have been much sought after, not least because of the greater freedom it entailed.

Second, there was the man who cut the trees, a dangerous and highly skilled job, swinging a heavy axe on a springy platform about twelve feet above the ground. The axe-men were not only skilled, but they also worked singly or in pairs, rather than in a gang. Their work was certainly very arduous, but, given the fact that it required great physical strength and a skill that would take a long time to acquire, the axe-men may have achieved some satisfaction, pride, and status in their work. Certainly they could be differentiated by skill from others in the gang whose task it was to trim the tree after it had been felled, to clear the rough track down which it was to be drawn to the riverside, and to roughly square the trunks at the river's mouth. Another important occupation was that of the cattlemen, whose job it was to feed and work the cattle used in trucking the huge trunks. Finally, there were the people, probably women or youths, who prepared the food and looked after the provisions of the labourers.

An early 19th century account stated: "The gangs of negroes employed in this work consist of from ten to fifty each; few exceed the latter number. The large bodies are commonly divided into several small ones, a plan which it is supposed greatly facilitates labour" (Henderson 1809: 47). A major difference is apparent here between the division of labour and work experience of slaves in Belize compared to those on sugar plantations: while most plantation slaves worked in large gangs, sometimes numbering a hundred or more, the slaves involved in mahogany extraction worked in small groups of ten or twelve, and in the extraction of logwood their groups could be even smaller.

The much smaller size of the gangs involved in timber extraction, and the isolation in which the gangs worked, may have inhibited the spread of solidarity among large numbers of slaves but it probably increased the solidarity within the gang, whose members would soon come to know and depend on each other closely. The smaller size of the gangs also reduced the masters' need for supervising the slaves and, though there was certainly differentiation among the slaves in terms of skill, there was little or no differentiation in terms of power. The foreman, whose job was chiefly that of integrating the productive activities of the gangs at the mahogany works, probably had some authority, but the whip-wielding drivers, ubiquitous on the plantations, were "not known to any Gang"[10] in Belize.

Apart from the occupations directly connected with the extraction of timber, slaves were engaged in two other activities: domestic work and the cultivation of provisions. Though the masters of Belize did not possess the armies of domestics that some Jamaican planters owned, they had slaves whose job it was to clean the house, sew, wash and iron clothes, cook and serve food, and to tend their children. Sometimes the women were required to perform sexual as well as domestic roles; some of the black or coloured concubines became mistresses of the houses, supervising the activities of domestics. These "housekeepers" had a rather insecure position in the home and an ambiguous social position in the community, so it is not surprising that there is evidence of their cruel treatment

Table 2: Occupations of the Slave Population of Belize, by Age and Sex, 1834

Occupations	Male, Age in Years								Female, Age in Years								Total
	0-9	10-19	20-29	30-39	40-49	50-59	60+	Total	0-9	10-19	20-29	30-39	40-49	50-59	60+	Total	Total
Woodcutter	1	88	158	144	244	121	39	795	...	...	...	...	...	...	...	...	795
Waiting boy or girl	56	42	2	...	...	...	...	100	40	14	1	...	...	...	...	55	155
Laborer	...	2	4	2	9	13	8	38	...	...	...	...	...	...	...	...	38
Carpenter or carpenter's boy	...	5	12	5	5	2	1	30	...	...	...	...	...	...	...	...	30
Plantation man or woman	1	2	...	...	4	11	19	37	...	...	3	2	1	1	4	11	48
Sailor or boatman	...	3	3	3	...	3	1	13	...	...	...	...	...	...	...	...	13
Cattleman	...	3	3	1	1	1	1	10	...	...	...	...	...	...	...	...	10
Footman	5	3	1	...	...	...	...	9	...	...	...	...	...	...	...	...	9
Washerwoman	...	...	...	...	...	...	...	...	...	9	52	37	47	14	1	161	161
Housemaid, servant, or domestic	...	2	...	...	...	2	...	4	6	48	47	10	6	4	4	125	129
Chambermaid	...	...	...	...	...	...	...	...	2	30	12	1	...	9	...	45	45
Cook	...	...	...	...	...	...	...	...	...	4	34	38	28	9	4	117	117
Seamstress	...	...	...	...	...	...	...	...	10	17	18	6	2	...	...	53	53
Drudge	...	...	...	...	...	...	...	...	...	2	3	3	8	9	5	30	30
Other	...	2	4	2	3	1	2	14	2	...	2	1	1	3	...	9	23
No occupation	140	1	...	...	...	...	3	144	122	1	...	...	...	...	...	123	267
Total	203	153	187	157	266	154	74	1,194	182	125	172	98	93	40	18	729	1,923

Source: Slave Register, 1834, BA.

of domestic slaves,[11] such treatment being the housekeepers' way of emphasizing social distance from the slaves despite their physical proximity.

The third occupation engaged in by slaves was the cultivation of provisions for consumption in the settlement. From the 18th century on, slaves were occupied in "making plantations", an expression used to this day in Belize to refer to the cultivation of small plots of ground-foods, vegetables, corn, and other subsistence crops. Unlike the organization of labour in the sugar plantations of the Caribbean, where there were various jobs of varying difficulty associated with sugar production, so that jobs could be allotted to women, children, and the infirm within the plantation, the tasks involved in logging were, without exception, arduous. In order not to lose the labour of those slaves who were unfit for the more demanding jobs of cutting and hauling trees, the masters sometimes put them to work growing provisions.[12] Of the 48 slaves who were listed as plantation labourers in the 1834 Slave Register none were men in the most physically mature age range of sixteen to thirty-nine years; most of them were fifty years old or more.

That the masters encouraged the slaves to grow provisions in order to cut the costs of maintaining their labour force is supported by an observation made in 1806 that "the slaves have pieces of ground allotted them for cultivation, which enables the most industrious, to make an agreement with their Masters in lieu of Provision."[13] These arrangements would be more necessary in times of war, when there would be a tendency for the price of imported food to rise and for the reliability of regular supplies to decrease. Though some slaves engaged in cultivation because they were required to by their masters, most of the plantation grounds were cultivated on the slaves' initiative. A settler described in 1788 how the slaves were "ever accustomed to make Plantation as they term it, by which means they support their wives and children, raise a little Stock and so furnish themselves with necessaries etc."[14] Though it can be assumed that most of the produce grown by slaves on their own account was for the consumption of their families, they also participated in a rudimentary marketing system whereby some of their produce was taken into the town of Belize for sale.

Though it is not possible to obtain a clear picture of the extent of the plantation grounds, Henderson wrote that "Every Settlement at Honduras has its plantain walk... the pine-apple and melon, being very commonly interspersed between the rows of plantains." He also mentioned that the banks of the Sibun River, which today is one of the chief areas of small farms producing for the Belize City market, were "thickly studded with plantations" (Henderson 1809: 42.). It must be emphasized, however, that these plantations were only for subsistence, no cultivation of export crops being undertaken in this period.

Table 2 shows the occupations and the marked sexual division of labour among the slaves in 1834. Only young children and, to a lesser extent, older men and women, shared similar employment; the children waited at table and the older people worked as plantation labourers employed in cultivating provisions. Among the men the chief employment was woodcutting, mainly in the extraction of mahogany, which accounted for over 80 per cent of all the males aged ten years or more, and over 87 per cent of all the men in the most physically mature age range of twenty to fifty-nine years. Even some of the other occupations for men, such as carpenter and cattleman, were part of, or closely associated with, the business of mahogany extraction. Eight men were stated to be the managers or captains of woodcutting gangs, seven of these being fifty years old or more. Other male occupations represented were labourers (38), sailor or boatman (13), footman and other domestic (13). There were also five blacksmiths or blacksmith's boys, two draymen, two penkeepers, one cooper, one bank keeper, one stove boy, and one butcher. The slave women, with the exception of eleven plantation women, were employed in domestic work, primarily as housemaids, chambermaids, or domestic servants (170), washerwomen (161) cooks (117), seamstresses (53) or drudges (30). There were also five nurses, three bakers, and one vendor among the women.

One feature of the employment patterns of the slaves, revealed in Table 2, is the transition from one occupation to another undertaken by the slaves as they grew older. Young boys and girls experienced their first work in the domestic realm where, waiting on the master's table, they would be taught to be subservient in their relations with the master. The majority of the boys would then become "attached to the Mahogany works" as assistants, a few of them becoming assistants to black-smiths or carpenters. The physically mature men were almost all in woodcutting, but as they became older or infirm they were more likely to be shifted to agricultural or some other less arduous labour, only about half of those men aged sixty years or more being woodcutters. Among the female slaves the transition was from one kind of domestic work to another: from waiting girl to housemaid, chambermaid, or seamstress, and then, as they attained their twenties, to the more skilled or heavy work of cook, washerwoman, or drudge.

The patterns of employment experienced by the slaves, men and women, must have appeared as a binding and unalterable necessity. Alternatives, particularly for the women, were few. Some of the men could hope to become captains of gangs or huntsmen in mahogany extraction or to acquire a skilled trade. For most of the slaves, however, their only experience remained woodcutting for the men and domestic work for the women.

Culture

Family Life

For most slaves in Belize work was arduous and frequently dangerous, the physical conditions of camp life were extraordinarily rough and uncomfortable, and the camps were isolated and inhibited the development of stable family life. Despite this, there is evidence that some of the slaves participated in fairly stable and extended familial relationships. There is also evidence that the masters used the attachment of slaves to their families as a means of social control, possibly threatening the women and children with punishment and certainly holding the families as a deterrent to the men's desertion (Burdon 1935: v. 1, 239). The domestic slaves in Belize, primarily women, were often subjected to ill-treatment and occasionally the most appalling tortures (Bolland 1977: 66, 82-83).

The 1834 Slave Register recorded many relatives, sometimes of several generations who, belonging to the same master, may have had the opportunity of living together. For example, Quashie Cunningham, a sixty-seven year old slave, was owned by Sarah Keefe along with seven of his children, ranging in age from thirty-seven to twenty-three years, and nine grandchildren, aged between eleven and three years. That some of the slaves lived in stable conjugal relationships is indicated by the family of Sam Burn and his wife Jane who were listed with five of their children and one grandchild. Jane also had an older daughter by a previous relationship who, with her three children, was owned by the same master. The largest family reported in the Register consisted of the twenty-eight slaves of the estate of Sarah Goff, all of whom were related. The eldest was a thirty-seven year old mahogany cutter, Sammy Goff, who had eleven cousins and sixteen second cousins. This appears to be a long-established family, dating back to the 18th century when a slave woman had a large number of children who were the parents of Sammy Goff and his cousins.

The existence of such large groups of related persons, maintaining contact over several generations, provided an opportunity for the transmission of African cultural traditions through the century of the settlement's existence prior to the abolition of slavery.

African Cultural Survivals

Since the slaves of the Caribbean, unlike their masters, could not communicate with their homelands, their only contact with Africa was through later arrivals. While it seems likely that many of the slaves imported to the settlement in the first years of the 19th century were born in Africa, and could therefore reinforce African cultural traditions, the flow of such slaves was reduced to a trickle after the abolition of the slave trade in 1807, and not all of those few who were subsequently imported would have been African-born. Between 1816 and 1825 forty slaves were imported, mostly from Jamaica, [15] and 459 Africans, "liberated" from Spanish and Portuguese slave ships, were landed at Belize in 1836,[16] but many of these died soon after arrival. The maintenance of African cultural traditions depended chiefly upon such factors as socialization in the slaves' families, the preponderance of African-born slaves in the slave population, and the persistence of tribal solidarity among both the slaves and the free blacks.

Religion is one area within which African customs survived, as, for example, in the practice of obeah. The whites were concerned with suppressing obeah which they believed, sometimes correctly, to be associated with revolt. The practitioners of obeah claimed exceptional knowledge of charms and fetishes, which were used for a number of purposes including medicine, and an ability to manipulate or control the world. The obeah-men acquired a reputation for involvement in revolts as they were frequently leaders within the slave community. A regulation banning the practice of obeah on pain of death was passed in Belize in 1791, indicating the settlers' fear of the influence of the obeah-men upon their slaves at the time of the St. Domingue revolt (Burdon 1935: v. 1, 195-6).

To many Africans death and burial constituted the most important phase of the human cycle and were consequently accompanied by significant ceremonies. Given also the common African belief that at death one's spirit rejoined one's ancestors, it is understandable that death, as a release from slavery and a return to Africa, was celebrated with feasting. As described in 1830: "Wakes...are recreations of vivacity amongst the people...where the house of mourning and the house of feasting are identified as one and the same" (*Honduras Almanack* 1830: 17-18). Concerning music and dance, there are a number of brief records, though because of the bias or ignorance of the reporters they are of little descriptive value. In 1790, for example, "a favourite custom among the Slaves to amuse themselves, by dancing about in the streets,"[17] was remarked upon and, about the same time, "negroes diverting themselves playing the gombay"[18] were reported. The use of gombay or goombay drums was essential in African music and dance but, because their use disturbed the white settlers, they were frequently suppressed.[19] The timber camps were isolated, the slave gangs were small, and much of the trucking of logs was done at night, so the slaves must have had few opportunities for communal recreation during most of the year. There is a reference to a slave owner who inspired "the Negroes when at work to make him the burden of their songs,"[20] probably satirical in nature, but the slaves' greatest opportunity for communal recreation occurred at Christmas, between the long seasons of arduous labour in the isolated camps. The militia was held in readiness during the holidays, partly because of the whites' fear of concerted desertion or revolt, but also because "the different African tribes" occasionally engaged in "faction-fights" (Gibbs 1883: 52). The regrouping of Africans on a tribal basis, itself a phenomenon of cultural survival, was also a means for the persistence of other aspects of African culture.

The survival of elements of the African cultural heritage occurred despite specific acts of repression, directed against African religion, music, and dance, and also despite the whole structure of slavery. The economic and political organization of the settlement was created by the masters and forced upon the slaves. Though some of the free blacks attempted to recreate some tribal political organization, this had to operate within the limits imposed by the British administration and the settlement's political economy.

Missionary Influence

The white settlers paid little attention to religious affairs, either their own or their slaves', during the 18th century. Though the Anglican chaplain baptised about three thousand persons, half of them slaves, between 1812 and 1829,[21] the Anglicans were not very concerned with the education of the slaves. Superintendent Arthur complained in 1822 that "The Religious Instruction of the Slaves as well as of adults of the lower class, generally has been almost systematically opposed."[22] Burials of slaves were more rarely solemnized by the chaplains and only three marriages between slaves were recorded between 1812 and 1823.[23] The chaplain's fee was certainly an obstacle and, under pressure from the Colonial Office, the Public Meeting finally passed a law abolishing all fees for the marriage or baptism of slaves in 1829.

The first Baptist missionary arrived in 1822, followed three years later by the first Wesleyan. The latter had been instructed to take the gospel to the slaves in the mahogany camps, but, deciding that was not feasible, he centred his congregation, like the Baptists and Anglicans, in the town of Belize. The missionaries were active in the area of education; the only activity denied them was that of conducting marriage ceremonies, as only Anglican marriages were considered legal. The effect of their activity is hard to evaluate. The number of baptisms among the free coloured, free blacks, and slaves, is impressive but many of them may have been simply nominal.

The fact that the missionaries did not spend time in the camps may mean that they did not become involved in social issues. Certainly these missionaries, unlike their counterparts in Barbados and Jamaica, did not experience the settlers' hostility and persecution to any extent. While missionaries on these islands were blamed for inflaming the slaves in the 1820s such charges were unknown in Belize where the missionaries were generally permitted to preach without hindrance, possibly because they had less influence among the slaves or because their preaching was conservative. Though the influence of the established church and the dissenters seems to have been less in Belize than elsewhere, their intention of replacing African religion with Christianity was largely realized over the years.

Slavery and the Law

Slave Laws

The earliest statement concerning the slaves' status in law is an assertion, made in 1803, that the "Consolidated Slave Law of Jamaica is adopted in this Settlement, so far as the local situation thereof will admit."[24] Given the fact that the consolidated slave laws of Jamaica, passed in 1800, were "largely a codification of what was already prevalent in custom," (Patterson 1967: 77) it is hard to evaluate to what extent these laws, the product of a plantocracy, could be adopted in the different situation of Belize. The difference in the organization of slavery in Belize did not give rise to a corresponding legal code (possibly because of the anomalous constitutional status and the absence of an unequivocal executive authority in the settlement) but it did modify the application of the Jamaica slave laws.

Though a Slave Court had been established in about 1787, it was only "for the trial of Slaves for offences not amounting to felony,"[25] the laws failing to make provision for dealing with other offences by slaves until the establishment of the Supreme Court in 1819. In 1821, in view of the fact that "doubts have arisen in the minds of several of our Subjects settled in Honduras, whether an Act of the Legislature of our island of Jamaica, commonly called 'the Consolidated Slave Law', is considered in force in our Settlement of Honduras" and that "there are no other laws whatever for the protection of the Slave Population known or promulgated in our said Settlement," Superintendent Arthur proclaimed the Jamaica consolidated laws to be in force in Belize (*Defense of the Settlers...*, 1824: 67). It appears that there was generally a very incomplete codification of slave laws, or of application of the Jamaica laws, in Belize and that individual cases were frequently treated on an *ad hoc* basis, at least until the 1820s.

Manumission

One noteworthy feature of the law in Belize was that someone in actual possession of liberty did not require written evidence of manumission but would be assumed to be free unless it could be proved otherwise. It was stated that in cases of disputed freedom the "*onus probandi* would lay with the person objecting," that the courts were guided by "the principle of general law and equity," and that if a future case were to be brought against the same "person of colour," by a second objecting person, then "the court would receive the evidence of the former action."[26] Moreover, it was stated that once a free person received value for the purchase of a slave's freedom, whether or not he signed a manumission, he would lose his right to the slave, "although it might require the decision of the court."[27]

Among the means by which slaves could be manumitted were self-purchase, purchase by others, bequest by will and testament of the owner, or gift of the owner. Of the 169 slaves who obtained their freedom between 1 January 1826 and 31 December 1830, 11 per cent purchased their own freedom, 18 per cent had their manumission purchased by others, 29 per cent obtained manumission by bequest, and 38 per cent were freed by gift.[28]

Manumissions were granted in Belize for almost as long as slavery had existed there, (Burdon 1935: v. 1, 69, 118, 167, 197-9) but no records are available on manumissions until the 19th century. According to the early censuses 178 slaves were manumitted between 1807 and 1816 and 50 between 1817 and 1820.[29] Another report stated even higher figures: 201 manumissions between 1808 and 1816, and 62 between 1817 and 1820.[30] In the 1820s the rate of manumission increased, 141 slaves being freed between 1821 and 1825,[31] and 169 between 1826 and 1830.[32] In sum, about six hundred slaves, or about one-fifth of the total slave population, were manumitted between the abolition of the slave trade and the abolition of slavery.

About 57 per cent of the slaves manumitted between 1808 and 1830 were female. Between 1826 and 1830 less than a quarter of the slaves manumitted were adult males (41 adult males, 68 adult females, and 60 children being freed in those five years[33]), despite the fact that adult males constituted the majority of the slaves. Adult white males outnumbered adult white females by at least two to one, so many of them took slave women as their concubines, subsequently freeing them and their offspring. The fact that the most common forms of manumission were by means of gift or bequest of the owner also suggests that many of these manumissions secured the freedom of mistresses and their children. A surprising number of slaves in Belize were able to purchase their own freedom, however, and often at considerable expense: one slave, for example, paid £450 to obtain his freedom in 1829.[34]

The result of this high incidence of manumission and the greater likelihood for women and children to be manumitted was the rapid increase of the freedman population (especially of women and "coloured" children) which equalled the number of slaves at the time of emancipation.

Punishment

Little is said in the Commissioners' report of 1829 concerning the types of punishments inflicted upon slaves, though it was stated that the owner may legally, and simply on his authority, inflict corporal punishment to the extent of thirty-nine lashes on his slave for misconduct or ill behaviour, and that owners had the power to imprison their slaves at their own expense, though the duration of such imprisonment would be at the discretion of the court. On the question concerning possible differentials in punishment for the same offence committed by a free person or a slave, it was reported that "free black persons and slaves are liable to the same punishment",[35] thereby indicating that different punishments would be considered suitable for free persons of mixed race or whites. There are many indications of inequalities in punishments administered by the law, examples of severe, even savage, treatment of blacks and of lenient treatment of whites. On the one hand, many of the punishments imposed upon slaves were explicitly intended to be exemplary, rebellious slaves being put to death "by burning, gibbeting and other methods of torture"[36] as a deterrent to other slaves. On the other hand, the excesses of the masters were rarely considered suitable subjects for exemplary punishment. While a slave who merely injured his owner could be hanged, the owner receiving compensation for his loss of property, a master who subjected his slave to cruel punishments far beyond the legal limits was treated leniently by his peers, though many such cases would never reach a court.[37] The settlements chaplain between 1812 and 1824 stated that "the necessary means of protecting slaves from oppression and cruelty are withheld, and every attempt to shield them from barbarous usage is considered an invasion of the rights of the owner; and, to such an extent is this carried, that even in cases of the most flagrant abuse and injustice, it is almost impossible to convict a master of cruelty, or to recover for the injured slave either right or remuneration" (Armstrong 1824: 59).

Rights

The Commissioners' report is somewhat more informative on the subject of slaves' rights than it is on punishments given by the courts. On the important question of property, it was stated that, by custom, the slaves of Belize could possess property for their private use and that, in cases where property acquired by or bestowed upon a slave was withheld by the owner, the slaves could seek redress to recover such property, except in matters of debt. In cases of injury to a slave an action of damages could be undertaken by an owner to compensate him for injury done to his slave, but, if the owner himself caused such injury, the slave had recourse only to criminal action. Since slaves could only sue through their owners, the problem for the slave in cases where their owners abused their person or their property was to find someone willing to advocate their case for them.

With regard to the sale of slaves, though it was stated to be "the custom of the country" to sell slaves in families, "there is no law in existence to prevent the sale of slaves individually."[38] Consequently, if a slave should be separated from his or her immediate family through sale, such sale would be contrary to custom, but the slave could have no legal recourse to prevent the separation. Finally, with regard to the controversial question of the competence of the slaves as witnesses and the admissibility of slaves' evidence in the courts, it was stated that, while their testimony could be received in cases directed against "persons of their own class," they were "not considered competent witnesses against white persons."[39] Such a disqualification would make it still more difficult, if not impossible, for slaves to achieve redress against their masters in cases of injury or the withholding of their property.

In summary, though the slaves possessed certain limited rights and experienced relatively high rates of manumission, their legal status remained one in which they were the property of their masters. Consequently, the slaves were afforded little in the way of protection by the law, their rights were vaguely defined, and most limitations upon the masters' treatment of the slaves were customary rather than legal in nature.

Slaves as Property

Ownership and Value

Slave ownership in Belize was highly concentrated. A small group of settlers owned many mahogany works and a high proportion of the slaves. The 1816 census showed that only 11 of the free heads of families owned 1,013 slaves, while 108 owned 185 slaves and 125 owned no slaves. At the two extremes of the distribution of slave ownership, 3 per cent of the free heads of families owned 37 per cent of the slaves, while 62 per cent of the free heads of families owned less than 7 per cent of the slaves. The 1820 census of the slave population recorded that 211 owners possessed 2,653 slaves, an average of twelve slaves each. The five biggest owners, however, possessed 669 slaves, or over a quarter of the total, while 31 per cent of the owners possessed a mere 4 per cent of the slaves. That the concentration of slave ownership increased is indicated by the 1835 census which showed 3 percent of the free heads of families owning 40 per cent of the "apprentices" while 81 per cent owned only 7 per cent of the "apprentices."[40]

In other words, while most of the free men owned a few or no slaves, most of the slaves were owned by masters who had large estates with many slaves. In fact, since land tenure was insecure because of the Spanish claims to sovereignty, the masters' estates consisted of little more than their slaves. In comparison with planters who invested in land and expensive physical plant, most of the Belizean masters' capital was invested in the persons of their slaves.

Partly because of the premium on strong and healthy workers and partly because of remoteness from slave markets, slaves had always been valued highly in Belize. In 1809 it was stated that a "seasoned" male slave was worth between £200 and £300 (Henderson 1809: 60) and some of the slaves who purchased their own freedom paid £200 or more, one paying as much as £450 in 1829.[41] While the average price for a slave, including children and the aged and infirm, was about £120 in the 1820s, the prices ranged from 10s for an old man to £610 for "Blacksmith Joe", clearly a skilled man. An estate of thirty-one slaves, four of whom were described as "very old" realized £9,710 in 1820, an average of over £300 per slave.[42] When the value of the slaves in the settlement was assessed in 1835 it was estimated to be £230,840, or about £120 per slave, and the portion of the £20 million of compensation money which was set aside for the proprietors in Belize was £101,958 .19. 7 1/2.[43] The rate of compensation per slave in Belize was £53 . 6. 9 1/2, higher than for any British colony.[44]

Treatment

Given the high monetary value placed on the slaves. it may be expected that, in general, the masters would have taken more care of their "property", especially in view of the fact that, with no legal freehold title to their land, their investment in slaves constituted most of their capital. Henderson claimed that "in no part of the world, where slavery prevails, can the condition of beings so circumstanced be found of milder or more indulgent form. The labour they undergo bears no proportion to that which they sustain throughout the islands: nor is it more to be compared with what they experience in the States of America" (Henderson 1809: 59-60).[45] Henderson estimated the annual cost of providing each slave with food (including 5 lbs of salt pork and 7 lbs of flour per week), clothing, and other items, to be about £36 Jamaica currency, or over £25 Sterling. While his account of the expenses incurred in maintaining slaves indicates an unusual generosity on the part of the masters, it appears to be a statement of the "ideal" provisions and it is doubtful that such an ideal was often attained. In periods of economic hardship, due to war or depression in trade, the masters would certainly require their slaves to tighten their belts, and even in peaceful and prosperous times there would be many ways by which the cost, and also the material conditions, of slavery could be lowered.

In plantation societies the masters were often reluctant to devote any potential sugar land to the cultivation of subsistence crops and while that was not the case in Belize the masters still had to consider whether the diversion of slave labour to crop production was economically worthwhile. Whereas the masters were eager to find ways to reduce the cost of maintaining their slaves and frequently allowed, or even encouraged, the slaves to produce their own provisions, the same pattern of dependency upon imported food supplies was established in the settlement as in the insular colonies.

While there is an impressive unanimity in the 19th century accounts with regard to the material provisions of the slaves, the accounts of slave treatment are somewhat more contradictory. Claims were made regarding "the good treatment, the extraordinary good provision, and the attachment the slaves show to their owners",[46] thereby asserting that good relations existed between masters and their slaves. This view was contradicted by Superintendent Arthur who made "some observations upon the extreme inhumanity of many of the lower class of settlers residing in the Town of Belize towards their slaves," and drew attention to "the increasing severity and cruelty which is now practised with impunity"[47] because the offenders could not be punished under the current legal system. Having ascertained that, "in many cases, the Slaves were severely oppressed", Arthur proclaimed the Consolidated Slave Law of Jamaica to be in force in Belize. "Encouraged by the Proclamation...the numbers [of slaves] who came forward in a few days filled me with no less astonishment, than the fraud and injustice which had so long been secretly practised towards them."[48] Several specific cases of "extreme inhumanity" were recorded[49] and the settlements chaplain stated that "there are instances, many instances, of horrible barbarity practised there" (Armstrong 1824: 61).

It would appear that, in general, the settlers in Belize treated their slaves with greater consideration for their physical welfare than did their planter counterparts in the Caribbean. Since the slaves had virtually no legal protection, and were thus subject to the whims and customs of their masters, it remains to be explained why these masters, who were as capable of cruelty as any others, were generally more restrained in their treatment of their slaves.

First, the settlers of Belize, who had no legal title to land, had most of their capital invested in their slaves[50] who, being largely imported through the Jamaican slave markets, were expensive, as was their upkeep on largely imported provisions. With the difficulty and expense of obtaining new slaves, especially after the abolition of the slave trade, the settlers had a financial interest in keeping their slaves well. In addition, of course, the very nature of the arduous work and rough conditions experienced by the slaves in the timber camps meant that only strong and healthy slaves could be of any value to the settlers.

Second, the fact that most of the Belize settlers seem to have considered Belize their home may have had some effect upon their attitude to their slaves. In the Caribbean islands many of the planters were intent on making a quick fortune in sugar by the gross exploitation, and consequent exhaustion, of both land and labour. Many planters stayed on their estates only long enough to be able to employ a managing attorney, whereupon they would return to England to live in luxury as absentee landlords. The attorneys and overseers who were in charge of the slaves generally lacked any concern for their welfare and were intent only to show immediate profits. The Belize settlers, on the other hand, had less contact with Britain and consequently they were more likely to see their future as dependent upon the upkeep of their property in the settlement, that consisted primarily of slaves.

Third, and most important, was the effect of the slaves' own actions, past and anticipated, upon their masters. Contrary to the frequently stated claims concerning the slaves' "affection for their owners,"[51] the slaves' actions, including such drastic measures as abortion, suicide, murder, desertion, and revolt, demonstrate that they did not share their masters' view of the institution of slavery.

Slave Responses

Revolts

The practices of suicide and abortion were often a reaction of the slaves against their situation, and cases of the destruction of masters' property and the taking of masters' lives are quite frequently recorded. The most important evidence from the historical records concerning the slaves' reactions to their situation, however, lies in the existence of four slave revolts and of countless and continual desertions of slaves from Belize.

One of the earliest references to slaves in Belize, dating from 1745, is an appeal for military assistance in the face of Spanish threats and it expressed a concern about the loyalty of the slaves, who already outnumbered the whites.[52] The white settlers, always a tiny minority, were constantly haunted by the spectre of slave revolts. The lack of any permanent police in the settlement meant that the settlers had no power, apart from an occasional warship from Jamaica, to suppress disorder. During the economic crisis of the 1760s and 1770s, when the logwood trade was severely depressed but not yet superseded by mahogany, the slaves, who were undoubtedly forced to bear a good deal of the hardship engendered by the crisis, rebelled at least three times. In the absence of any police power, even the small scale revolts of 1765 and 1768 exposed the helplessness of the settlers and threatened the existence of the settlement.[53] The biggest slave revolt, lasting five months, occurred in 1773.

Though there are no reported revolts in the late eighteenth or early nineteenth centuries the settlers were continually apprehensive about the possibility of such revolts developing and they tried to exclude what they defined as dangerous slaves from the settlement. In 1791, for example, the settlers were said to be "panic struck" when a French ship carrying over two hundred of the St. Domingue rebels arrived. It was decided that "they should not be permitted to land so infectious a cargo."[54] In 1796 the Magistrates prohibited the landing of five Jamaican slaves who were suspected of having been maroons[55] and in 1800 a Public Meeting discussed the settlers' "apprehension of internal convulsion and the horrors of St. Domingo" (Burdon 1935: v. 1, 282).

Though there is no evidence that the slaves ever joined the Maya in revolt, the settlers were apprehensive of such a possibility. In 1817, "the exposed and unprotected state of the settlers, surrounded by vast hordes of Indians who are all in the constant habit of breaking in upon their works" was feared for placing the settlers "entirely at the mercy of the Slave Population."[56] The Magistrates feared that "a very small Gang of desperate runaway slaves, who would join and lead these Indians, must instantly overpower us and the destruction of every British subject would be inevitable."[57]

The last slave revolt in Belize occurred in 1820 on the Belize and Sibun rivers. Superintendent Arthur reported that the settlers were "earnestly praying for immediate protection" because "a considerable number of slaves had formed themselves into a Body in the Belize River, and being well armed, and having already committed various depredations the most serious consequences were to be apprehended."[58] Arthur immediately declared martial law to be in force and sent troops up the rivers. His inquiries discovered that "the Negroes who had first deserted and had excited others to join them, had been treated with very unnecessary harshness by their Owner, and had certainly good grounds for complaint."[59] On 3 May, about ten days after the revolt began, Arthur offered rewards for the apprehension of two black slaves, Will and Sharper, "reported to be the Captains and Leaders of these Rebels," and offered "a Free Pardon to any of the other Runaways, who will at this time voluntarily come in and deliver themselves."[60] This inducement to divide the rebels may have succeeded since, on 22 May, about a month after the revolt began, martial law was ended as "there no longer exists any Combination amongst the slaves".[61]

Escapes

The other major evidence of slave discontent is the continual complaints from the settlers that the neighbouring Spaniards gave asylum to runaway slaves. The organization of timber extraction made escape relatively easy. In the eighteenth century, most of the slaves who escaped went north into Yucatán. This was partly because the south and west of the area that is now Belize were unexplored, but also because the Spaniards had outposts just across the Rio Hondo and the Commandant at Bacalar offered freedom and protection to the runaways.

When the settlement expanded to the west and south early in the nineteenth century, the slaves went still further, through the bush into the Petén or by boat down the coast to Omoa and Truxillo. Shortly after the neighbouring Spanish territories became independent in 1821, they abolished slavery and the complaints that slaves were escaping to these republics increased. In 1823, for example, it was stated that in a little over two months thirty-nine slaves had "absconded" and fled to the Petén which "is believed to be well known to many of the Negroes, it has also been long known that Negroes who have absconded some years ago during the War are residing there."[62] A complaint from Superintendent Codd to the Petén authorities drew the response that there was "a Town of black People" which was joined by those who "emigrated from your Establishment" and who "already enjoy the privileges of Citizens."[63] In 1825 the settlers were desperate, "having just learnt that 19 slaves have left their employments up the river in a body, and taken the road to the Town of Petén at the head of the River, and 12 to Omoa...instant ruin stares us in the face."[64] A Colonial Office official commented in 1830 that "Honduras is now in the center of countries which have declared Slavery illegal, and if we persist in maintaining it we must look for a rapid depopulation of the settlement by the slaves passing the border line, and returning no more."[65]

Maroons

The slaves, in their periodic revolts and continual escapes, demonstrated dissatisfaction with their situation and frequently threatened the very existence of the settlement. The geographical conditions in Belize certainly favoured the slaves and some of those who escaped created independent Maroon communities on the fringes of the settlement area. In 1816, reference was made to such a community "near Sheboon River, very difficult to discover, and guarded by poisonous Stakes" (Burdon 1935: v. 1, 184). The following year, Superintendent Arthur reported that "a considerable body of runaway Slaves are formed in the interior"[66] and, in 1820, he referred to "two Slave Towns, which it appears have long been formed in the Blue Mountains to the Northward of Sibun."[67] Apart from the settlements of escaped slaves in the neighbouring countries, then, there were maroon communities in the Belize area, particularly near the Sibun River, a tributary of which is still called Runaway Creek.

While these maroon communities sometimes communicated with the slaves and, as in 1820, provided a refuge for revolted slaves on the run, they were never the basis for any organized or protracted guerrilla action against the white settlers. As a response to slavery, revolt was not such a pressing alternative in Belize when freedom could be obtained by slipping away into the bush of the interior or over the borders of the settlement. Though the masters deplored the frequent desertion of their slaves, the facility with which the slaves could withdraw may well have functioned as a safety valve (from the masters' viewpoint) in letting out the most rebelliously inclined of the slaves, and so reducing the likelihood of insurrections. Indeed, the revolt of 1768 can perhaps be more accurately described as an armed thrust by the slaves to force their way out of Belize, and even the 1773 revolt ended with the survivors forcing their way across the Rio Hondo. Given the favourable geographical conditions and the great numerical superiority of the slaves, the fact that they never actually took over the settlement can best be explained by the availability of freedom beyond the bounds of British jurisdiction.

Another factor which reduced the likelihood of successful revolt is that the units in which the slaves worked were small, the slaves working in small groups which were isolated from one another. Such a pattern of settlement, encouraging solidarity within each group but inhibiting communication between groups, would favour small scale revolts and escapes but would hinder the organization and coordination of a large scale insurrection, such as occurred on the plantations elsewhere in the Caribbean.

Still another factor which detracted from the development of a massive slave revolt was the very limited identification the slaves had with the Belize area as a possible permanent home. Only a minority of the slaves were Creole, most being Africans of diverse national origin who had been transported to the Caribbean, where some would have stayed for a while before being resold, taken to the Mosquito Shore or Belize, and then continually shifted from one temporary camp to another. The limited time which most slaves had spent in Belize and the migratory nature of their settlement patterns must have inhibited any identification with the area which, had it been present, may have encouraged the slaves to take over the settlement. The slaves, however, were concerned not with taking over a territory but with avoiding slavery and, where the latter could be more easily accomplished by withdrawal than by confrontation, slave revolts were less likely to occur.

Effect upon the Masters

The slaves' propensity to revolt and the often demonstrated facility with which they escaped were among the chief factors which inhibited the masters from ill-treating their slaves. That the settlers themselves recognized this is frequently indicated: for example, George Hyde, a leading free coloured merchant and slave owner, stated in 1825 that "As for punishments or ill-usage, you are aware (if ever so deserved) we dare not inflict it, so easy is their retreat to the Spaniards" (Crewe 1850: 321).

The situation in the timber camps, in which one or two white men lived in remote isolation with between ten and fifty slaves, all of whom possessed machetes, axes, and sometimes muskets which were used for hunting, must have made the masters cautious about rousing their slaves' anger. The fact that slaves possessed arms was the object of frequent comment. In 1788, for example, it was stated that "it has always been a Custom with us to allow our Negroes Firearms",[68] and twenty years later it was noted that "the whole of the slaves of Honduras are permitted to use arms, and possibly a more expert body of marksmen could no where be found" (Henderson 1809: 73). Superintendent Arthur, soon after his arrival in 1814, reported with amazement how some slaves "leaving their Works in the interior of the Country came down in a body to the Town of Belize to dictate who should be their masters...the several Thousand Slaves in this Settlement...by some unfortunate mismanagement, have been allowed to be provided with Arms, and therefore it requires additional attention to keep them quiet and peaceable, and certainly to give them no just grounds for discontent".[69]

The extent to which the treatment and conditions of slaves were different in Belize than elsewhere was partly the product of the different economic function of slavery and its consequent mode of organization but it was also a product of the slaves' own responses to their situation. The slaves, who knew the territory better than their masters, possessed a capacity for affecting their masters' behaviour and thus were able to modify the institution of slavery itself.

Conclusions

The fact that slavery in Belize was a means of controlling labour for purposes of timber extraction resulted in some important differences from the nature of slavery in a plantation system. These differences occurred especially in the organization of work, the various occupations, the size of the production unit, the division of labour, and the working conditions. However, these important differences in the social organization of slavery in Belize did not themselves create an altogether different system of slavery. Belize, though not officially a colony, was nevertheless part of Britain's Caribbean empire and some of the laws and customs pertaining to and affecting slavery in Belize stemmed from the tradition of the slave system in the British West Indies; for example, the attempt to apply the Jamaica slave laws and the activity of Protestant missionaries. The settlement at Belize was so small, and so dependent upon Jamaica and the rest of the British colonial system, that its version of slavery was inevitably affected by the cultural traditions and legal structures which had been well established in the islands. While this study of slavery in Belize supports the view that economic factors are paramount, it also indicates that the consideration of cultural and legal traditions should not be neglected.

Finally, and possibly most important, the system of slavery was not the perfectly organized and calculable system of labour control desired by the masters but was, on the contrary, frequently an unstable institution. First, there was the important factor of demographic instability: that the population did not reproduce itself meant that the system could be sustained only by the continual importation of new slaves. Second, the slaves repeatedly reacted against the iniquitous institution, sometimes threatening its existence, but always, through their actions, modifying the way they were treated by the masters. Through their assertive responses, the slaves, despite the oppressive system of slavery, were able to maintain a degree of control over their family and community life and made important contributions to the development of Belizean culture.

The masters, in Belize as elsewhere, attempted to make the system of slavery a total institution by demoralizing and dehumanizing its victims and considering them merely as property. The creativity of the slaves, in Belize as elsewhere, ensured that it would not be so, however. Their refusal to be defined as chattels and their continual struggle through generations to assert their essential dignity as people constitutes one of the great victories of humanity.

Notes

01. An earlier version of this paper was presented at a seminar of the Division of Social Sciences at Colgate University in December 1976. The author benefitted from the comments of those present, especially two guests, Orlando Patterson and Michael Craton. I wish to thank them for their contribution and also to thank Arnold Sio for the excitement of our continual discussions on slavery, from which I learn so much, and Assad Shoman for his perceptive criticisms of the earlier version of this paper. Though they have improved this paper a great deal, I must be held responsible for any errors which may remain.

Much of the material presented in this paper has appeared in a different form in Bolland 1977, and grateful acknowledgement is given to The Johns Hopkins University Press for their permission to use this material herein: Copyright © 1977 by The Johns Hopkins University Press.

2. The view that "slavery in British Honduras was, as has always been claimed, much less oppressive than elsewhere" (Waddell 1961, 14) is insupportable. None but the victims of oppression can evaluate the various kinds and degrees of oppressiveness. Studies of slave systems can compare the organization, treatment, conditions, and responses of slaves but should not make judgements about relative oppression.

03. James Stephen to Lord Glenelg, 4 October 1838, CO 123/54.

04. Superintendent Codd to R. Wilmot, 23 February 1823, CO 123/34.

05. "General Return of the Inhabitants..." 22 October 1790, CO 123/9.

06. Unsigned letter to Gov. Dalling, 3 September 1779, CO 137/75.

07. "General Return of the Inhabitants..." 22 October 1790, CO 123/9.

08. Br. Gen. Montresor to Gov. Coote, 22 October 1806, CO 123/17.

09. Superintendent Despard to Lord Sydney, 17 August 1787, CO 123/5.

10. Montresor to Coote, 22 October 1806, CO 123/17; see also Maj. Gen. Pye to Earl Bathurst, 26 July 1822, BA, R.2: "The Name of Driver is here unknown...".

11. See, for example, Supt. Arthur to Bathurst, 7 October 1820, CO 123/29.

12. See "Remarks upon the Situation Trade etc..." by ex-Supt. Barrow, 1 May 1809, CO 123/18.

13. Montresor to Coote, 22 October 1806, CO 123/17.

14. Richard Hoare to Robert White, 25 August 1788, CO 123/7.

15. P. C. Codd, "Return of Slaves Imported and Exported", 15 December 1823, CO 123/34, and 31 December 1825, CO 123/37.

16. Act. Supt. Anderson to Glenelg, 10 August and 20 December 1836, CO 123/48.

17. Thomas Graham, "Journal of my Visitation..." 27 October 1790, CO 123/9.

18. William Usher's affidavit, in Despard, "A Narrative of the Publick Transactions..." 8 March 1791, CO 123/10.

19. Magistrates to Dyer, 25 January 1809, CO 123/18.

20. Pye to Bathurst, 25 July 1822, CO 123/31.

21. For 1812-23, return of baptisms by Rev. Armstrong, 16 December 1823, CO 123/34; for 1825-29, return from the church register by Rev. Newport, 19 October 1829, BA, R.2.

22. Arthur to Pye, 3 April 1822, BA, R.2 and CO 123/31.

23. Return of burials and marriages by Armstrong, 16 December 1823, CO 123/34 and return from the church register by Newport, 19 October 1829, BA, R.2.

24. "The Laws Regulations and Customs of Honduras...as abstracted from the whole...,' 18 March 1803, CO 123/15.

25. Report of the "Commissioners of Inquiry into the Administration of Criminal and Civil Justice...on the Settlement of Honduras", 3, 24 February 1829, CO 318/77.

26. Ibid., 93.

27. Ibid., 94.

28. Superintendent Cockburn to Lord Goderich, 25 April 1831, CO 123/42.

29. Censuses of 1816 and 1820, GRB.

30. Return of manumissions by George Westby, 15 December 1823, CO 123/34.

31. Return of manumissions by Westby, 31 December 1825, CO 123/37.

32. Cockburn to Goderich, 25 April 1831, CO 123/42.

33. Ibid.

34. Ibid.

35. Commissioners' report, op. cit., 95.

36. Despard, "A Narrative of the Publick Transactions..." 8 March 1791, CO 123/10.

37. Contrast, for example, the cases recorded in Burdon 1935, v. 1, 210 and Arthur to Bathurst, 21 October 1816, CO 123/25.

38. Commissioners' Report, op. cit., 94.

39. Ibid., 94.

40. Censuses of 1816, 1820, and 1835, GRB.

41. Cockburn to Goderich, 25 April 1831, CO 123/42.

42. "Sales negroes Est. of P. C. Wall;" 28 August 1829, CO 123/40.

43. 7 July 1835, CO 318/117.

44. In Bermuda the compensation per slave was £20.13.8 1/4. The only comparable compensation rates were in the newer colonies with developing plantations, Trinidad and British Guiana, where they were £50.1.1 1/4 and £51.17.1 1/2 respectively.

45. See also Arthur to Bathurst, 7 November 1816, CO 123/25.

46. Montresor to Coote, 22 October 1806, CO 123/17.

47. Arthur to Bathurst, 7 October 1820, CO 123/29.

48. Arthur to Bathurst, 10 January 1822, in *Defense of the Settlers*... 1824, 68.

49. See, for example, the case of Michael Carty, Arthur to Bathurst, 21 October 1816, CO 123/25.

50. "The chief property of the settlers of Honduras... must be supposed to consist in slaves"; Henderson 1809: 59.

51. Barrow, "Remarks..." 1 May 1809, CO 123/18.

52. Inhabitants to Maj. Caulfield, 8 June 1745, CO 137/48.

53. Joseph Maud to Gov. Lyttleton, 7 October 1765, CO 137/62 and Allan Auld to Lord Hillsborough, July 1768, CO 137/63.

54. James Bartler to Dyer, Allan & Co., 26 November 1791, CO 123/13.

55. Magistrates meeting, 13 September 1796, MMA 2, GRB.

56. Minutes from the public record, 25 February 1817, CO 123/26.

57. Magistrates to Bathurst, 26 February 1817, CO 123/26.

58. Arthur to Bathurst, 16 May 1820, CO 123/33.

59. Ibid.

60. Proclamation, 3 May 1820, CO 123/33.

61. Proclamation, 22 May 1820, CO 123/33.

62. Codd to Bathurst, 8 March 1823, CO 123/34.

63. Leon Baldison to Codd, 15 November 1823, CO 123/34.

64. Magistrates to Codd, 28 January 1823, CO 123/36. See also Codd's report in which he stated that the slaves, having "almost a total absence of all respect" for their masters, were discussing whether to continue escaping or to take over the settlement. Codd expressed anxiety about the reliability of the black soldiers and militia in the event of a slave revolt and requested white troops; Codd to Bathurst, 18 February 1825, CO 123/36.

65. Stephen to Horace Twiss, 13 October 1830, CO 123/41.

66. Arthur to Fraser, 12 June 1817, CO 123/26.

67. Arthur to Bathurst,16 May 1820, CO 123/29; since there are no mountains north of the Sibun River the communities must have been to the south where there are inaccessible caves and gorges.

68. Hoare to White, 25 August 1788, CO 123/7.

69. Arthur to Bathurst, 2 December 1814, CO 123/23.

3. African Continuities and Creole Culture in Belize Town in the Nineteenth Century

I

> The streets, especially near the bridge, are pretty constantly thronged with a medley of passengers of many different races, among which may be recognized various tribes of Africans, the Carib, the Mosquitoman, and the Spanish Indian as well as the European and the Belize Creole, as they style themselves (Crowe 1850: 34).

The pattern of human settlement in colonial Belize[1]—shaped by the economy—was very different from that prevailing in the sugar colonies. The systems devised by the British colonizers to control land and labour, both before and after 1838, were comparable to those elsewhere in the West Indies (Bolland 1981; Green 1984; Bolland 1984), broadly characterized under the rubric "plantation society". However, the "reconstituted peasantry" (Mintz 1961) that was such a typical response to the plantation system did not emerge to any great extent in nineteenth century Belize. Indeed, so far as Afro-Belizean people were concerned, farming and village life were almost completely absent until late in the nineteenth century. Such Creole Belizeans, as they generally refer to themselves, resided almost entirely in Belize Town when they were not in seasonal logging camps.

In 1839, the year after Emancipation, Patrick Walker and John Herbert Caddy travelled up the Belize River on an expedition to the ancient Maya centre of Palenque. They described the evolution of a mahogany camp into a more permanent hamlet. "Should the locality turn out a good one likely to give several years cutting, a regular village springs up and the wives and families of the gang take up their abode during the season, which commences soon after Christmas or after the termination of the wet weather. And at last it becomes the home of many, who take advantage of the Plantations and clearances" (Pendergast 1967: 49).

Walker and Caddy identified such communities at Tiger Run and Duck Run, the latter just below present-day San Ignacio being then "the highest inhabited spot" on the Belize River (Pendergast 1967: 52). These communities were not exclusively Creole, however, as they were said to include Spanish or Mestizo refugees from Guatemala who worked as labourers in the mahogany camps. Some more settlements emerged in the latter half of the nineteenth century along the Belize River, some of them Creole, some Maya, and others, like San Ignacio, which became the chief village in the region, with a mixed racial-ethnic composition. However, seasonal movement between Belize Town and the temporary logging camps was still the norm for most Creoles in the century following Emancipation.

Though Belize Town was itself not much more than an overgrown village until well into this century, this unusual pattern of settlement seems to have had particular consequences for the persistence and change of aspects of the African cultural heritage. At any rate, it is in this largely "urban" social context that the Belizean Creole variant of Afro-Caribbean culture developed. It is my hope that this paper will contribute to the comparative study of the relations between cultural and social change in the development of Afro-American cultures.[2] Before examining African continuities and the development of Creole culture, I will outline the history of the pattern of settlement of Belize.

II

Although the origins of the British settlement in Belize remain obscure, it appears that British buccaneers used the tricky coastline as a base from which to attack Spanish ships from about the middle of the seventeenth century. In the 1650s, and 1660s, some of these buccaneers changed from plundering Spanish logwood ships to cutting the wood themselves in various parts of the Yucatán Peninsula. The dye obtained from logwood—used in the European woolen industry—was the chief *raison d'être* of the British settlement in Belize for at least a century (Joseph 1977). The shift from buccaneering to logwood cutting and more permanent settlement was encouraged when the great powers agreed to suppress piracy in the 1670 Treaty of Madrid. Conflict between Britain and Spain over the right to cut logwood and to settle in Belize continued through the eighteenth century, however, and the British on several occasions were forced to leave. Until the last of these evacuations, in 1779, the chief British settlement was on St. George's Cay, but from the time of the resettlement that took place after the peace of 1783 the principal establishment was located at the Belize River mouth. This settlement grew into Belize City. In the nineteenth century, Belize Town, which in 1881 consisted of 5,767 persons (about 21 per cent of the colony's population), remained a small town. It was, and still is, the centre of concentration of Belize's Creole population: over 60 per cent of the 45,584 inhabitants of Belize City today are Creole.[3]

Whatever the date at which Africans first appeared in Belize, they certainly outnumbered the white settlers by the middle of the eighteenth century. A description of the settlement in 1779, a few days before St. George's Cay was captured, stated there were about 500 British settlers and 3,000 slaves. After the resettlement, 2,214 people, three-quarters of them slaves, were evacuated to Belize from the Mosquito Shore. Some of these were settled in Convention Town, which was established on the south point of the Belize River mouth. Censuses taken in 1790 indicate that there were about 2,200 slaves and about 400 "free people of colour" in a total population of less than 3,000.[4] Most of these people were engaged in cutting logwood and mahogany up the various rivers and creeks, principally the Belize, Sibun, New, and Northern rivers, but their principal settlement, to which the woodcutters returned at the end of each logging season, remained Belize Town (Bolland 1977: 25-48).

The economy largely determined this pattern of settlement. Woodcutters were required to spend several months living in isolation in temporary makeshift camps in the forest. By the late eighteenth century, a small group of between twelve and twenty "old Baymen", as they styled themselves, owned over half of all slaves in the settlement and had allocated vast tracts of land to themselves. This "monopoly on the part of the monied cutters"[5] was unsuccessfully challenged by Superintendent George Arthur in 1817, though he did manage to proclaim all unclaimed land to be Crown Land, henceforth to be granted only by the Crown's representative (Bolland and Shoman 1977: 34-42). Prior to Emancipation in 1838, the number of "free people of colour" in Belize had increased substantially until they were almost half of the population, but in addition to the usual forms and processes of discrimination the extraordinary degree of economic monopoly made them almost entirely dependent upon the "forestocracy". After apprenticeship was abolished, the majority of the population remained poor and dependent largely because they were landless. While the forestocracy were confirmed in their possession of virtually all the accessible land in Belize, land that they had acquired gratuitously, Crown land was not to be freely granted after 1838 for fear that allowing the ex-slaves to obtain land might "discourage labour for wages".[6] The result of this policy was that no Crown land was sold in the period up to 1855, and by 1868 the total amount sold was said to be "utterly insignificant".[7]

The inability of the ex-slaves to obtain suitable land, combined with the undeveloped internal market system and a method of labour control that combined advance payments and truck practices to create virtual debt servitude, meant that small farming was not a practical means of livelihood. In Belize, therefore, despite the apparently favourable man/land ratio, a peasantry did not develop after Emancipation as it did in Jamaica and British Guiana. The slaves

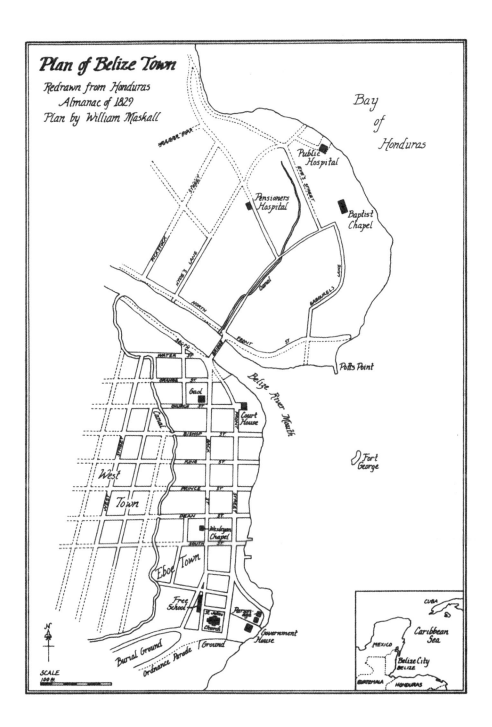

Plan of Belize Town

Redrawn from Honduras
Almanac of 1829
Plan by William Maskall

Bay
of
Honduras

Public
Hospital

Pensioners
Hospital

Baptist
Chapel

Polls Point

Belize River Mouth

Fort
George

Gaol

Court
House

West

Town

Eboe Town

Wesleyan
Chapel

Free
School

St. Johns
Church

Parson
age

Government
House

Burial Ground

Ordnance Parade Ground

N

SCALE
100 M.

CUBA

Caribbean
Sea

MEXICO

Belize City
BELIZE

GUATEMALA

HONDURAS

81

of Belize had been accustomed to growing provisions such as plantains, rice, and ground foods in temporary provision grounds near the mahogany camps, but this was largely undertaken to supplement their rations. Such seasonal or shifting cultivation was compatible with the economy of timber extraction—indeed, it is more accurate to say that agriculture was largely restricted to this form by the predominant economy—but it did not encourage the development of a settled agricultural system. The forest workers, both during slavery and after, had little time or opportunity to devote to farming. Even though the provision grounds were usually on the river banks, the time needed to transport produce to the market in Belize Town and, even more, to return upriver, was generally prohibitive. As a result of all these factors, the growth of rural communities after Emancipation in Belize was severely retarded (Ashcraft 1973: 80-85).

There is evidence of maroon communities in Belize during the time of slavery,[8] but they do not appear to have survived. Most Creole villages (as distinct from Maya, Garifuna, and Mestizo communities) were established late in the nineteenth or in the twentieth century. Owing to the almost complete absence of roads until the 1930s, the older Creole villages are generally on the coast (such as Placencia) or on the rivers (such as Burrell Boom). A report from the Acting Magistrate of the Western District in 1883 stated that "The only permanent element in the population may be said to be the Indians, Mestizos, and refugees from the neighbouring Republics", but he did refer to several small settlements on the Belize River that had Creole inhabitants or mixed populations including Creoles. These communities included Cayo (now San Ignacio) with a Creole, Mestizo and Maya population of 270, Mount Hope (population 40), Negroman (20), Orange Walk (30), Rockdondo (96), Spanish Lookout (24), San Felipe (15), and Tea Kettle (14). The main occupations of people in these settlements were said to be mahogany cutting, agriculture, and stock-raising.[9] During the depression of the 1930s some villages were established on the Northern Highway (including Salt Creek, Rockstone Pond, and Santana) as a way of relieving the pressure from the unemployed in Belize Town.[10] The historical sociology of these Creole villages is as yet a closed book.[11]

In the middle of the nineteenth century, then, the only substantial and permanent Creole settlement was Belize Town, which in the 1850s consisted of about 5,000 people. According to the 1845 census, there were 399 whites and 9,410 "coloured", the latter category probably including some Maya and Garifuna (Squier 1858: 588). After 1845 the population increased very rapidly because of the large influx of refugees from the *Guerra de Castas* in the Yucatán, until by 1861 there were said to be 25,635 people in Belize, about half of whom were in the Northern District. We can safely assume that in the nineteenth century most people in Belize Town were of African origin and also that most of the people in Belize who were of African origin were based in that town. When the mahogany cutters came from the various camps into the town at Christmas the population almost doubled.

What kind of town was Belize Town in the middle of the nineteenth century? Despite its small size, it was socially and culturally heterogeneous. The 5,000 or so inhabitants were sharply differentiated by legal status (before 1838), race, ethnicity and class, as well as age and sex. The town was bounded by the sea on the north, east, and south, and divided through the middle by the Belize River. The site is low and swampy. Any dry ground was created by filling in the swamp with sand. On these inauspicious foundations, several sizeable public buildings were created, including Government House, the Court House, the Public Hospital, and the Anglican Cathedral, St. John's. The dwellings of the wealthier inhabitants were said to be "large and commodious" (Squier 1858: 589), and were mostly along the shore on North and South Front Streets. Much of the wealth of these inhabitants was derived from a flourishing entrepôt trade with the neighbouring republics, as evidenced by the large warehouses on the shore.

The majority of the people lived behind Back Street in more crowded situations, further from the sea breezes and close to the swamp, as is generally true today. One of these areas, between South Street, Back Street and the Burial Ground, was referred to as Eboe Town in a plan of Belize in the *Honduras Almanack* of 1829. An account of Belize in 1850 described Eboe Town as "consisting of numerous yards, flanked with long rows of what are called negro houses, being simply separate rooms under one long roof, which used to be appropriated to slaves, and now accommodate the poorer labourers" (Crowe 1850: 33).

Though I doubt very much that we will ever have a detailed and accurate account of the origins of Afro-Belizeans, it is clear that they were very diverse. Most slaves were brought through the West Indian Islands, "imported from Africa by the intercourse with Jamaica, no direct importation having ever taken place; but many of these people are creoles of the different West Indian Islands, and several have been brought into the Settlement, by their owners, from the United States" (Henderson 1809: 59). Though many were West Indian Creoles, others certainly came, via the slave markets, more or less directly from Africa. A complaint, lodged in 1769, that the Spaniards granted escaping slaves asylum in the Yucatán on the grounds of their supposed conversion to Catholicism, said that "many of them are New Negroes, that can't speak a single word of any European language, and Consequently not very solicitous about any religion",[12] presumably meaning European religion. The names of many of the slaves recorded in a 1790 census also indicate African birth, though they cannot be relied upon as an indication of their ethnic identity (these include, for example, Congo Will, Guinea Sam, Eboe Jack, Mongola Sam, Mundingo Pope, and Corromantee Tom). This census and several other references suggest that the majority of African-born slaves in Belize were from the Niger and Cross deltas in the Bight of Benin and from farther south in the areas of the Congo and Angola. Certainly, until well into the nineteenth century, Africans predominated in the slave population. In 1823 it was estimated that there were "near 1,500 Africans" in a slave population of about 2,500, "the remainder being Creoles and Descendants of Indians".[13] The African contingent in the population was reinforced when discharged members of the West India regiments, many of whom had been "recruited" in West Africa, were settled in Belize in 1817 and 1818. An attempt to augment the labour force in the 1830s with "liberated" Africans from Spanish and Portuguese slave ships was only partly successful. Some of those who landed died of cholera, drowned, or killed themselves, but at the end of 1837 some 357 of these Africans remained in Belize (Bolland 1977: 103).

In the middle of the nineteenth century, then, a large proportion of the population of Belize Town was African, of diverse ethnic origins, most of the rest of the people being Creole, born either in the West Indies or in Belize. Given the presence of this racially and culturally diverse population, distinguished also by class (and, prior to 1838, by legal status), we would expect that some very complex cultural changes occurred. While not denying the importance of life in the logging camps, it was primarily in the crucible of Belize Town that Belizean Creole culture emerged.

III

Any discussion of continuities of African culture and of the process of creolization in nineteenth century Belize must remain tentative and speculative. The fact that such a high proportion of the population of Belize Town was African is a clear indication that the Town was culturally heterogeneous, its people coming from diverse cultures and societies. Fragments of evidence indicate that elements of diverse African cultures persisted in Belize in the nineteenth century, but there is also evidence of a process of cultural change in which a new, Belizean Creole culture emerged.

Evidence of African continuities occurs in many aspects of the culture of Belize Town, including religion, music, folklore, and the festivals that took place at the end of the year. While not attempting to claim, much less to prove, the existence of any direct continuities between particular cultural phenomena reported in Belize and social or cultural forms from specific African homelands, the analysis of the persistent cultural elements for which we have evidence suggests a broad pattern of African cultural influence in the social context of Belize Town. More subtle and thorough ethno historical research may yet disclose specific "survivals" or "retentions" though we should bear in mind the wise observation that "direct formal continuities from Africa are more the exception than the rule in any Afro-American culture" (Mintz and Price 1976: 31).

In 1791 a regulation was passed in Belize to ban the practice of obeah,

> the wicked art of Negroes going under the appellation of Obeah Men and Women, pretending to have communication with the Devil and other evil spirits, whereby the weak and superstitious are deluded into a belief of their having full power to exempt them whilst under protection from any Evils that might otherwise happen (Burdon 1935: v. 1, 195-196).

Despite the threat of capital punishment for practicing obeah, the "wicked art" continued into the nineteenth century, though doubtless chiefly in secret. In 1816 a deserter from the Seventh West India Regiment was said to have great "influence over the poor Slaves by virtue of his Obeah performances", and his immediate execution was demanded as "the only means by which his pernicious principles can be eradicated from amongst the poor Slaves".[14] However, the authorities failed to eliminate obeah and by the middle of the nineteenth century, its practice was said to have spread to the whites (Crowe 1850: 324). In this and in other instances that we will see it is apparent that the process of creolization was one that affected white as well as black Belizeans.

Another example of this occurs in a description of a wake which is a mosaic of African, European, and Creole cultural elements. Interestingly, this is a wake for a slave-owner, presumably of British origin.

> If a slave-owner died, all his dependents and friends came together to be feasted; and the wife or mistress and her children prepared the house and provided provisions and plenty of ardent spirits. The corpse, dressed in its best clothes, was laid upon a bed and *waked* during the whole night. Cards, dice, back-gammon, with strong drink and spiced wine, helped to beguile its watches, during which the loud laugh and the profane oath were unrestrained. In the negro yard below, "the sheck'ka" and the drum "proclaimed the sport, the song, the dance, and various dreem"...[by] the different African nations and creoles, each in parties... Sometimes a tent was erected, where rum, coffee, and ginger tea were dispensed to all who chose to come and make free. After a night thus spent, the corpse was carried in the morning to the churchyard, the coffin being borne by labourers, who in their progress used to run up and down the streets and lanes with their burden, knocking at some door or doors, perhaps visiting some of the friends of the deceased, professing to be impelled by him, or to be contending with the spirit who opposed the interment of the body. At length some well known friend came forward, speaking soothingly to the dead, and calling him Brother, urging him to go home, and promised him rest and blessing. They then moved all together towards the grave, and the sheck'ka's jingle, the voice of song, and latterly, the funeral service of the Established Church were mingled together in the closing scene (Crowe 1850: 324-325).

Several aspects of this wake deserve comment. First, the integration of games, strong drink, dancing, and general merriment in the wake is a widespread feature of Afro-American culture. Second, the reference to "different African nations and Creoles, each in parties", implies that the cultural attributes of people in Belize remained diverse, reflecting their various origins, in the mid-nineteenth century. Third, the custom of carrying the corpse from house to house, visiting friends of the deceased, was widespread in West Africa as well as Afro-America. The bearers of the corpse were believed to be controlled by his spirit who could reveal the cause or source of his demise. This part of the funeral rite was therefore a kind of divination, a way of "interrogating" the deceased to give his spirit an opportunity to disclose whether he had enemies. Such divination would have been familiar to most Africans, and this account shows that it was being learned by Creoles in Belize, perhaps by white as well as black Creoles. Finally, the music used in the ritual, if not yet a synthesis, juxtaposed African and European elements, drums and sheck'ka with the Anglican funeral service. Such wakes, described as "recreations of vivacity amongst the people… where the house of mourning and the house of feasting are identified as one and the same" (*Honduras Almanack* 1830:17-18), were important and frequent contexts for the juxtaposition, mingling, and synthesis of different cultures in Belize Town.

Another example of behaviour that was influenced by religion derived from Africa refers to free blacks. "It is not rare to meet with black persons who possess an utter aversion to spirituous liquors, and can by no means be prevailed upon to taste a beverage in which they know anything of the sort to be a component part" (*Honduras Almanack* 1830:6-7). The suggestion that this aversion derived from "national usage, or original intercourse with Mahometan connexions", was reasonable, as many of the slaves brought by the British out of the Niger delta area in the late eighteenth century could have been Muslim or have been influenced by Islam in the interior. This reminds us how complex is the religious heritage derived by Belize out of Africa.

The boundaries between religion, music, and dance were indistinct in Africa, where music and dance were frequently an intrinsic part of religious rituals. It is hard to say in what ways, specifically, this relationship persisted in Belize, though it surely did at a general level. In other words, though we may not be able to specify the continuity of particular cultural *forms*, there does appear to be a continuity of common assumptions, values, and even motor habits, about social relations and the nature of the cosmos. Some of these are probably institutionalized in musical religious behaviour, albeit in a complex and changing way that is extremely difficult to decipher. There is plenty of evidence, though it is fragmentary and imprecise in nature, that musical instruments, styles, and events that were derived from African sources persisted in Belize. The use of gombay drums was frequently reported, often in complaints by white settlers. In 1806 several of these settlers complained about

... a very large assemblage of Negroes either free or Slaves ... who have resorted to certain appointed Huts situated in different parts of the Swamps on the South side of this Town, whose apparent motive for which is Dancing. Whatever may be their real motive for such meetings, certain it is these nightly revels are productive of much noise and occasion much disturbance in the Neighbourhood.[15]

The Superintendent himself complained about the slaves being accustomed "to beat Gumbays or other Instruments sounding like drums, and to be strolling about the Streets at all hours of the Nights."[16] Soon after, the slaves, who had engaged in "their Country Plays on musical Instruments until 12 o'clock ... were in the first instance limited to 9 every night ... to which restriction they punctually submitted, tho' not without murmuring."[17]

Despite such restrictions and suppression, these nocturnal meetings survived. A description from 1830 recognized the meetings as

being importations from the coast of Africa; large parties meet at night, at some appointed negro yard, where they commence dancing to the beat of the drum, and the music of their voices .... There can be nothing more calculated to impress a stranger with surprise, than the different formations of their drums and the variety of their dances (*Honduras Almanack* 1830: 18).

The relatively large numbers of blacks, both African and Creole, and their dense settlement pattern in the confines of Belize Town, made possible such "large parties", providing another social context for the creation of Belizean Creole culture.

The greatest opportunity for communal recreation and cultural creativity occurred between the long seasons of intense and arduous labour in the isolated logging camps. The fact that this holiday season occurred between Christmas and Epiphany has led to it being called a Christmas holiday, though little about it would suggest that the Afro-Belizeans were celebrating feast days in the Christian calendar. Three nineteenth century accounts show how persistent was this event, one that seemed to bring together all the blacks in a street festival of music, songs, dances, feasting, and boat races. The first account dates from 1809:

The morning of Christmas-day is invariably ushered in by the discharging of small-arms in every direction, every thing now from established custom being free and unrestrained; and the master's house (where the festivity commences) and whatever it contains is now open to all. The members of the several African tribes, again met together after a long separation, now form themselves into different groups, and nothing can more forcibly denote their respective casts of national character than their music, songs, and dances. The convulsed rapid movements of some, appear inconceivably ludicrous; whilst the occasional bursts of loud chorus, with which all are animated, contributes greatly to heighten the singularity of the entertainment.

The endurance of the negroes during the period of their holidays, which usually last a week, is incredible. Few of them are known to take any portion of rest for the whole time; and for the same space they seldom know an interval of sobriety. It is the single season of relaxation granted to their condition; and that it should be partaken of immoderately may therefore appear not altogether so extraordinary.

At this season water-sports are also common, and Dory-racing affords a very general amusement; and on these occasions large sums are freely betted both by owners and slaves. This species of diversion has no small share of utility attached to it, as it contributes to render the latter highly expert in a kind of exercise that is inseparably connected with the labour in which they are principally engaged (Henderson 1809: 76-77).

The second account is from 1830:

At Christmas, the slaves enjoy a saturnalia which continues without interruption for the space of a fortnight. During this time there is an entire relaxation from all toils; negroes of all conditions join in sets, and perambulate the streets from morn till night, with colours flying and music playing, to which they keep time in graceful movements, waving their flags and umbrellas to the measured beats of the drum (*Honduras Almanack* 1830:17).

The third account, published in 1883, attests to the lively traditions created half a century earlier, though the author exaggerates when he claims that the slaves had three to four weeks' holiday:

At Christmas, when the season's work of cutting, hauling, manufacturing and bringing out was over, the slaves were allowed from three weeks' to a month's license to enjoy the pleasures of town in Belize, according to the respective ideas of what was enjoyment peculiar to the several tribes. These congregated in several bodies, and followed the African rites they had brought with them, but all displaying the same wonderful endurance in undergoing the fatigues of dissipation that they undoubtedly did in sustaining those of toil—"keeping it up" day and night. Amongst other questionable results deducible from slavery-times, this of keeping festivity going all night as well as all day, clings to the celebration of the Christmas holiday still. Music and dancing and the extravagant consumption of gunpowder by discharging it from their shot-guns, were common to all the tribes. Pitpan-races on the river formed a much more interesting and agreeable feature of the carnival, and a prettier acquatic sight cannot be witnessed in any quarter of the globe....On race-days the largest pitpans are manned by crews of from twenty to forty paddlers, appropriately dressed and representing rival mahogany firms (Gibbs 1883: 75-76).

Several aspects of these accounts deserve comment. First, the fact that people organized in "sets" or groups distinguished by their different "national character". Such groups are a common feature of Afro-American street festivals from Jamaica to Brazil. Frequently they represent formally organized "nations" that maintained a degree of ethnic distinctiveness and were generally involved, during the street festivals, in a degree of rivalry in costumes and dancing, and sometimes fights.[18] Second, each of these sets emphasized its own particular "music, songs, and dances," some of which seemed "ludicrous" to the English observer because the movements, being of African origin, were so strange to him. The use of drums, the "bursts of loud chorus", and the flag-men in the street dancing, are all of African derivation. Third, though the accounts stress the variety of African tribes and rites, this celebration was the major occasion on which they came *together* along with Creoles and, presumably, other Belizeans. There would thus be an intensified flow of cultural exchange during this period of heightened contact even while each group was emphasizing its distinctiveness and trying to recreate its own particular heritage. It was a period when the usual discipline was relaxed, as is evident by the guns being fired in the streets and the absence of sobriety. This frenzy of energy, of "'keeping it up' day and night", was surely a special opportunity for cultural creativity, during which some new, Belizean features developed. One of these was the dory or pit-pan races on the river. These may have begun by being organized by the sets as another form of rivalry, but became "sponsored" by the mahogany firms. The masters would encourage such events because competition between gangs of slaves developed skills and feelings of teamwork that were valuable to the business of timber extraction. In this way a new Belizean tradition became established.

Yet another cultural influence in Belize Town at Christmas time is the John Canoe dance. Known in Jamaica since the eighteenth century and perhaps earlier, John Canoe or Jonkonnu is a masked and costumed street dance performed at the Christmas season. The music, instrumentation, and characters appear to be derived from both English and African sources, and the dance is widely performed in the Afro-Caribbean (Bettelheim 1979). In Belize it is performed by the Garifuna, who call it *wanaragua*. Garifuna men began dancing John Canoe in Belize Town sometime in the nineteenth century, dancing in small groups and going from house to house (Kerns and Dirks 1975). What is unusual about this for the Garifuna is that they make a point of coming out of their own villages to perform John Canoe for a non-Garifuna audience and since the nineteenth century this has been another strand in the complex cultural tapestry of Belize Town. The occasion of Christmas has for a very long time provided a major opportunity for a culturally heterogeneous population to exercise their own particular traditions, to observe those of others, and to create new, distinctly Belizean variants.

The Garifuna, while contributing a very distinct element to the street festival of Belize Town, were only temporary visitors to that community. As a distinctive cultural group with strong African links they were unique, but perhaps not all that unusual in mid-nineteenth century Belize Town. An observer remarked on the fact that the free blacks, who just before Emancipation constituted almost half the population, were organized in "tribes" or "nations" and tried to maintain their ethnic identity and customs, even to recreate some sort of political organization:

> The Blacks . . . present almost as many varieties as there are countries whence they come; and seem to uphold their original systems, prejudices, superstitions, and amusements, to as great a degree, as they can be allowed consistently with the regulations of civilized society. . .
>
> As they have come to this and other neighbouring regions from various places, so they maintain, as far as in them lies, the customs of the countries whence they came; and hence their habits in a great measure continue. In order to preserve themselves distinct and to uphold their customs, each nation selects one from their body to whom they give the title of king. This is observed by almost every tribe or nation; consequently we have a variety of sable monarchs, who exercise a certain species of lordship over their respective subjects, and receive, in return, the most marked attention and respect (*Honduras Almanack* 1830: 6-7).

In 1850 it was stated that there were in Belize "Congoes, Nangoes, Mongolas, Ashantees, Eboes, and other African tribes" (Crowe 1850: 50), an indication that tribal identification persisted well after Emancipation. The area that was known as "Eboe Town, a section of the town of Belize reserved for that African tribe" (Gibbs 1883: 79), was reported to have burned down in 1819, but was still referred to by that name in 1850.

The African slaves and free blacks of the Caribbean, unlike their masters, could not easily communicate with their homelands, but they tried to maintain a sense of identity through keeping some of their original customs in reconstituted social groups. In addition to acts of repression directed against particular cultural features, such as obeah and drumming parties, the whole structure of slavery and colonialism militated against the persistence of African cultures. The flow of Africans into the settlement was reduced to a trickle after the abolition of the slave trade in 1807. Though, as we have seen, some Africans came to Belize from the West India regiments and from liberated Spanish and Portuguese slavers, the maintenance of African traditions depended heavily upon the sense of tribal solidarity among free blacks, often reinforced at the Christmas festivals, and upon the continuance of traditions in black families. Though there was no law to protect the families of slaves, it was considered contrary to custom to sell slaves in such a way that families would be broken up. Since the expense of importing and maintaining slaves in Belize was greater than in the sugar colonies, some slave owners may even have encouraged the development of stable families. Familial stability would not only have encouraged the slave women to have and care for children, but it would also be a way of tying the men to the town of Belize and discouraging them from escaping into the interior. Some of the slaves, certainly, enjoyed a fairly stable family life and sometimes had the opportunity to maintain quite large kinship networks.

The 1834 slave register, which states the relationships of slaves belonging to the same master, where such were known to exist, shows that some quite extended networks of kin were known, though this tells us nothing about households or domestic organization. The largest such network is that of twenty-eight slaves on the estate of Sarah Goff. The eldest was a thirty-seven year-old mahogany cutter, Sammy, who had eleven cousins and sixteen second cousins. This appears to be a long-established family, dating back to the eighteenth century when a slave woman had at least eight children who were the parents of Sammy's generation. In another case there were two generations of apparently stable conjugal relationships between slaves belonging to the same owner: Hannah, one of two children of Murphy and Mary Anne Black, was living with and had two children by a man named Glasgow.[19]

Of course, with regard to cultural persistence and change, such family groups and kin networks could, and probably did, work two ways. The existence of large networks of people who maintained contact over generations provided an opportunity for the transmission of African cultural traditions down through the century prior to Emancipation. At the same time, however, these networks constituted one of the important social contexts within which Creole Belizeans created a new culture. Through miscegenation, such networks were expanded to include whites, thereby linking the various groups in the slave society that were "implicated in the development of a single Creole culture" (Sio 1979: 272). Would that we knew more of the social structure and the cultural processes that occurred every day in these social networks.

Language and folklore are further examples of ways in which African influences persisted in Afro-Belizean culture. I will leave the study of the origins of the Belizean Creole language to those who are more qualified, but I am confident that Creole was well-established as the most widespread language of Belize by the end of the eighteenth century and that the peculiar concentration of the population in Belize Town must have facilitated its rapid development. Likewise with folk tales and proverbs, both of which, though told in Belizean Creole, have roots in West Africa. Belizean Anansi stories and proverbs were adapted to the new environment and social context while continuing to express, and thus to preserve, traditional values and views of the world. Two examples of West African proverbs that are still in use in Belize must suffice. First, the Creole proverb, "W'en fish come fram riba battam an tell you alligeta hab bellyache, believe am," has West African sources: "When the Apopokyi fish comes out of the water and says,'The alligator is dead, then there can be no doubt" (in a Guang dialect spoken in Bosa, Ghana); "The Bra-alligator and his mother live in the river, and he came up to tell that his mother was dead. Would you then say that he is telling a lie?" (in Adangme, spoken on the Guinea coast and parts of Togo). Second, the Belize Creole proverb, "Neba call alligeta big mout' till you don cross di riba" appears to be a version of the Twi proverb, "When you have quite crossed the river, you can say that the crocodile has a bump on its snout" (Hellinger 1975: 29-31).

Skill with words and the ability to perform publicly have a premium in Afro-American cultures and Belize is no exception. The tradition of story telling, including Anansi stories, is said to be less common in Belize City today, when other sources of recreation have come to predominate, than in the past, though there are still some well-known raconteurs (Hadel 1973). Such story-telling occurred in the logging camps but it was surely more important in Belize Town where the women and children lived. Both African and Creole folklore must have been especially prominent during the Christmas season when men returned from the camps and families were reunited. Can we imagine how African men would adapt traditional tales to fit their experience in the bush?

Despite persistent efforts to retain African cultures, the fact remains that most Africans who came to Belize came as slaves, subject to the military and political power of the slave owners. As a colonial society based upon slavery, Belize was organized around a core of European-derived institutions— economic, political, military, legal, religious, educational—all of which were concentrated, to an extraordinary degree, in Belize Town after 1784. The 1829 plan of the town shows the location of Government House, St. John's Cathedral, the Wesleyan and Baptist Chapels, the cemetery, barracks, gaol, school, hospitals, and court house. All these institutions were established by the British settlers and many of them excluded not only the slaves but also the free people of colour during slavery. Nevertheless, these institutions interpenetrated with those of the Afro-Belizeans, resulting in the "acculturation" of the slave population and the subsequent development of Belizean Creole culture. It is worth repeating the words of the 1830 *Almanack* quoted above, that the free blacks could organize their "nations" only as far "as they can be allowed consistently with the regulations of civilized society", that is, within limits imposed by the colonial administration.

It is hard to trace and evaluate the effects of missionary activity upon the people of African origin in Belize Town. Though the influence of the established church and the dissenters seems to have been less in Belize than elsewhere, it was certainly the intent of the clergymen to suppress and eliminate African beliefs and practices and to replace them with Christianity. An Anglican clergyman was appointed to the settlement in 1794, but although the Cathedral register records that the rector baptized his own slaves and a few belonging to other slave owners, the Anglicans did not have much to do with the slave population. Instead, the Anglican church worked more closely with the military establishment, as a "Garrison church" (Lewis 1977). By the time St. John's was consecrated in 1824, the first Baptist missionary had arrived and he was followed soon after by the first Wesleyan. Like the Anglicans, the Baptists and Wesleyans centred their congregations in Belize Town and did little to take the gospel into the mahogany camps. These missionaries, unlike their counterparts in places such as Barbados and Jamaica, were generally permitted to preach without hindrance, though Anglican marriages alone were considered legal. Hundreds of slaves, free blacks and free coloured were baptized in the 1820s,[20] and some were given Christian marriages and burials. Many of these baptisms may have been simply nominal and may not reflect much real involvement with the Church or with Christianity. On the other hand, some of those who remained unbaptized may have been influenced considerably by Christian beliefs and practices. There does not seem to have been any equivalent of the Jamaican "native churches" in Belize, though doubtless some reinterpretations and syntheses of African and European religious elements occurred. More research needs to be done on the religious changes that took place in Belize in the nineteenth century, the chief social context for which was Belize Town.

IV

It has been justly said that "continuities between the Old World and the New must be established upon an understanding of the basic conditions under which the migrations of enslaved Africans occurred" (Mintz and Price 1976: 43). Among the particular conditions in Belize that differed from those pertaining in the sugar colonies is the fact that the Afro-Belizean population has always been a largely *urban* population, centred since 1784 in Belize Town. Though this town was not large, as it grew from about 5,000 people in 1850 to about 5,800 in 1881, it was, because of its peculiar setting, bounded by sea and swamp, very densely populated and the people were culturally very heterogeneous. These aspects of Belize Town distinguished it sharply from the pattern of community development centred around village life that was widespread in the sugar islands after Emancipation. How did the particular social conditions prevailing in Belize Town affect the development of Afro-Belizean culture in the nineteenth century?

Paradoxically, the social context of Belize Town may have both encouraged the retention of elements of African culture and also promoted the rapid emergence of a Creole culture. The way in which the free and slave, the European and African sectors of Belize intersected provided opportunities for

African continuities while, at the same time, providing a context within which Creole institutions and culture were created among whites as well as blacks, free as well as enslaved.

While the spatial organization of Belize Town, in terms of its street plan and the location of the principal buildings and residences, was determined primarily by the British settlers, the concentration of some groups of Africans into particular areas, such as Eboe Town, was surely determined by the Africans themselves. This phenomenon in which "urban slaves and 'free blacks' were formed into 'nations' with their own 'kings' and 'governors'," (Bastide 1971:9) has been observed in other urban parts of Afro-America, including Argentina, Brazil, and Peru. If it is true that the "comparative prevalence of African survivals...will to a large extent depend on the density of the black population in certain areas" (Bastide 1971: 12-13), then we would expect this feature of the social organization of Belize Town to facilitate continuities in African culture. As we have seen, large parties of Africans, both free and slaves, met regularly in "certain appointed Huts" or in "some appointed negro yard". In particular, we have seen that the period between Christmas and Epiphany was used by the "members of the several African tribes" to get together in their "different groups" or "sets", for cultural recreation. These activities would reinforce their sense of ethnic identity, often in rivalry with other "nations".

But we also have the other side of the coin. The very fact that such particular African "nations" rubbed shoulders with each other in such close proximity and on such a regular basis was a suitable social context for cultural flow between them, of course, but also with the British, West Indian, and Belizean Creole inhabitants of the town as well as Garifuna visitors. As there is no evidence to suggest that the "nations" were ever endogamous, we may assume that kin networks quickly linked together people who, in other contexts, viewed themselves as culturally distinct. Thus, ethnic mixing as well as miscegenation occurred, and it became increasingly difficult for successive generations to see themselves as anything but Creole.

In the middle of the nineteenth century, shortly after Emancipation, a large enough proportion of the population of Belize Town was African to permit the persistence of distinct "nations". As late as 1861, the census of Belize enumerated 894 people as African-born—about 3.5 per cent of the total population—but by 1901 there were only 110 people so described—a mere one per cent—compared with 1,093 from Jamaica and Barbados (Census 1946:xxix). The "Africanness" of such groups became impossible to sustain in the face of a prevailing Creole culture. At the risk of considerable oversimplification, one could summarize this change by saying that Belize Town, which in the early nineteenth century was an aggregate of ethnic groups and individuals, was by the end of the century a Creole community.

I hope this paper has stressed two points that should have more general comparative value. First is the need for considerably more ethnohistorical research into the relations between social contexts and processes of cultural change in particular instances. It is only on the basis of many more, and increasingly subtle and thorough studies that we can reformulate generalizations about "Afro-American acculturation", for instance. Second is the recognition of the "fundamental dynamism" (Mintz and Price 1976: 26) of Afro-American cultures. This is one generalizatin with which it would be hard to quarrel. Elements of African cultures survived the "middle passage", were maintained or recreated in Belize Town, and there helped for a while to preserve and sustain a sense of identity and solidarity among the various peoples of African origin. But these elements survived in a hostile context. The dominant Europeans continually repressed African cultural traditons, and the power structure of society—the most oppressive kind of society, based as it was on both slavery and colonialism— militated against the persistence of African social organization, whether economic, political, familial, or religious. It was in little niches and corners of this terrible social context that the dynamism of African cultures, the creativity of people of African origin, gave rise to a new and distinctive Belizean Creole culture.

Notes

01. Belize was known as British Honduras from the mid-nineteenth century until 1973 and, before that, as the Belize Settlement or the Settlement in the Bay of Honduras. The chief town and capital, until 1970, was Belize Town, redefined as Belize City in 1943. To avoid confusion, Belize is used throughout this paper to refer to the territory that has been and independent nation since 1981.

02. "The study of acculturation or cultural change cannot be complete without parallel study of social change.... The study of African Heritage in purely cultural terms is not adequately conceived and cannot by itself reveal the processes and conditions of acculturation" (Smith 1957: 35).

03. Nationally, Creoles were about 40 per cent of the population when this article was written (Statistical Office 1982). In the 2000 census Creoles were 24.9 per cent of the national population (Central Statistical Office 2000).

04. "List of the inhabitants of Honduras, taken by His Majesty's Superintendent, in January and February 1790..." CO 123/11: "General Return of the inhabitants of the Bay of Honduras, Free people of every description and Slaves, returned 22nd October 1790" CO 123/9.

05. Supt. Arthur to Lord Bathurst, 17 October 1816, CO 123/25.

06. Lord Normanby to Supt. Macdonald, 22 April 1839, BA R15.

07. Lt. Gov. Longden to Gov. Grant, 6 March 1868, BA R98.

08. Reference was made in 1816 to a maroon community near Sibun River, "very difficult to discover, and guarded by poisonous Stakes" (Burdon 1935: v. 2, 124), and Superintendent Arthur referred to "two Slave Towns, which it appears have been long formed in the Blue Mountains to the Northward of Sibun" (Arthur to Bathurst, 16 May

1820, CO 123/19). A tributary of the Sibun River, which flows northeast out of the Maya Mountains, is still called Runaway Creek, but the exact location of these maroon communities is unknown.

09. Alvan Millson to Colonial secretary, 7 December 1883, CO 123/172.

10. It was claimed that over 2,500 persons, a few of them Jamaican immigrants but most of them Belizean Creoles, were settled on the land betwwn 1934 and 1936, amounting to about 15 per cent of the total population at that time. See Gov. Burns to Secretary of State, 3 June 1938, BA 136.

11. Some of these villages have intriguing names, such as Spanish Lookout, More Tomorrow, Never Delay, Young Gal Bank, Teakettle, but less is known of the origins of these names than of those of Maya and Garifuna communities (Sanchez 1979). The ethnically heterogeneous western frontier village of Bullet Tree Falls was studied in 1977. Most of the villagers have Maya origins and the few Creoles in the village speak Spanish (Sullivan 1978).

12. Memorial to Lord Hillsborough, 1769, CO 137/65.

13. Supt. Codd to R. Wilmot, 23 February1823, CO 123/34.

14. Arthur to Major Fraser, 19 November 1816, CO 123/27.

15. Thomas Potts *et al* to Supt. Hamilton, 3 May 1806, CO 123/17.

16. Hamilton to Gov. Coote, 26 November 1807, CO 123/17.

17. Magistrated to Dyer, 25 January 1809, CO 123/18.

18. "It was found necessary to institute a guard to control the slaves during the annual Christmas holidays, the different African tribes, no doubt, occasionally indulging in faction-fights" (Gibbs 1883: 52).

19. Examples of "slave families", derived from the 1834 slave register, are in Rolland 1977: 201-205.

20. "Return of Baptisms..." by Rev. John Armstrong, 16 December 1823, CO 123/34. "Return from the Church Register..." by Rev. Mathew Newport, 19 October 1829, BA R2; Bolland 1977: 104-105.

Part 2

Colonization and the Maya in the Nineteenth Century

4. The Maya and the Colonization of Belize in the Nineteenth Century

Introduction

The Owl of Minerva Spreads its Wings only with the Falling of the Dark

It has been stated that "there is no record of any indigenous population and no reason to believe that any such existed except far in the interior [of Belize]. There are traces of extensive Maya Indian Population . . . all over the Colony . . . but this occupation was long before British settlement" (Burdon 1931-1935: v. 1, 4). Sir John Alder Burdon was the governor of British Honduras from 1925 to 1931. His view that the area was uninhabited at the time of British settlement was convenient because it removed some of the stigma attached to the process of conquest, dispossession, and colonization. Stephen L. Caiger, an amateur historian and colonial apologist, wrote of the Maya as "aboriginals" but asserted that they "had abandoned the Belize district long before the seventeenth century. Afterwards, however, hearing of the mild rule of the logwood-cutters as contrasted with Spanish arrogance and cruelty, they percolated over the frontiers from Mexico and Guatemala, in such large numbers that today these Indians compose more than one sixth of the total population, with a culture, industrial life, and a Reservation of their own" (Caiger 1951: 126-127). Caiger, who wrote during the period of emerging nationalism in Belize (Shoman 1973), was arguing, first, that the British occupation did not displace any indigenous population and, second, that the Maya chose the "mild rule" of the British.

It is only now, when the sun is finally setting on the British Empire, that it is possible to perceive and understand the meaning of the colonial myths. Historical events can be interpreted only when enough further events have unfolded for the total historical framework, within which the earlier ones occurred, to be revealed. The meaning of history, therefore, progressively

101

unfolds itself, and it is only toward the end of a historical epoch that we can achieve sufficient wisdom to penetrate the gloom of preceding events. Now, for example, it is possible to expose the ideological nature of Caiger's shadowy argument. The view that Maya-British relations in Belize were nonantagonistic, while convenient from the standpoint of colonial ideology, is contrary to the historical record.

This article presents evidence to demonstrate that the territory now known as Belize was definitely occupied by Maya who were displaced and dispossessed by the British, that relations between the Maya and the British were generally antagonistic in nature, and that the rule of the British, neither mild nor chosen, was imposed upon the Maya in the nineteenth century by force of arms. Finally, this article examines the changing image held by the British of the Maya and relates the changes to phases of the colonization process.

Early Encounters between the Maya and the British Woodcutters

The first British settlers who arrived on the coast of Belize to cut logwood, about the middle of the seventeenth century, have left no record of contact with Maya for the first century of their occupation, though we know from Spanish records that Maya did live in the interior during that century (Bolland 1974). There is such a paucity of early British records that evidence of early contacts is unlikely to be unearthed. The first British settlers were pirates and adventurers, probably mostly illiterate, who, unlike the Spanish missionaries, would not be inclined to keep accounts of their encounters with the indigenous people. Moreover, if any accounts existed, they are unlikely to have survived, as the constant harassment of the early settlement by the Spaniards provided little security for historical records. For example, when St. George's Cay, the British settlers' principal residence, was captured by Spaniards from Bacalar on September 15, 1779, it was recorded that all "the Books and Papers of the Merchants and principal Inhabitants should be put into Chests . . . and delivered to . . . Mérida."[1] Just prior to this attack, however, a description of the state of the settlement had mentioned the presence of small numbers of Maya in the area: "The Indians who live near the English are so inconsiderable that it is unnecessary to take any notice of them."[2]

Up to this time there would have been little cause for contact, the British obtaining most of their logwood near the coast, where it could be easily loaded on their ships, and the Maya probably preferring to retire and keep out of their way. As the accessible timber became exhausted, however, the British penetrated farther inland, and in the 1770s the demand for mahogany created by the English luxury furniture industry enticed the British woodcutters into the Maya forests of what is now central and northwest Belize. As the frontier of British exploitation moved inland, contacts between the two peoples increased, the Maya forcing the British to "take notice" of them.

From maps of the late eighteenth and early nineteenth centuries it is observed that the frontier of the British timber reserve at that time lay from the Rio Hondo south through New River Lagoon and Roaring Creek to the Sibun River.[3] The Maya who lived to the west of this line responded to British encroachments upon their territory with vigorous military action. Thus an "attack of the Wild Indians"[4] was reported as having occurred on the New River in 1788, and in 1802 a detachment of troops was requested to "be sent up river to punish the Indians who are committing depredations upon the Mahogany works" (Burdon 1931-1935: v. 2, 58). Unfortunately it is not recorded which river was involved in that case, but a request in 1807 for "arms and ammunition for gangs working up the River at Hogstye Bank, who have been attacked by Indians" (ibid.: v. 2, 101) is more helpful in locating the frontier, for Hogstye Bank was a little above Orange Walk on the Belize River, probably close to Roaring Creek.

Though they ultimately failed to check the expansionism of the British, these Maya were certainly seen by the British as a serious threat to their settlement. Capt. George Henderson, who was stationed in Belize with the Fifth West India Regiment at the beginning of the nineteenth century, stated that "not many years past, numerous tribes of hostile Indians often left their recesses in the woods for the purpose of plunder. This they often accomplished; and if resistance were offered, not infrequently committed the most sanguinary murders. The habitations of these people have never been traced. Their dispositions are peculiarly ferocious . . . the dread of the military, whom it has been found expedient frequently to dispatch in pursuit of these fugitives, has latterly operated as a very effectual check" (Henderson 1809: 18-19). Contrary to Henderson's assurances, the Maya continued to fight back, despite the employment of regular troops against them. As late as 1817 "the exposed and unprotected state of the settlers, surrounded by vast hordes of Indians who are all in the constant habit of breaking in upon their works" was feared as placing the British settlers "entirely at the mercy of the Slave Population."[5] Supt. George Arthur also reported in 1817 that "we are surrounded by Tribes of Indians who occasionally commit great depredations upon the Cutters."[6] Though "vast hordes" can be assumed to be an exaggeration resulting from fear, there can be no doubt that the number of Maya encountered by the British was no longer "inconsiderable" as it had been in 1779. Neither can it be doubted that the relations between the Maya and the British, far from being as cordial as has been suggested, were extremely hostile and antagonistic.

The cultural identity of these Maya is in doubt, however. They may have included some Tipú Maya[7] and, possibly, refugees from Spanish oppression in the Petén and Yucatán (the Maya revolt at Quisteil under Jacinto Canek had been savagely suppressed by the Spaniards in 1761). Though we cannot be certain regarding the origin or identity of these Maya, they were probably living in small towns, similar to Tipú, and in little villages and homesteads scattered around the upper Belize River valley and in the bush and forest to the north. Their political decentralization meant that they were unable to mount a massive attack, but it also meant that they could not be decisively beaten. How many Maya there were in the Belize area early in the nineteenth century cannot be estimated, and no attempt was made to enumerate them in the early censuses.

The British settlers' fears of a link between the Maya and the African slaves proved groundless, no mention being made of the Maya when a slave uprising occurred on the Belize River in 1820. By that time, in fact, the Maya seem to have been on the wane; and in the 1820s and 1830s, unable to overcome the woodcutters' invasion, the Maya had retired deeper into the forests and rarely appeared to the British settlers. Walker and Caddy, in their expedition to Palenque in 1839, described Duck Run (just east of present-day San Ignacio) as "the highest inhabited spot" up the Belize River, and there they employed three Indians to accompany them to the Petén They referred to the presence of "wild Indians in the vicinity, who . . . at various times emerge from the secret recesses of the Forest for the purpose of plundering" (Pendergast 1967: 52, 159), Maya settlements in the upper Belize River valley having by then been pushed back to the limits of present-day Belize.

For the first century after the arrival of the British little or no contact took place between them and the Maya. During most of the eighteenth century we can assume that the Maya in the west of present-day Belize were relatively unaffected by the British woodcutting operations near the coast (though the British occupation would have disrupted their traditional maritime trade) and that they continued to live in small villages or isolated homesteads throughout the area. Only when the British penetrated farther inland in search of mahogany late in the eighteenth and early in the nineteenth centuries were these Maya settlements seriously affected. The British, whose sole concern was then the extraction of timber, perceived the Mayas' swidden agriculture as a threat to the forest reserves, while the Maya viewed British expansionism as a threat to their territory and their independence.

The fresh evidence presented here proves not only that the British displaced the Maya in the territory of Belize but also that the Maya resisted the rule of the British in this period, fighting frequent skirmishes along the frontier of British occupation. Despite their spirited resistance, the Maya were forced back into the forests of the interior. When they reemerged later in the nineteenth century from "the secret recesses of the Forest" into which they had been driven, they were decisively beaten by the British, who then incorporated them into the social structure of the colony as a dominated and dispossessed people.

The Resurgence and Defeat of the Maya, 1847-1872

The resurgence of the Maya of Yucatán that began in 1847 was paralleled by a revival of anticolonial activity among the Maya in the west of Belize. A newspaper report of June 12, 1847, states that, while Bacalar was threatened in the north, "on several occasions recently we have heard of depredations being committed on the property of the Mahogany Cutters in the Belize River, and in one or two instances attacks on individuals, by what are called the 'wild Indians.' We learn that some two or three weeks since, a party of them attacked and plundered several of the store-houses of the gangs employed on the Eastern and Western Branches, and fears are entertained that unless some effectual means are at once resorted to, this system of pillage will be continued."[8]

A raid on a mahogany camp on the Rio Bravo was reported later in 1847,[9] and in March 1848 it was reported that "the Indians are surrounding and attacking the Gangs in the New River pilfering our working tools [and] destroying our cattle."[10] Another letter states that "we have engaged in the Mahogany Works in the New River Lagoon and Irish Creek about 100 Men with their families...Indians are supposed to have crossed from the Rio Hondo and are armed with bows & arrows, several arrows were fired at the people in charge of our provisions at Hill Bank...Indians were kept off by firearms in possession of the men."[11]

Though it was "supposed" that the last raid originated from north of the Rio Hondo, it is quite possible that this, and the raids of the preceding year on the Belize River and Rio Bravo, came from Maya settlements in the western forests. If there were Maya settlements in the Yalbac Hills area at this time, these three raids were directed toward the most advanced penetration of mahogany camps to the south, north, and east of that region. It can be surmised that this may have been an attempt, possibly in coordination with Maya groups north of the Rio Hondo, of Maya settlements in the Yalbac Hills region to preserve their territorial integrity against the continually expanding woodcutting frontier. However, the events then taking place in Yucatán were to profoundly influence the pattern of Maya settlement and the nature of their relations with the British in the west and north of Belize.

The Santa Cruz Maya, who were engaged in the prolonged war with the Spanish Mexicans known as the *Guerra de Castas* (see Reed 1964), made a few raids across the Rio Hondo into the northern districts of Belize but never attempted to lay claim to any of the territory. The Santa Cruz preferred generally to keep good relations with the British as they needed the supply of arms and ammunition that came to them from the merchants of Belize. The British colonial officials were frequently willing to turn a blind eye to this munitions trade, despite complaints from the Mexican government, as long as the Santa Cruz were the *de facto* rulers of the territory just north of the settlements border.

The British were very apprehensive of the dangers of alienating their powerful neighbours who had forcefully demonstrated their dislike of *los blancos* in Yucatán. Throughout the *Guerra de Castas*, therefore, the British and the Santa Cruz, with brief exceptions, perceived a mutual interest in keeping the Rio Hondo a peaceful channel of communication. Not so the Mexicans, however, who wished to cut off the war supplies of their enemies, the Santa Cruz Maya.

In 1853, apparently on the intervention of Supt. Philip Wodehouse, who had succeeded Col. St. John Fancourt in a mediating role between the Santa Cruz and the Mexicans, a section of Maya to the south and west of Santa Cruz submitted to the Mexican authorities. These Maya, known as *los pacificos del sur*, consisted of various groups, including the Xkanha, the Lochhá, and the Chichanhá, who formed and re-formed in a series of alliances, splits, and realliances between the two centres of power, the Mexicans of Campeche and the Maya of Santa Cruz. At one time, Pablo Encalada, the leader of the Lochhá, claimed control over all *los pacíficos*, with the support of the Mexicans but basing his authority on the "votes of the Indians in the different villages."[12] One group of Maya, the Chichanhá, located close to the northwest border of Belize, proved particularly independent of any such alliances, however.

Chichanhá was a Maya settlement with a long history. In 1695 the Maya of Chichanhá were discovered plotting to massacre the Spaniards who resided in their town. The leader was executed in the town plaza and many of the Maya scattered into the surrounding jungle (Villa Rojas 1945: 17). Said to have been reestablished in 1733, it was first referred to in the British records as "a considerable Town named Chechenhá" in 1826.[13] In 1813 it had been mentioned in a Spanish dispatch, two escaped Belizean slaves having been "sent by the alcalde of Chicanhá, Miguel Navaez," to Bacalar, but it is not clear whether "the authorities of Chicanhá" referred to were Maya or Spanish.[14] The Maya of Chichanhá had been among the first to sign a treaty of peace in 1851, but peace with the Mexican authorities meant war with the Santa Cruz. Jose Maria Barrera, founder of the cult of the Talking Cross, marched on Chichanhá with about five hundred men, burned the village, and captured the head, Angelino Itza (Reed 1964: 141). Through signing the treaty the Chichanhá Maya had gained no protection from remote Campeche or Mérida but had brought the wrath of the Santa Cruz upon themselves. By the treaty of 1853 for *los pacíficos del sur* were to fight against the Santa Cruz, Maya against Maya, the Chichanhá agreeing to furnish four hundred men for the Mexican cause. In particular, the Mexicans wanted the Chichanhá to cut the trade in war materials between Belize and Santa Cruz.

The Chichanhá Maya, led by Luciano Tzuc, raided the mahogany works of Young, Toledo and Company at Blue Creek in September 1856. They demanded rent for cutting on Mexican territory and ransom for the prisoners they had taken.[15] This action, which was repeated in May the following year, appears to have been motivated not so much by Mexican interests as by a desire for gain on the part of the Chichanhá themselves. In 1857 the Santa Cruz again attacked the Chichanhá, and the village divided, "nearly one half... of the whole force accompanied by women & children, under the guidance of Asunsion Ek march southward & settle in the territory of Guatemala and of British Honduras."[16] These latter Chichanhá Maya appear to have been motivated by a desire for peace, retiring from the struggles of Yucatán and settling in an area which was probably thinly populated by other Maya.

On May 15, 1857, Supt. Frederick Seymour reported: "On a visit which I recently made to the Northern & Western frontiers of this settlement I fell in with some Indian residents of British Honduras, who communicated to me the intelligence that several bodies of Indians of another tribe; the Chichenhas, numbering in the aggregate... 8000 individuals, forsaking the neighbouring province of Yucatán have immigrated to our side of the Hondo where they are employed in burning & otherwise destroying bush & mahogany trees with a view to the cultivation of the soil, contemplating permanent occupation."[17] Seymour himself stated an un-willingness "to make myself responsible for the accuracy of the numbers reported," and eight thousand is certainly an overestimation. At the time of Seymour's report these Maya were settling near "the remoter mahogany works" from New River Lagoon west to Booth's River and over the boundary in the Petén.

After Bacalar fell to the Santa Cruz Maya in 1858, the Chichanha lacked any buffer between themselves and their eastern neighbours. In 1860 the Santa Cruz burned Chichanhá, and the village disintegrated, Tzuc establishing the survivors at a new site nearer the border of Belize at Icaiché. In the meantime, Ek's group of Chichanhá drifted farther south, away from Tzuc, who seemed anxious to reestablish his authority over them. In 1862 a commissioner sent by Seymour found them in the Yalbac Hills area, just north of the Belize River valley.[18] Their main village was San Pedro, lying less than 10 miles northwest of Young Girl, and inhabited by about 350 people. Their villages extended northward, to include San José, Chunbal-che, and Naranjal, and Ek's authority extended west, beyond Chorro and San Domingo, to villages within the Petén. The population of ten of the villages was estimated by the commissioner to amount to over 900 persons.

The area into which Ek's Maya migrated may have been already populated, though we do not yet have sufficient evidence to prove a continuous Maya occupation since the seventeenth century. A distinction must be made between the Maya who may have already inhabited the area (though not necessarily uninterruptedly since Tipú) and those who migrated with Ek from north of the Río Hondo and who may have borne no relation whatever to the Tipú Maya. That Ek may have settled in an area that was already inhabited by Maya is indicated by a reference to the village of "San Pedro on the River Belize" shown in a Guatemalan map of 1832[19] to be in the vicinity of Ek's village. Moreover, in 1834 it was stated that the Belize River became navigable at San Pedro,[20] which would place this village close to the branch, north of the old site of Tipú. So, while it cannot be denied that there *may* have been some continuity between Tipú and the nineteenth-century settlements, first, there is no evidence to support such a claim, and, second, we do know that considerable numbers of the Maya in that area had migrated from the north.

Ek's group had moved into the last area of western Belize that had not been penetrated by the woodcutters—the Yalbac Hills region. British settlers, the sole goal of whom was the extraction of timber, had always restricted themselves to camps on the rivers and creeks, down which they could float the huge mahogany logs to the coast. The frontier of their exploitation, for it was hardly a settlement in any permanent sense,[21] had moved west from New River Lagoon and Roaring Creek since the early nineteenth century. By the middle of the century, the mahogany cutters had penetrated the northwest up the Rio Bravo and Booth's River, and the west along Labouring Creek to Yalbac and up the Belize River as far as Duck Run, near present-day San Ignacio. The Maya settled just beyond this frontier, in the Yalbac Hills region, but they were close enough to the mahogany camps to make the mahogany cutters and the colonial administrators apprehensive. Superintendent Seymour attempted to control these new immigrants and to bring them under the authority of the colonial administration by appointing Asunción Ek as their *comandante* and appointing other individuals in the various villages as alcaldes, giving them all symbols of their offices.[22] Though, in fact, this amounted merely to a recognition of Ek's own previously established authority among the Maya, Seymour attempted to make them dependent upon British protection. The superintendent's intention was only fulfilled with difficulty, however, after a period of struggle and armed conflict.

The Icaiché Maya had been led, since the death of Tzuc in 1864, by Marcos Canul, a man who showed little respect for British authority and did not recognize British territorial claims in the northwest of the colony. Canul's raid on a mahogany camp at Qualm Hill on the Rio Bravo in April 1866 was considered very serious by the timber companies and the colonial administration. Two men had lost their lives, rent was demanded for the use of land considered to be British territory, and a considerable ransom was demanded for the prisoners taken in the raid.[23] Six months later the administration was afraid that the Icaiché Maya were about to join those in western Belize, thereby threatening the Belize River camps. It appears that Canul was under some pressure from both the Santa Cruz and the Lochhá Maya in the north,[24] while Ek expressed apprehension of the approach of the Icaiché,[25] probably fearing that he would be displaced if the two groups of the Chichanhá Maya became reunited. In any case, a hasty march on San Pedro by one Capt.

Peter Delamere actually precipitated the very realliance it had been intended to prevent. The San Pedro Maya, feeling they had somehow earned the disapproval of the British, could only turn to Canul for support. Canul and his troops arrived in San Pedro early in December, promptly demanded rent from a mahogany camp,[26] and protested to Lt. Gov. John G. Austin "that English troops had been scouring the country... with a view of molesting the Indians."[27] A detachment of British troops was sent up the Belize River under the command of Major McKay, but on the morning of December 21 they were routed on their way to San Pedro by the combined Maya forces led by Canul's second-in-command, Rafael Chan.[28] The British casualties were five dead and sixteen wounded, and the civil commissioner, Mr. Edward L. Rhys, was abandoned in the precipitate retreat and never heard from again. Though the situation appeared serious to the British at the time and caused considerable panic throughout the colony,[29] the repercussions were in fact to prove far more serious for the Maya.

After troop reinforcements arrived in Belize early in 1867, a field force of over three hundred soldiers, complete with incendiary rockets, was organized and led by Lt. Col. Robert William Harley. Entering San Pedro without opposition on February 9, they burned the village to the ground. San Pedro had been a village "of some 50 houses most of them well built and substantial, beside larger buildings, which were of a solid construction, such as the Fiesta House, Chapel, etc.—but nothing of San Pedro now remains except the Chapel, its population...was not less than between 3, and 400 people."[30] Harley went on to destroy "the rich and ample provision grounds of San Pedro covering a large extensive plain, about 3 or 4 miles from the Town...as also their corn houses."[31] The British troops also destroyed the Maya villages of Santa Teresa, San José, Naranjal, Cerro, Santa Cruz, and Chunbal-ché, burning the adjacent corn and provision grounds and the granaries, in order to drive the Maya out of the district.[32] This they appeared to have done, the area remaining sparsely occupied for a while, but soon the Maya drifted back, rebuilding and reoccupying some of their old villages.

Canul kept up his struggle against the British during the next five years. In April 1870, Canul and his men marched into Corozal and occupied the town, and on August 31, 1872, leading about 150 men, Canul attacked the barracks at Orange Walk (New River). After several hours of fighting, the Icaiché were unable to dislodge the garrison, so they retired. Canul, who had been fatally wounded, was carried over the Hondo where he died on September 1, 1872.[33] That was the last serious attack on the colony, and more peaceable, but still uneasy, relations continued between the Icaiché Maya and the British throughout the 1870s.

In 1875 it was reported that the Icaiché Maya had joined those of San Pedro at Hololtunich and laid claim to the whole of the north bank of the Belize River down to Black Creek.[34] In 1879 the Icaiché made another raid across the Rio Hondo, but by this time their strength had diminished. On October 13, 1882, there was a meeting at Government House, Belize, between General Santiago Pech, head of the Icaiché Maya, and Governor Harley. Pech began by stating that "he had Alcaldes, appointed by him, stationed at Holotonich, San José and San Pedro, and had always understood that his jurisdiction extended to those places."[35] But Harley, threatening to maintain a trade blockade with the Icaiché, managed to extract from Pech a declaration of willingness to respect the boundaries claimed by the British.

The British, having resolved the problem posed by the Icaiché in 1882, no longer found it necessary to maintain their unofficial alliance with the Santa Cruz Maya. Following the submission of the Icaiché and intense diplomatic pressure from the Mexican government, British relations with the Santa Cruz deteriorated, and in 1886 Great Britain and Mexico reopened negotiations for fixing the northern frontier of the colony. The Mexican conditions for entering into negotiations were that the British should stop supplying Santa Cruz with arms, whereas the British conditions were that Mexico should control both the Santa Cruz and the Icaiché Maya and prevent Indian raids upon the colony. When the treaty was signed on July 8, 1893, the first article concerned the location of the boundary and the fourth was purely procedural. The remaining two articles concerned the mutual control of the Maya near the frontier—an agreement to prohibit the supply of arms and ammunition to the Maya and to prevent the Maya within each territory from raiding the other (Humphreys 1961: 145-147). In this way the governments of Mexico and Great Britain reached a mutual agreement concerning the "pacification" of the Maya on their common border.

The Maya who had migrated to the Yalbac Hills in the mid-nineteenth century were a splinter from one of the several groups of the Maya of Yucatán who had been divided against each other during the *Guerra de Castas*. But this group, the San Pedro Maya under Ek, had avoided one area of conflict only to be drawn into another. Escaping the conflict between the Spanish Mexicans and the Santa Cruz Maya, which had developed into a fraternal struggle between groups of Maya, Ek and his followers were unable to remain neutral in the conflict between the British and the Icaiché Maya, despite the fact that they had settled in a relatively remote region. The realliance between the San Pedro Maya and the Icaiché Maya was a temporary affair, at first precipitated but later destroyed by British military action. When the San Pedro Maya were joined by the Icaiché, they were able to win the battle of San Pedro in 1866, but they were to lose the subsequent war. Driven out of the Yalbac Hills area in 1867, these Maya, upon their return, were dominated by the British colonialists, while the Icaiché Maya were beaten back across the northern border during the following five years.

The Place of the Maya in the British Colony

There were four phases of Maya-British relations in nineteenth-century Belize. The first of these went back into the eighteenth century, at least to 1788, and lasted until about 1817. During this period Maya settlements in the interior of Belize, which may have been occupied more or less continuously since the Spanish visits to Tipú in the late seventeenth century, were encroached upon by the intruding British mahogany camps. The Maya, in a series of small but persistent raids upon these camps, resisted the British occupation. The second phase lasted from 1817 until 1847, three decades during which little was recorded of the Maya who had retreated into "the secret recesses of the Forest" in the interior. The reemergence of the Maya of western Belize in 1847 occurred simultaneously with the resurgence of the Maya of Yucatán. The third phase, from 1847 to 1872, was characterized by periodic and violent military activity throughout the western and northern parts of the colony, resulting, in 1867 and 1872, in decisive defeats of the San Pedro and Icaiché Maya. The remainder of the nineteenth century, constituting the fourth phase, witnessed the consolidation of British jurisdiction over the Maya within Belize and the incorporation of these Maya into the colonial social structure.

The images held by the British of the Maya changed considerably during the nineteenth century, and it is possible to associate these changing images with the different phases of the colonization process. Thus, during the first phase, when the Maya undertook vigorous and spirited resistance against the British woodcutters, they were perceived, in the words of Captain Henderson, as a "hostile" and "peculiarly ferocious" people who "not infrequently committed the most sanguinary murders" (Henderson 1809: 18-19). In other words, the image of the Maya which the British held in the early nineteenth century was that of a warlike and hostile people, the "vast hordes" of whom were feared and had to be checked by the military.

During the second phase of colonization, when the Maya were secluded in the unknown interior, the image of them changed dramatically, as is apparent from this anonymous description in the *Honduras Almanack* for 1830:

With respect to the Indians, the real aborigines of the South American continent ... they are in general a timid, inoffensive race; they seem to be guided as much by instinct as by reason; they travel independent either of track or of guide, through woods and bush impervious to others, and perform their journeys with a rapidity and correctness of direction, that almost set other modes and marks at defiance. A small bag of maize, slung over their shoulder... is all the subsistence they need; and thus, in a state of nature, they wander... over wilds unknown to other men, and through forests.... Their greatest luxury is composed of rind of limes with corn and allowed to ferment, which they term Pesso; this, with a mixture of a little honey, forms a beverage of which they are particularly fond. They are almost without exception addicted to drunkenness to an excessive degree, but appear to be entirely free from vindictive or malicious propensities (*Honduras Almanack* 1830: 11-13).

By this time, then, the Maya, though still perceived as "savage," are somewhat ennobled. This Rousseauian vision of the noble savage "in a state of nature," at peace with his primitive and wild environment, contrasts greatly with Henderson's emphasis. After more than a decade of peaceful relations (or, more precisely, an absence of relations), the Maya in 1830 were perceived as "timid," "inoffensive," and "free from vindictive or malicious propensities."

In the second half of the nineteenth century, as relations between the Maya and the British became closer, the British image of the Maya became more complex. In particular, the changing perception of the Maya after 1847 is related to the actions of the Maya throughout Yucatán and the changing character of British colonialism in Belize, as the *raison d'être* of the settlement shifted from forestry toward agriculture.

In the last quarter of the eighteenth century the demand for mahogany by the English luxury furniture industry sent the British woodcutters farther up the rivers and creeks of the interior, thereby rousing the Maya to resistance. Similarly, the demand for mahogany to be used for coach construction in the European railway boom of the 1830s and 1840s led to a further expansion of woodcutting, the export of mahogany rising from 4.5 million feet in 1830 to 8.5 million feet in 1837. In 1846, the year before the report of a recurrence of raids upon the camps up the Belize River, mahogany exports peaked at almost 14 million feet.[36] It is surely not the result of chance that the periods of increased mahogany production, which entailed the penetration of the interior by the woodcutters, coincide with the reports of Maya raids upon the most advanced mahogany camps.

Although from about 1850 the mahogany trade entered a more or less permanent depression, the big landowners and the colonial administrators in the next decade remained primarily concerned with timber production, a concern which affected their perception of the Maya. Thus, when the immigrants from Chichanha moved south into western Belize in 1857, Superintendent Seymour made a point of insisting that they "must not be allowed to destroy the trees which alone give value to the land on which they are squatted,"[37] the exploitation of Belize's timber resources remaining the sole *raison d'être* of the British settlement's existence at that time. Seymour perceived these immigrants, whose swidden agriculture may have affected the valuable trees, chiefly as a nuisance. Nevertheless, he also wanted "to persuade them to accept work & wages in the interior,"[38] believing that by incorporating them into the labour force "much ultimate benefit to the settlement" might ensue.[39]

The image of the Maya as a potential agricultural wage labourer, which became the dominant image in the last half of the nineteenth century, had been foreseen as early as 1835 when a memorandum "relating to the labour which might be made available for the proposed cultivation of the soil in [British] Honduras" suggested the importation of labour from "the adjoining countries":

> but a further supply could be obtained from the adjoining countries. Those which are contiguous to Honduras although not densely populous, are still well peopled. The population is native consequently they are inured to the climate. They are poor and therefore would be disposed to go where the wages would be good. The intercourse between Honduras and those countries is now so great that considerable numbers of the people have already hired themselves to the Mahogany cutters, and work on their Banks.... Already there is an extensive and lucrative trade carried on with Belize by the Spaniards from the Northern town and port of Bacalar, in poultry etc.; and there can be no doubt that if inducements were held out to them, the native Americans would come up to Belize in great numbers.[40]

When the Maya came to Belize "in great numbers," however, it was not as a result of any "inducements" being offered them but, rather, in order to escape the strife of the *Guerra de Castas*. Moreover, far from the Maya being imported in order to cultivate the soil, their pioneering agricultural efforts were often viewed initially, as by Seymour, to be a nuisance. It was only after the Yucatecan refugees in the Corozal area themselves began to cultivate, and even export, sugar that the big landowners began to consider the agricultural potential of the soil and, consequently, to perceive the Maya, as agriculturalists who were "inured to the climate," as their potential labourers.

In 1847 the superintendent had to report that "of Agriculture in British Honduras little that is satisfactory can be said." He reported that, though "two or three individuals have recently applied themselves to the manufacture of rum," sugar was still "almost exclusively derived from the Town of Bacalar in Yucatán." He concluded that "the existing body of Merchants & Mahogany Cutters" would probably never invest capital in the cultivation of the soil, despite the fact that "sugar cane grows luxuriantly."[41] The prospects for agricultural development were thus very dim in 1847 at a time when mahogany exports were at their peak.

However, as a result of the chaos and bloodshed of the *Guerra de Castas*, thousands of Maya and Mestizos fled south into Belize. Many of these refugees returned to Yucatán, but a large number remained and settled, some, as has been described, in the west, but most in the north. The report on the Blue Book for 1856,[42] which estimated a total permanent population of about twenty thousand, stated that over a quarter of the people, or about 5,500, were in the Northern District, and most of these would have been Yucatecan refugees. In 1857 it was reported that the town of Corozal "now in the sixth year of its existence already possesses 4500 inhabitants"[43] and that the population of the Northern District, excluding Indians, was between 10,000 and 12,000. "Tickets of residence" were issued at Corozal to 2,000 adult male immigrants in 1857, it being estimated that they were only a quarter of the refugees.[44]

In 1858 a census taken by the fathers of the Society of Jesus "of such towns villages & mahogany works as are partially or entirely inhabited by Roman Catholics"[45] showed the enormous growth of villages in the Northern District, populated by Yucatecan refugees. Corozal, which contained 4,500 people, "Yucatecos principally but some Indians & Creoles," and San Estevan, populated by 1,300 "Yucatecos" were the second and third largest towns in the country. A number of villages, such as San Pedro, Sarteneja, Punta Consejo, Lowry's Bight, Orange Walk, San Antonio, and Corozal Chico, each contained 200 or more persons, mostly from Yucatán. Though many of the Maya who came into the Northern District settled as domestic servants and agricultural labourers in Mestizo communities, it was at about this time that the Maya villages of Xaibe and Patchakan were settled (Jones 1971: 10). In the first of the regular modern censuses, taken in 1861, the total population was said to be 25,635, of which 13,547, over half of the total, lived in the Northern District,[46] a high proportion of them having come from Yucatán.

The Maya and mestizo refugees who came to Belize in the decade or so after 1848 had been, for the most part, small-scale cultivators in Yucatán. The value of their continuing agricultural activity and their potential value as labourers was recognized as early as 1852 by the superintendent: "They have already commenced the cultivation of Sugar, Corn, Tobacco, and other articles for which there must always be great demand in this market; and looking to the almost entire absence of agricultural undertakings in the other Districts, as well as to the general scarcity of labour which exists here, it cannot be disputed that the retention of these settlers, and their general absorption into the permanent population of our territory, is a matter of great importance to this community."[47] Four years later, in 1856, Superintendent Stevenson urged support of the Northern District, "the first…in which there has been any attempt at establishing villages, peopled by small and independent cultivators." He spoke of them growing "considerable quantities" of rice, corn, and vegetables, for which "we are at present wholly dependent on neighbouring countries." Since any break in the fragile friendly relations with those neighbours would create problems of supply, Stevenson concluded, "It requires but little foresight to encourage Agricultural Industry, wherever it can be profitably pursued."[48]

The *Guerra de Castas* introduced uncertainties in this supply situation, and, since the Yucatecan refugees no doubt included some of the very people who had been engaged in such trade with Belize, the superintendents perceived it to be in the interests of the settlement to allow and encourage them to continue to supply the market from within the settlement itself. Moreover, when the

Yucatecans began to produce sugar, as well as vegetables and other subsistence crops, the superintendent was plainly overjoyed at the development, for sugar was a tropical export crop *par excellence*. In 1856 Stevenson reported that, apart from subsistence plots, agriculture had never been successfully pursued.

> But within the last few years—the cultivation of the cane has been attempted by the recent Spanish and Indian Settlers in the Northern District, who, by their own rough means have succeeded very fairly in establishing small but rather profitable plantations near Corosal on the margins of the principal Rivers in that district,—and, although in no one place is there a large field of cultivation or anything like scientific agriculture or Manufacture, yet the result has shown...a pressure on the Revenue on "Spirits" and "Sugar". The aggregate amount produced and sent in small quantities from time to time to Belize being very considerable.[49]

The following year Stevenson reported that eight hundred acres were under cane cultivation in the north, and that "the wants of the Settlement, in the two articles of Sugar and Rum, will soon be more than fully supplied by the Northern District alone."[50] In fact, production increased so that, later in 1857, the new superintendent was able to report: "The first shipment to Europe of sugar the produce of Honduras was made, to the extent of a hundred barrels, about a fortnight ago, in the ship 'Byzantium' for Liverpool. It is but very recently that our planters were able to satisfy the demands of our own market."[51]

The Yucatecan refugees, with their little *ranchos* on rented land, had shown that sugar could be successfully cultivated and exported, and before long the big land-owners followed in the footsteps of these small farmers, their tenants, and took over the business. This development was foreseen by the settlement's treasurer, who predicted in 1860 that agricultural enterprises "will soon be valued by Capitalists, now that the capabilities of the Soil have been practically tested by small Planters."[52] Thus the big landowners, who were then suffering from the depression in the mahogany trade, became agricultural entrepreneurs, forcing some of their tenants into wage labour and quickly dominating the production of sugar.

Between 1862 and 1868 the export of sugar from Belize was more than quadrupled, from less than 400,000 pounds to 1,706,880 pounds.[53] Lt. Gov. James R. Longden stated that, in 1867, 3,000 acres of land were under cane, that 868 tons of sugar were produced, 544 tons being exported, and that 53,914 gallons of rum were produced, of which 4,800 were exported.[54] In 1868, 1,033 tons of sugar were produced, of which 762 tons were exported.[55] In the report on 1868 it was stated that "there are Ten Estates, devoted to the cultivation of Sugar, on which steam machinery has been erected...the present acreage is only a small part of that which it is intended to cultivate." These ten estates with steam machinery had an estimated total of 1,683 acres in cane, of which 1,176 acres were in the north and 507 in the south. By far the biggest sugar producer was the British Honduras Company, whose four estates at Santa Cruz, Trial Farm, Tower Hill, and Indian Church had an estimated 746 acres in cane. The report added: "Besides these ten large Estates there are 32 small estates or Milpas cultivated partly in Sugar and partly in Indian corn by the Spaniards who immigrated into the Northern District from Yucatán. On these 'Milpas' as they are called the extent of land in cane varies from 5 acres to 110 acres. In the whole of the Milpas together there are 1,015 acres of cane land giving an average of nearly 32 acres to each Milpa."[56] There can be no question but that, within a decade of the first export of sugar from Belize by the Mestizo *rancheros*, the production and export of sugar had become dominated by the five companies which had steam machinery on their extensive estates.

The system of production on the *ranchos* was quite different from that on the plantations. Whereas the former utilized traditional swidden techniques of cultivation, associated with the Maya *milpa*, animal power, and simple processing equipment, the plantations used a short-term fallow system, steam power, and more sophisticated machinery. Both plantations and *ranchos* cultivated sugar cane and subsistence crops, such as corn and vegetables, though one may expect that the development of the prime concern of the enterprise from subsistence toward cash crops was associated with increase in the size of the production unit. Only a little space of the smallest *milpas* was devoted to cash crops, but the largest plantations were primarily involved in the production of sugar.

The growing dominance of the plantations over the *ranchos* and *milpas* caused changes in the cultural ecology and social structure of the Northern District. Much of the traditional Maya culture in craft production, for example, was neglected as the Maya became increasingly dependent upon goods bought from the company store. Many of the Maya and Mestizos became a rural proletariat dependent entirely upon the wages, in cash and goods, provided for plantation work. Others, however, became part proletariat and part peasantry, their low cash wages being under-written by their continued subsistence agriculture on small plots of rented land. So long as the population remained small and the expansion of sugar production did not strain land resources, this arrangement suited the employers who could thereby reduce the wages and simultaneously collect rents.[57] With the consolidation of agricultural estates in the 1860s therefore, the Maya and Mestizo settlers were perceived by the big landowners chiefly as a potential source of cheap labour for the developing plantation system.

Within two decades of the reemergence of the Maya onto the colonial stage in Belize, the very foundations of this stage had changed dramatically, thereby creating a new situation into which the Maya became incorporated. The export of mahogany, which had been the basis of the settlement's economy since the

1770s, declined rapidly after its peak of nearly 14 million feet in 1846. In 1868 only 3 million feet of mahogany were exported,[58] and in 1870 only 2.75 million feet were exported,[59] the lowest recorded annual figure since the beginning of the century. But mahogany declined in value as well as in volume, so that in 1866 the 5,167,167 feet of mahogany exported, valued at 4 1/2d. per foot, was worth £96,884, but only two years later the price had dropped to 2 1/4d. per foot, so the 3,006,619 feet exported in 1868 was worth only £28,187. The effect of this great fall in demand for the colony's staple product would have been completely catastrophic had it not been for a temporary increase in the volume of logwood exported. Nevertheless, the value of logwood was also declining, so that the combined value of logwood and mahogany, which together accounted for 82 per cent of the total value of the colony's products exported in 1868, dropped from about £140,000 in 1866 to a mere £56,000 in 1868.[60]

It was in this context of a drastic decline in the value and volume of the colony's chief exports that agriculture was first seen as a serious alternative economic basis. Though an agricultural company had been formed in 1839,[61] it was unsuccessful in encouraging and promoting agricultural activity. It was not until the Yucatecan refugees demonstrated the agricultural potential of the land, particularly after they first exported sugar in 1857, that the big landowners, experiencing difficulty with the mahogany trade, looked to sugar production as an alternative. And as they looked to sugar production, the landowners perceived the Maya and Mestizo immigrants as their chief potential labour supply.

A report of 1859 had distinguished between the Maya and the Mestizo refugees in terms of their characteristic economic activities. The Maya were said to be either employed in mahogany gangs or engaged on their own account in logwood cutting, "which has passed principally into their hands," and in *milpa* farming and pig raising. The Mestizos, on the other hand, were described as those "who, with a sprinkling of Indians, are our sugar growers." The report, heavy in its degree of racial stereotyping, concluded that the Maya, "more robust than the Spaniard, less addicted to pleasure than the negro... are admirably adapted to the monotonous drudgery of logwood cutting."[62]

In the 1860s, when sugar estates were expanding in the north, the question of a labour supply became of great concern. In 1864 Lieutenant Governor Austin reported that there were 2,883 people on the Rio Hondo and 10,664 on the New River and that "of these 3933 are pure Indians, 1129 Spanish and 6737 Mixed, and consequently with exception of the wood cutting gangs which are migratory, & consist to a great extent of Creoles, there is but little labour available in the rivers, save for the Yucatecan & Indian villages scattered here and there on the banks."[63] Austin commented that both "Medical & Magisterial supervision in the New River... are even now lamentably deficient," and he expressed his desire "of placing the rights of employers & employed generally on a more satisfactory basis. I had several opportunities of observing how at such a distance masters could be successfully defied by their people, & how in many ways the labourer was completely at the mercy of his employer."[64] It is apparent from the report of Edwin Adolphus, the magistrate at Corozal, on "the general treatment of the Indian labourers" five years later that "Magisterial supervision" meant enforcing "the rights of employers; 'not of the employed. *All* of the 286 cases decided by him under the colony's labour laws in 1869 consisted of discipline imposed upon the employees: 245 for "absenting themselves from work without leave," 30 for "insolence and disobedience," 6 for "assaults on masters and bookkeepers," and 5 for "entering into second contracts before the expiry of the period of former ones."[65]

Though the magistrate clearly functioned in his legal capacity as an instrument of discipline for the employers against the employed, his report on labour conditions is not uncritical of the behavior of the employers and particularly of the advance and truck systems whose use had been extended from the mahogany cutters to the Maya and Mestizo agricultural labourers. Adolphus stated that the *mozos*, or "Indian labourers," are, "without exception, always in debt to their Employers," and he described the causes and effects of their indebtedness:

> During the annual fair, held in Corozal at Christmas, when much carousing takes place, the greater part of the mozos squander their money advances for the following year: the advances in goods are usually supplied after Christmas on their proceeding to work.
>
> The system of advances to which they have become so accustomed, and without which the Indians cannot be got to hire, is the main drawback to their regular attendance to work; for, knowing at the commencement of their engagements that they already are in debt, the chief incentive to labour is thereby removed. The Employer, though able of course to cause the idle to be arrested and punished by the Magistrate, is frequently deterred from so doing by reason of the great probability that, on liberation from gaol, the recently punished Indians will take the earliest opportunity of crossing the border into Yucatán, but a few miles distant, where the Indian Commandants gladly receive them.... There are at present scores of runaway mozos living on the opposite bank of the Rio Hondo, who are largely indebted to their former masters, some of whom have actually been ruined by this practice. Another reason that they are so seldom imprisoned for misconduct, as compared with the black laborers, is that they are paid by the task and not by the month as are the latter...
>
> The Spanish system of hiring, or as I may truly call it semi-slavery, was originally brought to this Colony by the Yucatecans when they took refuge here, some twenty years back, after having been driven out of Bacalar by the Indians. It is still practised to a great extent. The Indian laborers, all being overwhelmed with debt, become regarded, in course of time, as a portion of the value of the

various ranchos or Estates on which they live and work, and actually themselves imagine, in many instances, that they have no right to leave the same unless they satisfy their Master's heavy claims against them, which belief is naturally of course much fostered by the employers, as it is their principal security for the payment of the servants' debts... but if the mozo fails to obtain, within a limited period, a new master, who will pay the debt for him, he unhesitatingly returns to the old service under the impression that there, and nowhere else, is he obliged to work... it is always clearly understood between the Indian and the Ranchero when the latter pays the debt of the former, that before he can leave his new Master's service he must repay either in cash or by labour the heavy money advance made... a complaint by an Indian against his master is a matter of very rare occurrence indeed.[66]

The debt peonage created by the advance system, combined with rents for annual tenancies in a context of land monopolization, and a truck system in which "they must receive the greater portion of their wages in goods" amounted to a situation of "semi-slavery." But Adolphus was wrong in placing the responsibility for the introduction of this system upon the Yucatecan refugees. Though a similar system had been practiced in Yucatán, it also existed in the settlement long before the immigration of the Yucatecans. The combination of the advance and truck systems had been utilized by employers to control the Creole labourers in mahogany gangs even before, but particularly after, emancipation in 1838. In fact, Adolphus stated that "the Creoles and Caribs receive about the same advances as the Indians, from three to four months—half goods, half cash," but that their contracts were attested before a magistrate. When breaking the contract, they were likely to be brought to the Summary Court, charged with "non-performance of tasks, disobedience, absenting themselves from their work, sick and idle time etc." (ibid). The Creoles and Caribs were actually more likely to be punished for such labour indiscipline because escape was more difficult for them than for the Indians. Thus we see that the prevalence of escape, the deterrent which had to some extent inhibited the masters' treatment of slaves, also inhibited the employers of the mozos in the 1860s.

The living conditions of Maya and Creole labourers were said to be similar: "Their houses, or rather hovels, are... entirely devoid of any [of] the slightest appearance of comfort." Adolphus stated that the Creoles and Caribs received more substantial rations than the mozos, "four pounds of salt pork or fish and fifty plantains per week," but that they also received "nominally much larger tasks than Indians." According to Adolphus, "The Indian labourers... are much sought after," and he gave four reasons: first, "cheapness"—their rations consisted of only twelve quarts of corn per week; second, they were considered to be "tractable and obedient... more easily managed than the Creoles and Caribs"; third, "they finish their work in a better style than the other labourers although they perform less"; fourth, "they will work at night willingly where but seldom the blacks can be got to do so. In fact they will attend for weeks together, during the night, at the mill without murmuring" (ibid.).

The problem facing the employers was the organization of a plantation labour force from among people whose experience had been either one of slave labour in the mahogany forests or primitive subsistence cultivation. While the labourers could be made thoroughly dependent upon their employers through the imposition of rents and the use of the advance and truck systems to induce indebtedness, such dependency did not ensure their regular attendance or disciplined behaviour at work. The employers seem to have preferred the *mozos* for plantation labour because they perceived them as more amenable to discipline, though less susceptible to punishment, than the blacks. The employers, judging that the blacks would quit at the end of their contract whether they remained in debt or not, did not extend advances exceeding the value of their labour, with the result that the blacks were generally free from debt at the termination of their contracts. "The black labourers...knowing full well that, at the expiry of their contracts, they cannot be detained cause, but too frequently, considerable trouble by impertinence and disobedience," while the *mozos*, encouraged to believe that they had "to continue working in the respective estates until the debts they have contracted are liquidated," were more easily intimidated and disciplined (ibid.). However, it was thought that there was a limit on the punishment it was profitable to apply to the Maya, as a "runaway *mozo*" was of no value to a plantation.

The magistrate at Orange Walk on New River, Robert T. Downer, wrote a similar report of labour conditions in 1869. He emphasized, however, that the Mayas' "love of independence" and "reluctance to enter into written contracts of service" made them "not so easily imposed upon, as some persons are inclined to think....Those that seek employment, or are prevailed upon to undertake it, are perhaps barely equal, numerically, to those that remain at home."[67] Downer also described wages, indebtedness, and the functioning of the truck system:

The average rate of wages paid to Indian labourers varies with the nature of the work they are required to perform. For cutting logwood, which is their principal occupation, they are paid at the rate of three dollars per ton with rations, or four dollars, they feeding themselves. The mule drivers, or those employed in bringing out the logwood, are paid at the rate of ten dollars and sometimes as high as twelve dollars per month with rations. For ordinary labor, such as working on the ranchos, etc. they are paid according to the work done... average at the rate of from $7 to $8 per month, and rations....

There is...a considerable percentage charged upon goods supplied to a laborer...the Indian laborer is scarcely ever out of debt...even where an estate labourer signs for all cash, he generally places himself in the same position as one who hires "half and half," by taking from the Estates' store such goods as he stands in need of.[68]

The wages were not only low, but were also frequently paid partly in rations, or "half and half," a practice which was obviously to the advantage of the employer. But even when the labourer was paid entirely in cash, the charges for goods at the estate's store would be excessive, thereby benefiting the employer and leading inevitably to the indebtedness and further dependency of the employees. Though the Maya were often perceived as "tractable," "obedient," and "easily managed," they did repeatedly demonstrate their "love of independence." Consequently it suited their employers to develop mechanisms of labour control so that the Maya *mozos*, "being overwhelmed with debt," would come to regard themselves as "a portion of the value of the various ranchos or Estates on which they live and work..."[69]

When, in 1857, Superintendent Seymour considered the Chichanhá Maya immigrants to be merely a nuisance to the mahogany business unless they could be persuaded to become wage labourers, "British Honduras" was still not officially a colony, little interest existed in agricultural development, and even the registration of land titles had not been instituted. Within the next decade, however, all this was to change and the place of the Maya within the colonial structure had to be more defined and systematized. The north and west of Belize were being colonized by the British in the last half of the nineteenth century, and a suitable administrative system had to be devised. Thus, even before the declaration of colonial status in 1862, an act was passed in Belize "to provide for the more speedy Administration of justice in the rural districts of British Honduras" giving a legal basis to the position of alcalde, which had been adopted from the Spanish colonial system.

The settlement of the Maya in the north and west of Belize in the third quarter of the nineteenth century took place within the discriminatory restrictions of a colonial framework. Thus, the zeal with which the British crushed the San Pedro Maya in 1867 is in part explained by their desire to revenge the rout of the preceding year, but it was also caused by the desire to secure the extremities of the colony for the settlement of potential immigrant Confederate refugees from the American Civil War.[70] Most of those immigrants who came stayed only a few years in the south of the colony, but the policy of attracting white settlers remained. This policy was not based solely on a desire to develop agriculture but also on the hope that the number of whites in the population, which in 1881 was a mere 375, or 1.4 per cent of the total (Gibbs 1883: 158), would increase. The Maya, who were trying to develop the interior of Belize for their own agricultural purposes, were thus the victims of a racial scheme of colonization. They were perceived in the colonial scheme, not as the agricultural pioneers that they in fact were, but merely as a potential source of "tractable," "obedient," and "easily managed" labour for foreign-owned plantations.

In 1867 Lieutenant Governor Austin issued the following regulation: "No Indian will be at liberty to reside upon or occupy, or cultivate any land without previous payment or engagement to pay rent whether to the Crown or the owner of the land."[71] The following year, in a lengthy "Report on the Land Question," Lieutenant Governor Longden discussed what could be done with the Maya villages which had been reestablished in the western district: "Several of these villages are situate upon the lands claimed either by the British Honduras Company or Messrs Young Toledo and Company, but whenever they are situate on Crown Lands I think the villages and a sufficient surrounding space should be reserved *in the hands of the Crown* for the use of the Indians,— no marketable titles being issued to them to enable them to dispose of such lands."[72] Thus it was made clear that, whereas the largest landowners of the country, who only a few years before had obtained firm titles to their vast lands, were not to be disturbed, the Maya should not be allowed to own land but were to be confined to reservations, the latter being created by the Crown Lands Ordinance in 1872.

The Maya, although made the objects of this discriminatory colonial scheme of things, were also significant subjects of Belizean history in the nineteenth century. They were, of course, pioneer settler-agriculturalists in the west and north of the colony, thereby having an effect, in part by their example, upon the economy. But more dramatically, the military activities of the Maya had an impact upon the politics of the colony in the late 1860s, the result being a major constitutional change.

In the late 1860s the expenses of administering the colony had increased, largely as a result of having to pay for the military expeditions against the Maya, at a time when the economy was severely depressed. As a result the public debt, being "chiefly for military expenditure" (Gibbs 1883: 155), rose to about $150,000 by 1870. The great landowners, whose mahogany camps in the west and northwest had been attacked and were continually threatened by the Icaiché Maya under Marcos Canul, were at last moved by this state of affairs to allow the Legislative Assembly to impose a land tax in 1867. However, its operation was limited to only two years to meet the immediate emergency, and it was based on terms which were actually very favourable to the big landowners.[73] In the particular crisis of 1866-1867 the great mahogany companies were willing to support a temporary measure for raising revenue by the taxation of land, but they had no intention of continuing to pay such a tax.

The Legislative Assembly, which determined the colony's revenue and expenditure, was controlled by the great landowners and the merchants. Though the landowners were also involved in commerce, some antagonism existed between them and the other merchants of Belize Town. Whereas the former resisted the taxation of land and favoured an increase on import duties, the latter preferred the opposite. Moreover, the merchants of Belize Town felt relatively secure from the Maya attacks and were therefore unwilling to contribute toward the military expenditure necessary to resist them. At the same time the landowners were unwilling to bear the expense themselves and held the view that it was unjust to require them to pay taxes for lands that were given inadequate protection. These conflicting interests produced a stalemate in the Legislative Assembly, which failed to authorize the raising of sufficient revenue.

Unable to agree among themselves but pressed by the necessity to raise additional revenue, the members of the assembly attempted to convert British Honduras into a crown colony in 1869 so that the imperial government would bear more of the burdens of defense. In 1870 the assembly agreed to surrender its privilege of self-government in return for greater security against the persistent Maya threat, in much the same way as the Jamaican assembly had abolished itself after the crisis of the Morant Bay rebellion in 1865. The Legislative Assembly having "committed political suicide" (Gibbs 1883: 152), the new colonial constitution was inaugurated in April 1871. A year later Canul was killed, and the Maya threat was annulled.

The fact that the Maya had made themselves the subjects, as well as being the objects, of Belizean history, introduced a new complexity into the colonial image of the Maya. Though white colonizers wished to perceive the Maya only as agricultural wage labourers, the Maya had thrust themselves into the colonial consciousness as a military force with which the colonizers had to reckon. The British in the latter half of the nineteenth century tended to hold two conflicting images of the Maya—one of the "tractable," "obedient," and "easily managed" agricultural labourer and the other of an independent fighter whose resistance to colonial rule commanded at least a modicum of respect.

An ambivalence in the perception and characterization of the Maya had developed shortly after the outbreak of the *Guerra de Castas*. Frederick Crowe, who was attached to the Baptist mission in Belize, wrote of the Maya in 1850: "In disposition, their leading characteristics are docility and timidity. When aroused, however, they are fierce, cruel, and implacable. Generally industrious, though not aspiring, they often amass wealth .... In their dealings they are shrewd, but not dishonest, and their word may generally be relied on. Long subjection has taught them a cringing servility and low cunning, probably foreign to their original character" (Crowe 1850: 42-43). In 1850 the Maya were still seen as "noble savages," alternately docile and fierce, timid and cruel, and it was not until the development of agriculture had created a greater need for labour and the expansionist British had encountered organized Maya military resistance that the images of the Maya as tractable plantation labourers and hardy warriors emerged. Thus, in 1883, Gibbs wrote two descriptions which illustrate the ambivalent colonial images of the Maya in the late nineteenth century. On the one hand, he emphasized their potential as cheap plantation labour: "The Indians ... are baptized, but mix up idolatrous rites and superstitious beliefs with the Christian creed and ceremonies... They live industriously and inoffensively in villages scattered over the district, cultivating their patches of maize and pulse, their pigs and poultry.... The indigenous Indian ... might be made available to some extent could he be induced to quit his scattered village-homes, and this is perhaps the cheapest labour to be procured" (1883: 162, 176). On the other hand, Gibbs, who had been the commissariat officer in the field force which destroyed the Maya villages in 1867, wrote of the Maya troops with a degree of respect:[74] "The 'Indios bravos' ... are trained to arms and discipline, are capable of enduring much fatigue ... are wiry, hardy, and courageous" (ibid.: 140).

With the wisdom that comes with hindsight, we can see that these images of the Maya, like the preceding ones, are something less than half-truths. They are distorted stereotypes of a colonized people, produced by the circumstances of a historically specific social situation.

Summary and Conclusions

The British settlement at Belize was first established as a base from which to export timber, and Belize grew as the centre of the exploitation of the country's timber reserves using African slave labour. When the settlement's *raison d'être* shifted from the export of logwood to that of mahogany in the last quarter of the eighteenth century, the British woodcutters, penetrating farther inland, encountered resistance from the Maya. Displaced by the British occupation, the Maya remained in the forests of the interior until the middle of the nineteenth century when, simultaneously with the *Guerra de Castas* in Yucatán, they once more resisted the colonial invasion.

The history of the Maya in the Belize area in the second half of the nineteenth century is inextricably linked with that of the larger Mesoamerican context, particularly the migrations and military activities connected with the political changes and shifts in the loci of power north of the Rio Hondo. But the Maya within Belize were also affected by, and themselves in turn affected, major developments in the colonial political economy. With the decline of the timber trade after mid-century, the land itself began to be perceived by the colonizers as being intrinsically valuable, and the interior was seen as a potential site of agricultural development, especially after the Yucatecan refugees successfully exported sugar in 1857. In the 1860s the western and northern frontiers of the colony had to be "secured" and the Maya "pacified" in order to make the interior attractive as an area for white settlement. In the colonialists' racialist scheme of things, only white settlers, whether humble homesteaders or big planters, were

124

considered to be valuable from the point of view of agricultural development or to be reliable in relation to defense.

Within this evolving colonial framework, the Maya, who had first been driven back and kept away from the valuable mahogany trees, came to be perceived as potential agricultural wage labourers to be exploited by immigrant white capitalists. The Maya, in this scheme, had to be "induced to quit his scattered village-homes" and denied the right to own land, in order to deprive them of an independent means of livelihood and make them dependent upon their employers. Defeated in military action in 1867 and 1872, dispossessed and denied the right to own land by colonial legislation, many Maya did become dependent upon wage labour. For the last century, therefore, the Maya have been integrated into the capitalist-colonialist society of Belize as a defeated, dispossessed, and dependent people.

Notes

01. Edward Felix Hill, "An account of the Spaniards landing at and taking of St. George's Key, by the subscriber, who was then on the place, and an inhabitant," 1 October 1779, CO 137/76.

02. Unsigned letter to Governor Dalling, 3 September 1779, CO 137/75.

03. See, e.g., two maps: Thomas Jefferys, "The Bay of Honduras," 20 February 1775, CO 123/14/ 1, and H. C. Du Vernay, "A sketch of the British settlement of Honduras and course of the southern coast to the River Dulce," 9 March 1814, CO 123/23.

04. Thomas Graham, "Journal of my visitation of part of the district granted by His Catholic Majesty for the occupation of British settlers...," 27 October, 1790, CO 123/9, and Edward Marcus Despard, "A narrative of the publick transactions in the Bay of Honduras from 1784 to 1790;" 8 March 1791, CO 123/10.

05. Minutes from the public record, 25 February 1817, CO 123/26.

06. Arthur to Major Fraser, 12 June 1817; see also Magistrates to Earl Bathurst, 26 February 1817, and Arthur to Bathurst, 12 June 1817, CO 123/26.

07. Thompson's statement suggesting that "British logwood cutters working on the Belize River in the eighteenth century employed Indians...[who] were probably descendants of the Maya of Tipú culture" (J.E.S. Thompson 1970: 71) is misleading. The Indian slaves used by the British in the late eighteenth and early nineteenth centuries were brought from the Mosquito Shore when it was evacuated in 1787, and they were not indigenous to the Belize area (see memorandum from Despard to the committee, 18 August 1789, minutes of public meeting, 22 August 1789, CO 123/12). We have no record of the Maya having been enslaved by the British or employed by them in the eighteenth century, though some were employed in cutting logwood and mahogany later in the nineteenth century.

08. *Honduras Observer* and *Belize Gazette*, 12 June 1847.

09. Ibid., 30 October 1847.

10. Letter to Charles St. John Fancourt, 16 March 1848, BA, R. 28.

11. Letter to Major General Berkley, 17 March 1848, BA, R. 28.

12. Statement of Encalada's commissioners, February 1867, BA, R. 89.

13. George Hyde to Marshall Bennett, 12 February 1826, CO 123/37.

14. Manuel Melendez to Manuel Artazo, 15 March 1813, in Work Projects Administration 1939,120-121.

15. Stevenson to Maj. Gen. E. Wells Bell, 9 September 1856, and 16 October 1856, BA, R. 55.

16. Seymour to Gen. Edward John Eyre, 12 November 1862, BA, R. 81.

17. Seymour to Bell, 15 May 1857, BA, R. 52.

18. Rhys to Seymour, 3 November 1862, BA, R. 78.

19. "Departamento de Verapaz, Año de 1832;" CO 123/47.

20. Frederick Chatfield to Viscount Palmerston, 7 November 1834, CO 123/47.

21. This kind of frontier, which was not supported by extensive rural settlement, has been referred to as a "hollow" frontier (see Humphreys 1961: 17-18).

22. Rhys to Seymour, 3 November 1862, BA, R. 78.

23. See BA, R. 93, passim.

24. Delamere to Austin, 4 October 1866, and Encalada to Austin, 8 November 1866, BA, R. 89.

25. Ek to Austin, 9 November 1866, BA, R. 89.

26. J. Swasey to Young, Toledo and Co., 5 December 1866, BA, R. 89.

27. Canal and Chan to Austin, 9 December 1866, BA, R. 89.

28. McKay to Austin, 24 December 1866, BA, R. 95; R. Williamson to Austin, 26 December 1866, BA, R. 89.

29. A later account stated that "the inhabitants, Governor Austin's family, at least included, if not himself, were all packed up ready to take to the shipping . . . . Christmas was anything but a holiday in Belize that year" (Gibbs 1883: 138).

30. Harley to Austin, 9 February 1867, BA, R. 95.

31. Harley to Austin, 15 February 1867, BA, R. 95.

32. John Carmichael, Jr., to Graham, 30 March 1867, and Harley to Austin, 7 September 1867, BA, R. 95; see also the account by Lt. Col. E. Rogers, "British Honduras: Its resources and development;" delivered before the Members of the Society at the Manchester Atheneum,14 October 1885 (Rogers 1885).

33. Maj. William Johnston to Gov. William Wellington Cairns, I l September 1872, and Serapio Ramos to Major Johnston, 15 September 1872, BA, R. 111.

34. Phillips and Co. to Graham, 22 March 1875, BA, R. 119.

35. Memorandum, 13 October 1882, BA, R. 93.

36. Figures from quarterly returns of exports from Belize, CO 123/41-42; Gibbs 1883: 93, 102.

37. Seymour to Bell, 15 May 1857, BA, R. 52.

38. Ibid.

39. Seymour to Bell, 17 June 1857, BA, R. 52.

40. Thomas Miller to William E. Gladstone, 23 February 1835, CO 123/47.

41. Fancourt to Gov. Sir Charles Edward Grey, 19 June 1847, BA, R. 25.

42. Stevenson to Bell, 2 March 1857, BA, R. 55.

43. Seymour to Gov. Charles Henry Darling, 16 November 1857, BA, R. 55.

44. Edmund Burke to Seymour, 2 November 1857, BA, R. 58.

45. Seymour to Darling, March 1858, BA, R. 55.

46. 8 April 1861, BA, R. 74.

47. Superintendent to Chairman, public meeting, 20 January 1852, BA, R. 20.

48. *Votes of the Honourable House of Assembly, sessions 1854-1859.* 22 January 1856.

49. Stevenson to Sir Henry Barkly, 5 April 1856, BA, R. 55.

50. Stevenson to Darling, 2 March 1857, BA, R. 55.

51. Seymour to Darling, August 1857, BA, R. 55.

52. Treasurer to Acting Supt. Thomas Price, 4 April 1860, BA, R. 66.

53. Longden to Gov. Sir John Peter Grant, 19 June 1868, and 17 May 1869, BA, R. 98.

54. Longden to (Grant, 19 June 1868, BA, R. 98.

55. Longden to Grant, 17 May 1869, BA, R. 98.

56. Ibid.

57. The maintenance of this form of land use and land tenure enabled the Maya to develop into small-scale cash crop producers when the plantations declined and also established a precedent for the coexistence of peasant-milpa and industrial-estate types of agriculture when the plantations were reintroduced in the twentieth century (see Jones 1969 for a discussion of these cultural ecological changes).

58. Longden to Grant, 17 May 1869, BA, R. 98.

59. Hooper's report, 1887, cited in Hummel 1921: 12.

60. Longden to Grant, 17 May 1869, BA, R. 98.

61. Col. Alexander Macdonald to Chairman, public meeting, 4 March 1839, BA, R. 16.

62. Seymour to Darling, 22 June 1859, BA, R. 65.

63. Austin to Eyre, 26 May 1864, BA, R. 81.

64. Ibid.

65. Adolphus to Longden, 15 January 1870, BA, R. 105.

66. Ibid.

67. Robert T. Downer to Longden, 27 January 1870, BA, R. 105.

68. Ibid.

69. Adolphus to Longden, 15 January 1870, BA, R. 105.

70. For example, one J. C. McRae, an ex-Confederate general, purchased a large tract of land up the Belize River in 1868; see Clegern 1967: 43.

71. 28 February 1867, BA, R. 96.

72. Longden to Grant, 6 March 1868, BA, R. 98.

73. Longden to Grant, 4 December 1867, BA, R. 98.

74. This emphasis on the martial qualities of the Maya was repeated a few years later in *Report of Indian Soldiery:* "The Indians are masters in the use of cover, and in the bush are redoubtable enemies" (Allen 1887: 3).

5. Alcaldes and Reservations: British Policy towards the Maya in Late Nineteenth Century Belize

I

Many anthropologists focus exclusively on fieldwork, with subsequent loss of historical perspective. This problem is of particular concern in those places that have experienced colonization, where the anthropologists' emphasis on reconstructing the "ethnographic present" too often fails to take adequate account of the consequences of colonial domination. The work of ethnohistorians and historical sociologists, lying somewhere between conventional history and anthropology, attempts to describe and account for the often extensive changes in indigenous culture that occurred in the colonial era. But this process of culture change was not a one-way street, as the concept of "acculturation" implies. Rather, the "native peoples who were the objects and subjects of these colonial control systems were caught up in a complex dialectic" (Cohn 1981: 241) in which they participated in shaping the colonial society, sometimes including even the institutions of colonial control.

An ethnohistorical perspective reveals how "lowland Maya society has maintained a remarkable degree of integrity and autonomy in the face of nearly overwhelming external pressure" (Jones 1977: xiii). In the area now known as Belize, such pressure came first from Spanish *entradas* and then, from the middle of the seventeenth century, from British conquest and colonization. Belize was a British colony in all but name at least since the eighteenth century, though not formally declared as such until 1862. When the British consolidated their Central American colony in the second half of the nineteenth century, they incorporated the indigenous Maya as a defeated and dispossessed people, sometimes on "native reservations." But the Maya continued to resist assimilation and domination.

In this paper I will show how the dialectic of British colonization and Maya resistance in Belize prompted the evolution of institutions and practices in the late nineteenth century that, while being rooted in the traditions and interests of both protagonists, were the product of the colonial situation itself. Under the pressure of Maya resistance, the British adopted a policy of indirect rule through the alcalde system. This was a Spanish colonial institution that originated in the *cabildo* or town council, and survived in Maya communities in Mexico and Guatemala into the independence period. Though, on the one hand, this system made British rule cheaper and more effective, on the other hand the Maya could use it as a foil against a more direct form of colonial control. It is especially interesting that the British extended the alcalde system and the reservations to the Garifuna, who are not indigenous to the region but are the descendants of the Caribs of the eastern Caribbean and Africans who escaped from slavery.

The institution of alcalde is possibly derived from the Postclassic Maya *batab* or "town chief" (Thompson 1977: 27, 36), who was generally assisted by a number of deputies. The Spanish colonial version of this "town council" was the *cabildo*, consisting of two alcaldes presided over by a *gobernador*. While it is "futile to try to trace the separate ancestry of each of the colonial offices" (Farriss 1984: 232), there were certainly "functional and structural continuities between the pre-Columbian and colonial Maya political systems at the local level" (Farriss 1984: 234-235). Utilized throughout Spanish America in both Spanish and native communities, alcaldes were traditionally military heads as well as judicial and administrative officers at the village level. In some instances, an *alcalde col* (*col* meaning milpa in Yucatec Maya) was responsible for allocating milpa sites, though this "may have been a title held by one of the two ordinary alcaldes elected each year rather than a separate office" (Farriss 1984: 273). The ability to control and allocate land and to settle disputes, many of which may have derived from questions of access to this essential resource, was an important aspect of the alcalde's power. The principle of rotation in office, which possibly occurred among the pre-Columbian *batab* lineages, was part of the finely graded system of the *cabildo*, so that individuals could "move up the political ladder and . . . fill the higher posts of alcalde before starting again at the bottom" (Farriss 1984: 345).

The Spanish were active in the Belize area for more than a century before the British arrived. Cortés may have passed through the southwestern corner of what is now Belize in 1525, when there were scattered settlements of Manche Chol Maya in that area. These were later forcibly removed by the Spanish to the Guatemalan highlands when Spain "pacified" the region in the seventeenth century. The chief Spanish incursions into Belize came from Yucatán, and they encountered stiff resistance in the sixteenth and seventeenth centuries from the Maya provinces of Chetumal, the capital of which was located near present-day Corozal Town, and Dzuluinicob, the political centre of which was probably

129

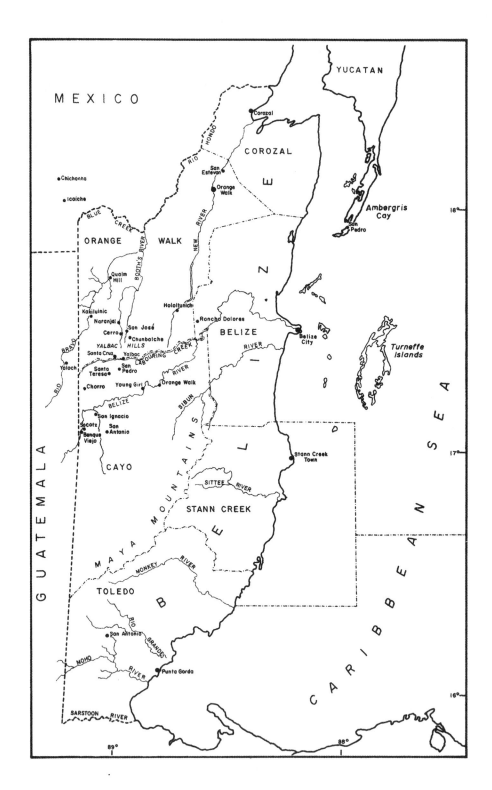

MEXICO

YUCATAN

COROZAL

Corozal

San Estevan

Orange Walk

Ambergris Cay

San Pedro

18°

Chichanha

Icaiche

BLUE CREEK

ORANGE WALK

Qualm Hill

BOOTH'S RIVER

NEW RIVER

RIO HONDO

Kaxiluinic

Naranjal

Cerro

San José

Chunbalche

YALBAC HILLS

Hololtunich

Rancho Dolores

BELIZE

Santa Cruz

Yalbac

LABOURING CREEK

BELIZE RIVER

Santa Teresa

San Pedro

RIO BRAVO

Yaloch

Chorro

Young Girl

Orange Walk

Belize City

Turneffe Islands

BELIZE RIVER

San Ignacio

Socotz

San Antonio

Benque Viejo

CAYO

MAYA MOUNTAINS

SIBUN

SITTEE RIVER

Stann Creek Town

17°

STANN CREEK

GUATEMALA

MONKEY RIVER

TOLEDO

San Antonio

RIO GRANDE

Punta Gorda

MOHO RIVER

SARSTOON RIVER

CARIBBEAN SEA

16°

89°

88°

130

Tipú on the Macal River. The Spanish *entradas* resulted in the usual devastating epidemics and the dispersal of much of the surviving population (Jones 1984). Nevertheless, there were still Maya in the Belize area throughout the seventeenth and eighteenth centuries.

For the first century after the arrival of the British, the Maya in the west of present-day Belize were relatively unaffected by British logwood-cutting operations near the coast, and they continued to live in small villages or homesteads throughout the area. When the British penetrated farther inland in search of mahogany late in the eighteenth and early in the nineteenth centuries, these Maya settlements were more seriously affected. The British, whose sole concern was then the extraction of timber, perceived the Maya's swidden agriculture as a threat to the forest, while the Maya doubtless viewed British expansionism as a threat to their territory and their independence. The result was frequent skirmishes along the frontier of British woodcutting for several decades, but, despite their spirited resistance, the Maya were forced back into the forests of the interior. The resurgence of the Maya of Yucatán that began in 1847 was paralleled by a revival of anticolonial activity among the Maya in Belize. In the second half of the nineteenth century, as the British consolidated their colony in Belize, they evolved new policies towards the Maya. This paper will describe and account for these policies, with special reference to the institution of the alcalde and the development of reservations.

The persistence of alcaldes in Belize to the present day shows that, through all the changes brought about during the colonial period, there are important continuities with Maya culture of the sixteenth and seventeenth centuries, and possibly even earlier. The dialectic of colonization and resistance in nineteenth century Belize resulted in the unusual adoption of an institution with Maya and Spanish roots into the British colonial system of local government, an institution that enabled the Maya to preserve a degree of autonomy in the colonial society.

II

In the 1830s and 1840s, the idea of "Trusteeship" over native peoples was powerful in the British Colonial Office, but there was some debate about its implementation. Lord Glenelg, who was Secretary of State for the Colonies from 1835 to 1839, and Sir James Stephen, the Permanent Under-Secretary of State for the Colonies between 1835 and 1847, were both officials in the Church Missionary Society and it was the missionary societies that supported the progress of Christianization as a keystone of Trusteeship. In 1836, the Aborigines Protection Society was formed and a Parliamentary Committee was established soon afterwards to formulate measures to secure justice, protection, civilization, and christianization for native peoples in British colonies. Whereas the missionaries concluded "that Europeans had no *raison d'être* among aboriginals except to christianize them" (Menezes 1977: 14), the Committee recommended a separatist policy. This debate about British policy towards native peoples continued in the middle of the nineteenth century, not only because there were differences of opinion in Britain, but also because such policies were experiencing a variety of pressures, the balance and outcome of which varied with particular local circumstances from one colony to another.

The demands of colonial settlers and the resistance of indigenous peoples constituted a dialectic which the Colonial Office tried to reconcile in terms of broad Christian and humanitarian principles along with a concern for the imperial interests and, not least, a need to keep within the limits of expenditure permitted by the Treasury. The result was often a series of pragmatic policies, or "rules of thumb," in which colonial interest and principles had to come to terms with indigenous customs and institutions. The most difficult position faced by the Colonial Office was when it had to curb the British settlers who were forcibly depriving native peoples of their lands, while at the same time helping the settlers to subjugate the natives whose resistance was thus provoked. In Natal and New Zealand, for example, in the 1840s and 1850s, the colonial settlers wanted imperial military assistance, along with a free hand to put down the natives and take their land. In British Guiana, where there was no need to grab land from the Indians, who stayed in the vast hinterland away from the coastal estates, and where there was a steady influx of immigrant indentured labourers after 1855, there were few clashes between the colonists and the indigenous people (Menezes 1977). Somewhere between these two extremes lay Belize, where colonial policy towards the Maya evolved in a pragmatic fashion. Before analyzing and accounting for the alcaldes and reservations, it is first necessary to summarize the sequence of events that provide the historical context for this evolving British policy.

A series of raids on British mahogany camps in 1847 and 1848, signalled the recommencement of hostilities between the British and those whom they called the "wild Indians." Events then taking place in Yucatán profoundly influenced the pattern of Maya settlement and the nature of their relations with the British in the west and north of Belize. Mexican control of Yucatán was as tenuous in the nineteenth century as Spanish control had been in the eighteenth century. In their numerous villages in this vast, inaccessible area, the Maya continued to resist conquest and assimilation in a series of "chiefdoms" that conformed to the centralized clusters of traditional Maya culture and political structure. A subgroup of the factious Chichanha Maya moved south to Belize in the 1850s, bringing this political system with them (Jones 1977). When the Santa Cruz burned Chichanhá in 1860, the surviving villagers, under Luciano Tzuc, moved to a new site nearer the border, at Santa Clara de Icaiché. Those who had previously moved into Belize, under the leadership of Juan Can and Asunción Ek, moved further south to the Yalbac Hills area, away from Tzuc who seemed eager to reestablish his authority over them.

Ek's group was not the only group of Maya to come to Belize in the turbulent years of the *Guerra de Castas*. From a small settlement consisting of about ten thousand people, mostly former slaves, the colony had expanded by 1861 to 25,635, some 4,675 of whom were said to be "pure Indians" and another 4,340 mixed, with the "Indian predominant."[1] But these various Indians were disunited, as was generally the case at this time. One of the groups that was most influential on British policy in Belize was a group of Icaiché Maya, led, since the death of Tzuc in 1864, by Marcos Canul. Between 1866, when he led a raid on a British mahogany camp at Qualm Hill on the Rio Bravo, and 1872, when he died of wounds received during an attack on Orange Walk, New River, Marcos Canul showed little respect for British authority and was considered a serious threat by the timber companies and the colonial administration.

Canul's was the last serious attack on the colony. Relations between the Icaiché and the British improved, but were still uneasy over the next few years. Rafael Chan, who had replaced Canul as the Icaiché chief, was seen by the British as a "peace-maker," but in 1877 it was reported that the Maya of San José and Chunbalché had "a defiant and threatening attitude."[2] Chan was succeeded by General Santiago Pech who, in 1882, declared his willingness to respect the boundaries claimed by the British. By a treaty signed in 1893 the governments of Mexico and Great Britain reached a mutual agreement concerning the "pacification" of the Maya on their common border. It now remains to be seen how the British colonial authorities developed the means of "pacifying" the Maya who had settled in Belize.

III

Soon after Ek's group of Maya moved from Chichanha into Belize, while Tzuc continued his "exactions and threats"[3] on the woodcutters, and while thousands of refugees from the *Guerra de Castas* were settling in uneasy proximity in the Northern District, the colonial administration produced "An Act to provide for the more speedy administration of justice in the rural districts."[4] In January, 1858, Superintendent Seymour addressed the Legislative Assembly:

> a Bill will be laid before you to legalize and define the position of the Alcalde in our several villages. You are aware that many congregations of houses and huts have sprung up, and are still springing up, at wide spread intervals over the country. In such cases, where the inhabitants are of Yucatecan or Indian race, and

133

accustomed to Spanish polity, my predecessors have allowed the people to elect and present to them certain individuals for appointment to a vague and indeterminate authority, with the title of Alcalde. The office is as unknown to our law as the designation is to our language, so I need hardly say that these supposed officers of justice have exposed themselves to an action in every case where their decision has been enforced by personal restraint. But unquestionable benefit has been derived from the unpaid services of these gentlemen, and I think it will follow that if one be cast in damages, the others will refuse to act, so I shall lay before you a Bill to provide for the appointment of unpaid officers, to whom the title of Alcalde will be continued. On them may properly be conferred a considerable amount of the summary police and criminal jurisdiction, with which Justices of the Peace are invested, and also a certain amount of authority in civil cases of petty debt, extending at the same time to the Alcaldes considerable protection for errors of judgment, and indemnity for past acts. I propose that the Alcalde should, as now, be nominated by the people and appointed by the Superintendent, with a power of suspension held over him by the Head of the Executive. These village officials should possess considerable authority in cases of riot, petty assaults, and malicious injury to property; the power to apprehend and transmit in custody to Belize or Corosal, for examination and possible commitment, persons charged on oath with serious felonies or misdemeanors, which would require for their conviction the verdict of a jury. Further, I propose that a summary punishing power should be given, within limitations, in cases of larceny not exceeding twenty shillings, where the person charged may plead guilty, and elect to be punished by the Alcalde rather than take his trial before a higher Court.[5]

This address has been quoted at length, not only because it summarizes succinctly the terms of the "Alcalde Jurisdiction Act, 1858," but also because it states the rationale for the Act, as seen by the head of the colonial administration. Several points should be stressed. First, this is a very pragmatic, if not opportunistic, response to a situation in which the ability of the colonial administration to maintain order and justice in the rural areas was hopelessly stretched. The administration possessed neither the personnel nor the means of transport to be able to enforce the law in all the new remote communities throughout the colony, especially among the thousands of immigrants in the north and west. Second, Seymour acknowledges that the institution of alcalde is alien to the Anglo-Saxon legal system and he tries to relate it to the traditional British office of Justice of the Peace. The office of alcalde is, I believe, the only non-Anglo-Saxon institution to have been incorporated into the administrative system of colonial Belize. Third, Seymour makes it clear that the alcaldes were already functioning; they were being selected by their communities, where they were administering justice and maintaining order. Indeed, to avoid possible embarrassment, the Superintendent proposed, in effect, to make their official status retroactive by indemnifying them for past acts. Strictly speaking, of course, they had no authority to judge and punish people prior to 1858, and were thus acting illegally and were susceptible to suits for damages.

Fourth, and most interesting from the point of view of this paper, is the proposal to redefine and limit the basis of the alcalde's authority, in such a way that a traditional institution becomes adopted, with some significant changes, into the colonial bureaucracy. As Seymour states, the alcaldes were *elected by the people* and, though he thought their authority was "vague and indeterminate," the office, and its duties and responsibilities, was presumably well known in these communities. Though Seymour and the legislators may have thought that they were simply clarifying and bringing order to this office, they were actually imposing British authority and legal concepts upon an institution that had firm roots in local custom, thereby creating a potential basis for conflict. Henceforth, it was made clear, the people may nominate their alcaldes, but the Superintendent will appoint, and may suspend, them. As the Attorney General expressed it, in justifying the Act, "The 'Alcalde' . . . receives a Commission, and with the Commission, the obligation to perform those duties with authority which he had hitherto gone through without authority."[6] There must be no doubt where real authority lies in a colony, namely with the Crown's representative, and all lesser authorities may be derived only from his.

The colonial administration saw the Act as "an experimental measure . . . introduced by the Government not as the result of any theory of judicial polity but out of sheer necessity as the only means of encountering a great and increasing difficulty."[7] Faced with the pressing problem of maintaining a semblance of law and order among the thousands of refugees in the north and west, many of whom were still prepared to fight each other or were engaged in hostilities with people across the border, the colonial administration could hardly repudiate the existing alcaldes whose activities provided a "practical benefit"[8] to the colony. The British adopted the alcalde system because they recognized that it worked. The Attorney General saw the alcaldes as having, under the new Act, civil jurisdiction over minor matters, and "with respect to Criminal matters he is neither a Magistrate nor a Constable . . . but a 'tertium quid' partaking of the nature and having to perform some of the duties, of both."[9]

When the Act was passed, on 19 March 1858, some significant changes were made in the conception of the alcalde as described in Seymour's address. No mention was made of the people nominating their alcaldes. According to the Act, the alcalde was to be appointed by the Superintendent from among those whom he judged to be "fit and proper" persons.[10] The alcalde shall then appoint his deputy, also "subject to the approval of the Superintendent;" and the Superintendent retained the power "to remove either the Alcalde or his Deputy for inability or misbehavior."[11] Though the Act used the traditional title of alcalde, it was clearly not formalizing the existing system so much as it was transforming it into a local judicial institution within the colonial system. It was decided to call the place where the alcalde exercised his jurisdiction a "Court" because, "when it was once determined to confer the authority, it seemed better to invest the recipient, with such dignity as should command respect; it was moreover thought that if ever this Settlement is to become a place of much importance, in this Act, would be contained, the principles of a County Court system."[12]

The alcalde's jurisdiction extended to civil disputes where the debt or damage claimed did not exceed $15, or beyond that if the parties agreed. Proceedings could only be heard in the absence of one party if that party had been given "reasonable notice of the claim made" and of the hearing.[13] The alcalde's order, which was to be final and conclusive, for payment of debt or damages, would specify appropriate modes of payment.[14] The sum so ordered was to be recoverable by execution against goods and chattels, if need be, the sale of such goods and chattels taking place no sooner than seven days after seizure, on the authority of the alcalde.[15] If the party was known to have the means to pay the debt or damages, but such goods or chattels were not "discoverable within the district of the Court," the alcalde could order up to ten days imprisonment.[16]

In criminal matters, the alcalde was empowered to "determine all cases of riotous and disorderly conduct, common assaults, and malicious injury to property," when the damage did not exceed $15. Upon conviction, on the basis of the testimony of credible witnesses or confession, the court could punish with a fine of between $5 and $25, or in default thereof, by up to seven days imprisonment.[17] In all cases the alcalde could summon witnesses to be examined orally on oath and could require the production of documents.[18] He was to keep a record of the particulars of cases coming before him and of such penalties as may have been inflicted, and was to send this record, at least every six months, to the Summary Court at Belize Town.[19] The Act made provisions for prisons,[20] and for the registration of foreigners under the Foreigners' Registration Act, 1847.[21] In serious criminal cases the alcalde was "to transmit the party charged . . . to Belize or Corosal . . . together with the witnesses in support of such charge" in order that the appropriate magistrate could investigate such charge.[22] Finally, the Act established indemnity to officers, unless their actions were willful and malicious.[23]

No indication was given by this Act regarding the law which was to be applied by the alcaldes. If, as is implied, they were to apply the common law and statute law of the colony, as colonial judicial officers, this may conflict with the customary principles and procedures of the Maya in the villages. In fact, British policy on this matter, as on the question of the selection and nomination of alcaldes, was sometimes unclear and changed from time to time. Nevertheless, despite these problems and potential conflicts, efforts were soon made to implement the Act.

On 3 May 1858, Superintendent Seymour reported that he had called at San Pedro, where "the Alcalde applied to me for instructions" concerning appropriate action vis-a-vis Mexican troops who "were immediately expected."[24]

The prevalence of frontier lawlessness and the problems of implementing the Alcalde Act were apparent in 1860, when acting-Superintendent Price reported some "atrocious murders committed by some 'Wild' Indians" near Labouring Creek and that one of the perpetrators had been lynched. "There was no local force disposable for the necessary prosecution of the enquiry and arrest of the offenders, that the Alcalde, Mr. Swasey, had exercised neither authority nor zeal in the affair, and that the inhabitants of the surrounding country, were in a state of considerable apprehension."[25] In this instance, the alcalde was the owner of a mahogany bank at Yalbac and, as he had only a Spanish copy of the Alcalde Act, which he could not understand, he was "wholly ignorant of the extent of the powers vested in him by the Act." Price took six days to reach Yalbac where, instead of dismissing Swasey from the office of alcalde, as was his first impulse, he cautioned him and made him swear to perform his duty.[26] It transpired that Juan Can, the alcalde of Santa Cruz, who spoke only Maya, had brought the perpetrators of the murder to Swasey "who was not prepared to act," so Can deported the suspects to Chichanhá for trial. Price pointed out that the settlement's entire police force consisted of 25 men (19 in Belize Town and 6 in Corozal), with none in the interior. His response to the lawlessness was therefore to try to expand the police force: "I shall endeavour, as an 'ad interim' measure, to excite the owners of mahogany works to recommend a fit person, as Alcalde, at every work, who shall have under his orders some 3 or 4 Special Constables.... What is especially required is the circulation throughout the country of a Mounted Constabulary."[27] His intention to create a greater police force and a network of alcaldes at every mahogany work, out of the British and Creole population rather than the Maya and Yucatecan population, indicated a major shift from the orientation of the Alcalde Act. Price himself seemed to recognize the danger of such direct policing by one racial-ethnic segment over another when he "took care to warn the assembled Creoles, that any act of oppression on the Indians would be severely punished."[28]

The problem for the British was not just that of having enough police. Many of the Maya alcaldes could speak only Maya, and most of the British and Creole mahogany cutters could not, though perhaps some of both groups could confer with each other in a little Spanish. How could Juan Can and Swasey have cooperated effectively in dealing with the murder suspects when they could not communicate with each other? And how could English-speaking, Creole alcaldes and constables, appointed by the Superintendent, administer justice among the Maya, without provoking real fears of oppression? In 1862, Seymour sent Edward L. Rhys as a commissioner to appoint alcaldes in the various villages of western Belize that were said to be under the control of Asunción Ek at San Pedro. The British recognized Ek as *comandante*, or chief authority, over all the southern Chichanha settlements, and Rhys presented alcaldes in the villages under his jurisdiction with commissions and staffs of office.[29] In so doing, it is obvious that the British commissioner was simply recognizing the authority of Maya alcaldes, who were already functioning within a traditional political structure.

Ek and his people maintained friendly relations with the British authorities for a few years, perhaps in order to obtain munitions to guard against interference from Tzuc at Icaiché. Ek was expected "to catch all runaways accused of murder or escape from the Belize gaol gang. To respect the mahogany trees. To keep the peace, and to punish Indians who ill treated women or committed theft."[30] But this first attempt at a more indirect rule, using Maya authorities rather than Creole police as Price had advocated, broke down in 1866. Factionalism emerged among the San Pedro leaders, partly over the issue of relations with mahogany gangs in the vicinity (Jones 1977: 149). A hasty march on San Pedro by British troops actually precipitated the very realliance between Ek's Maya and those of Icaiché that it had been intended to prevent. The Maya of the Yalbac Hills, feeling they had somehow earned the disapproval of the British, turned to Marcos Canul for support. Ek, who was perhaps seen as too friendly towards the British, was replaced as San Pedro's alcalde by Santiago Pech, who was more aligned with Icaiché. In December, the alcaldes of several villages around San Pedro turned up with their men to serve under Canul and his second-in-command, Rafael Chan. These combined forces routed 446 British troops outside San Pedro after a brief battle on December 21, 1866. What is particularly interesting for the purpose of this paper is that the various alcaldes of these Maya villages, in this confrontational situation, ignored the oaths of allegiance which they had presumably made to the commissioner. As traditional Maya political leaders, they joined the rebels against the British.

IV

In the late 1860s and 1870s, following a decline in the timber trade and a rising interest in agriculture, the colonial officials in Belize began to think of the Maya and Mestizo immigrants as a potential source of labour for plantations. In this changing context, the colonial authorities decided that the Maya should not own land. Instead, when Maya villages were located on Crown reserves, the alcaldes could allocate plots of land by permits, renewable annually. This land policy was to apply to the Garifuna, known to the British as "Charibs," as well as the Maya. Apart from a few instances, however, this policy of "native reservations" was not really implemented, and in the last years of the century it was virtually abandoned.

Just after the western Maya villages were destroyed in 1867, Lieutenant-Governor Austin issued the regulation that "No Indian will be at liberty to reside upon or occupy, or cultivate any land without previous payment or engagement to payment whether to the Crown or the owner of the land."[31] Austin's successor, Lieutenant-Governor Longden, addressed the issue of Maya land rights in his "General Report on the Land Question" in 1868:

> There are upon the Sibun River some villages inhabited by Indians and until last year there were similar villages in the Western district, San Pedro, Santa Cruz, Chambulche, San José, Naranjal. Several of these villages are situate upon the lands claimed either by the British Honduras Company or Messrs Young Toledo and Company, but whenever they are situate on Crown Lands I think the villages and a sufficient surrounding space should be reserved *in the hands of the Crown* for the use of the Indians,—no marketable titles being issued to enable them to dispose of such lands,—but the land being divided amongst them from time to time by the alcalde or chief man amongst them.[32]

Whereas the largest landowners in the colony had obtained firm titles to their vast estates only a few years before (Bolland and Shoman 1977: 72-77), the Maya were not allowed to own land but could only rent it or live on reservations. This discriminatory colonial policy coincided with some major changes in the political economy of Belize. In the context of a drastic decline in the volume and value of the logwood and mahogany exported, agriculture was seen for the first time as a serious alternative economic basis. After the Yucatecan refugees had demonstrated the agricultural potential of the land, and particularly after they first exported sugar in 1857, some big landowners who were experiencing difficulties with forest products looked to the plantation production of sugar. In the 1860s, when sugar estates were expanding in the north (while the population of that region declined from 13,547 in 1861 to 10,552 in 1871)[33], the question of a labour supply became a great concern. In 1864 Lieutenant-Governor Austin speculated about the 4,000 "pure Indians" and 6,700 "Mixed" Yucatecans who lived in the Rio Hondo-New River region as a source of labour.[34] The Maya were not to be allowed to own the land on which they situated their villages and *milpas*, because it would make them too independent.

It is in this context, in which an attempt was being made to promote plantation development for which an abundant supply of cheap labour was required, that the Crown Lands Ordinance of 1872 must be understood. A handful of large landowners held most of the privately-owned land in the colony and land prices remained high from the 1860s to the end of the century. Such Crown lands as were left after the landowners had made their vast claims were mostly peripheral and of poor quality, in the Maya Mountains region of the south.[35] By the Crown Lands Ordinance, lands already occupied by the Maya and Garifuna settlements were "reserved to them under the protectorate of the Crown,"[36] but, as Longden had recommended in 1868, they were not allowed to have titles to such land. The Act decreed that

> ...there shall be issued to the Indians or Charibs, through their Alcaldes or Headmen, or, if there be no Alcaldes or Headmen, then through the nearest Paid Magistrate, permits to occupy particularly defined portions of such lands during pleasure... renewable from year to year; and any or all of them may be cancelled by the direction of the Lieutenant Governor in the event of the vacation of the land by the holder or holders, or of his or their wilful neglect to renew the permit to occupy the same: Provided always, that such Crown Land held upon such permits shall not be transferable by sale, lease, or otherwise, without the written consent of the Colonial Secretary...provided however, that nothing, hereinbefore contained shall be construed to prevent the widow, or child, or next of kin, of any deceased holder of such permit as aforesaid at the time of his decease, from continuing to occupy such portion of land on the usual terms, or from obtaining a renewal of the permit from year to year.[37]

A register of such permits should be kept and the alcalde, headman, or magistrate should report the decease of a permit holder, the vacation of any portion of such reserved Crown land, or any attempt to fraudulently dispose of the same. The expense of the survey of such lands was to be borne by the public revenue. Another section of the ordinance was directed against squatting, of which Lieutenant-Governor Cairns said, "the evil is great, and its treatment must be severe."[38] Since most of the Maya villages were situated on lands held by the great landowners, this ordinance made Maya tenure more insecure and increased their dependency on the government.

Though the intent of the colonial policy was to make the Maya more dependent upon the government and more available as a wage-labour force, it was not too effective because, as in the case of the Alcalde Act, it was easier to pass a law in Belize Town than it was to implement it in the remote parts of the colony. This becomes apparent in the case of the communities of Benque Viejo and Succotz, on the Western Branch of the Belize River. These villages were settled, largely by refugees from Yucatán who first sojourned in northeastern Petén, in the mid-1860s (Mazzarelli 1972). Burned by raiders from Holmul in the Petén "some time before"[39] 1867, Benque Viejo and Succotz were soon reestablished. John Samuel August, a foreman for the mahogany firm of Young, Toledo and Company, moved from Duck Run to Benque Viejo in 1867 and, presumably "because of the opportunities for employment and for selling produce" (Jones 1977: 168), Maya continued to migrate to these villages from the Petén. In 1868, a faction from Yaloch on the Rio Holmul, led by Jose Justo Chan, moved to Benque Viejo, and in 1875 one Felipe Novelo settled there and "commenced a small sugar plantation and distilling."[40] Initially, he obtained a "license from an Indian Commandant," namely Asunción Ek, "but never paid for it; subsequently finding he was on English territory, he paid rent to the Colonial Treasury and has so continued."[41] When General Pech of the Icaiché claimed Benque Viejo as Mexican territory, Lieutenant-Governor Barlee advised Novelo "to take no notice of any further applications from General Pech."[42]

The Colonial Secretary, on a "journey across the unexplored portion of British Honduras," described Benque Viejo as an "Indian village," with Maya as its principal language and Chan its alcalde, in 1878. Along with Succotz, its population was "increasing rapidly" (Fowler 1879:5). In 1882, Benque Viejo was described as more "Spanish" than Maya in culture,[43] but Succotz has remained firmly Maya in identity to the present day.

In 1880, Barlee sought to incorporate these remote and semi-autonomous communities more firmly into the colonial scheme of things. He described Benque Viejo as a village with about 350 Indians and Succotz as having about 300 Indians:

> They are quiet and orderly and appreciate the advantages of English Law as compared with the unjust treatment they have received from Indian Rulers.
>
> Aware of this, and that they were mere squatters on Crown Lands, I communicated with the Alcaldes in these villages (Indians selected by me in that capacity) and pointed out to them the advantages of properly laying out these villages and locating each Indian on his own lot; where this was fairly understood, there was a general assent, and I ordered a Surveyor to proceed to these villages and mark them out in lots, avoiding interference with existing houses or lots, as much as practicable. The Surveyor has laid out 80 lots in "Benque Viejo" and 73 in "Soccott" [sic]; of these lots 68 were at once purchased in the former and 58 in the latter village, by existing occupants at two dollars; each lot averaged 100 x 50 feet and the majority of the purchasers have assumed the role of landed proprietors and commenced to fence in their lots. Each purchaser received a location ticket for his lot, numbered to agree with the plan of the village, and these location tickets will be duly registered. The total cost for survey was £40 and the sum already received amounts to £50 8 0.
>
> Irrespective of the money question, I believe that the effect of this step will be to induce many Indians to settle in the Colony, where they can obtain work at remunerative rates and that they will feel more sure as to their position and more independent of Indian Chiefs outside. The enterprise started by Mr. Lefebvre of planting coffee in this neighbourhood will probably be much furthered by these means.[44]

Barlee's action, which was approved by the Colonial Office, was consistent with the development of colonial policy in Belize. It would be interesting to know what the Maya thought about having to buy "location tickets" for plots that they had already occupied for more than a decade, but one can only speculate. Since ordinary Maya labourers received only $7 or $8 per month at this time, the cost of these tickets was quite significant. Perhaps they were glad to be "more independent of Indian Chiefs outside," but Barlee's goal was at the same time to make them more dependent on the colonial administration and available as labourers to local planters.

In 1884, the Colonial Secretary pointed out that a land ordinance passed in 1879 made no mention "of either Carib or Indian reserves, so that these natives are now subject to the same provisions as other people," and that Benque Viejo and Succotz were the only examples of places where land had been reserved for the Maya.[45] He was himself "strongly in favour of forming Carib and Indian reserves as a mere act of justice on the grounds of former recognitions of the claims of these natives."[46] Why had this change taken place? The answer seems to be not so much in terms of a change in colonial policy as in the fact that the existing policy regarding native land rights was impracticable.

In 1888, the surveyor general of Belize was still puzzling how to create Indian reserves and where they should be located. "There are as yet no reserves of land set apart for Indians in the Colony, although provision is made for such in the Crown Lands Ordinance 1886."[47] He proposed laying out Indian Reserves in three locations: between the two branches of the Belize River, to include Benque Viejo and Succotz (where he stated that the inhabitants had received "no regular grants nor strict legal title" for their town lots in 1880); a plot just east of New River mouth that was escheated to the Crown; and the area around San Antonio, a village in the south that had recently been settled by Kekchi Maya from Guatemala. It was subsequently pointed out that the proposed northern plot, the only available piece of Crown land in that region, was largely swamp and totally unfit for agriculture.[48] The point is simply that the thousands of Maya who came into the north and west of Belize in the 1850s and 1860s came into an area that, though largely uninhabited, was entirely claimed by the handful of large landowners who monopolized the private lands of the colony. Apart from the town plots of Benque Viejo and Succotz, and a little land in the vicinity, and the area of land around San Antonio in the remote south, the Crown possessed little land that was suitable for Indian reserves in those areas where the Maya lived.

At the end of the nineteenth century the whole attempt to create Indian reserves was reevaluated, not on a basis of new principles but, pragmatically, in the realization that the old policy had never really worked. The acting District Commissioner of Cayo reported on the reserves in his district in 1895: "The Indian Reserves of Benque Viejo and Succotz, especially Benque Viejo, are only so by name for the inhabitants chiefly consist of Spaniards from Petén . . . yet they are termed Indian Reserves and on that ground no British subject is permitted to carry on business there . . . . It would be better in every respect to open the towns of Benque Viejo and Succotz to British subjects."[49] He pointed out that the "Indians make their milpas indiscriminately all over Crown

Lands.... Yet it is most desirable that there should be allotted a certain portion of land marked out for the purpose of making these milpas."[50] Commenting on this report, Sweet-Escott wrote:

> The present policy of the Government lies in the abolition of the Reserves System...
>
> I have been unable to satisfy myself that any useful purpose has been served by the establishment of Carib and Indian Reserves, and, when townships or villages are established throughout the Colony, I think it will be found a wiser policy to throw open lots in such settlements to all comers irrespective of colour or nationality, to exact a fair rent for each lot, or to sell it by auction to any purchaser, and to require that all persons desiring to cultivate milpas on Crown Lands should apply in the usual way for the lease of the land in question.[51]

While the idea of reserves was being abandoned in the west, they were soon established in the south. In 1897, the District Commissioner of Toledo reported that, "The village of San Antonio was surveyed during the year and a parcel of land measuring two miles square was apportioned to the Indian Settlers, on the condition of payment of an Annual Rental of $1.00 from each family, and the upkeep and maintenance of the road, and its bridges from the Toledo Settlement to the Village."[52] Such rents, amounting to $108.00, were not insignificant to a largely subsistence-oriented community, and the gratuitous road work and bridge building relieved the District Board of expense.[53]

Governor Wilson, acknowledging that his predecessor had promised a "Report on Indian Reserves," that was never received, asserted in 1897 that "the present system is not satisfactory and requires complete revision and amendment."[54] In 1904, it was reported that the Maya had asked the District Commissioner of Cayo in 1899 to be told "the limits of the Reserve, but no reply was made to this enquiry" and "up to the present no steps have been taken to mark out such reserves, or, apparently, to make any Rules governing the settlements."[55] Once again, it was acknowledged that something needed to be done, but what should be done was not clear.

> The present situation appears to require action, but it is essential that any steps taken should be in pursuance of a definite policy to be gradually developed and pushed forward to a conclusion. I regret that I do not feel able to make any recommendation which would possess the merit of being based on special knowledge of the characters and idiosyncrasies of the Indians.... If it is decided to at once attempt to change the system of granting Reserves to the Indians, which has been for so long in contemplation but has not been fully given effect to, it would not seem to be a proper time to mark out such reserves and give emphasis to a policy which is about to be abandoned. On the other hand the present position of affairs is not satisfactory, and I think that any change made

should be very gradual and should not do violence to the traditions of the people.[56]

In minutes attached to this despatch, officials of the Colonial Office approved the idea that reserves for the inhabitants of Benque Viejo and Succotz should be roughly demarcated and that "the question of changing the system should await further enquiries and consultations with the Indians. The inhabitants of those two villages should however be warned that the marking out of a Reserve for them is only intended as an interim measure... and gives them no right to the enjoyment of the land in perpetuity."[57] The idea that the Maya should be consulted and their traditions taken into account was admirable, if belated. However, this correspondence reveals the endless dithering and indecisiveness on the part of the administrators in Belize and officials in London. The "interim measures" underline the fact that there was no "definite policy" regarding Indian reserves by the end of the nineteenth century.

In the absence of clear principles upon which any such policy could be articulated, a series of expedient actions by the colonial authorities had left the majority of the Maya without a secure system of land tenure. Reserves were maintained only in Toledo District; elsewhere most Maya were tenants or squatters. The British sugar plantations in Corozal District closed down by the end of the century and most of the American planters in Toledo left the colony. The Maya, who for a while had become a part-time plantation proletariat, reverted to small-scale food production, largely for subsistence, until a revival of mahogany and logwood extraction and the development of the chicle industry created a new demand for their labour in the early twentieth century (Jones 1971: 11-13).

V

Whereas the attempt to establish and implement a colonial policy on Maya land rights in the form of reserves on Crown land fell apart in the last decades of the nineteenth century, a reevaluation and renewal of the alcalde system was successfully undertaken in the same period. Although, as noted above, some alcaldes were given commissions in accordance with the Act of 1858, by 1884 the statutory scheme had broken down. Nevertheless, the traditional system, which existed prior to the Act, was functioning in many communities. On the one hand, it may be that the way in which alcaldes were operating within the traditional system was seen by the colonial authorities to be incompatible with their role, as defined by the Act, in the colonial system. The rebellious actions of the alcaldes in the Yalbac Hills region in 1866 was a serious blow to the colonial scheme. On the other hand, it appears that, in some instances, the colonial administration found it convenient to simply acknowledge an existing state of affairs over which it had little real control, as when Lieutenant-Governor Barlee referred to Benque Viejo in 1879 as an Indian village "presided over by an Alcalde recognized by this Government."[58] A few months later, Barlee was claiming that he "selected" the alcaldes in Benque Viejo and Succotz.[59]

A serious reevaluation of the alcalde system was undertaken by the colonial authorities, with the result that it was revised and renewed. Responsibility for the reevaluation may be laid with Henry Fowler, the Colonial Secretary who administered the colony in 1883 and 1884. He obtained reports from the District Magistrates and wrote a series of lengthy memoranda on the subject to the Colonial Office. He even wrote an articulate explanation of his new Indian policy.

At the end of 1883, the acting district magistrate of Cayo, the western district, reported on the various Maya villages and their judicial staff. Benque Viejo had two alcaldes and five special constables, along with a small court house and a lock-up; Chorro had two alcaldes and one volunteer constable and was constructing a court house and prison; San Antonio had one alcalde; Santa Cruz had one alcalde and one volunteer constable; San Francisco had two alcaldes, as did San José; San Pedro had two alcaldes and one volunteer constable, and was constructing a court house and lock-up; and Succotz had two alcaldes and two volunteer constables, along with a court house and lock-up. "The payment of salaries to the Alcaldes of the various villages causes great satisfaction, and the anticipation of a staff of office, and a flag to be hoisted before the Alcalde's house on Sundays and fiesta days makes them feel that they will not be inferior in display to their neighbours in the Republics. Without these advantages it would be difficult to exact any service from the Alcaldes, or to support their authority."[60] The system appeared to be working well, though there was some concern about how "to exact from them a strict adherence to the legal forms of the Colony" and "to draw them from their old traditions, and little by little to teach them our more exact methods of justice." There was also some anxiety about the fact that the constables, whose job it was "to restrain the inhabitants of their native villages," were elected "in accordance with the wish of the people." On the whole, however, the Maya were said to "have experienced the promised advantages of British Rule, and are learning submission to the exactions of its legal restraints."[61] This was a far cry from the situation just seventeen years earlier, when the Maya in this frontier region, led by the alcaldes, were in armed rebellion against British rule.

One of the costs of the rebellion for the Maya was the attempt by the colonial administration to rule them directly, using magistrates and Creole policemen. As Fowler expressed it, "Leaving them to their own devices, or attempting to govern them directly by means of Magistrates and negro policemen has not worked satisfactorily.... The mutual cynical feelings existing between the Indians and negro policemen render the exercise of this [direct]

145

jurisdiction expensive, inefficient, discordant, and of little avail in the endeavor to bring the Indians and Caribs under the favourable influences of the Government."[62] Quite apart from the issue of reducing expenses by keeping the colonial police force and judicial establishment small, Fowler was developing a rationale for indirect rule in 1884. He considered the Alcalde Act of 1858 to be "inoperative," and hence that the District Magistrates were "the only recognized authority" (this view does not appear strictly valid, as the 1858 Act was not repealed by the District Magistrates Ordinance, No. 8,1881). He voiced the opinion, shared by the Executive Council, that "the jurisdiction of the Alcaldes should continue to be of a paternal character administered according to native custom under the supervision of the District Magistrates, whose jurisdiction would remain intact to be appealed to and exercised when necessary."[63]

Among the reasons Fowler offered for a renewal of the alcalde system were the following:

> That the Government will have a responsible agent in each native village, with magisterial and police supervision provided at a cheap rate.
>
> That the natives would appreciate a jurisdiction exercised over them according to their native customs....
>
> That the natives can by the proposed means be brought under the legitimate influence and control of this Government and be converted from passive and indifferent subjects into loyal and willing settlers.[64]

In 1887, Fowler expressed most clearly the principle on which the new policy of indirect rule through alcaldes was based, namely "the principle, that the best way to manage the natives was through their own Chiefs and according to their own customs subject to supervision by an officer of the Government."[65] This principle, he explained; was based on his experience with natives in Vancouver Island, British Columbia, and in the Gambia and Lagos. Nevertheless, from what he went on to say, it is apparent that the new policy was also based on expediency, as the colonial administration really had no practicable alternative to indirect rule.

> The previous policy appears to have been to recognize only English ways and laws in the Colony and to place the natives under police control. This was impracticable, for the Indians were scattered about in small villages, the access to which was most difficult, so that no control was really exercised over them. Besides which, the negro constable...was not fitted nor did he attempt to influence them in any way beyond trying to frighten them and getting all he could out of them.... Financial difficulties prevented this policy being efficiently carried out, so that the Indians had drifted away from the influences of this Government and fallen under those of Indian chiefs living outside the Colony.

Spasmodic efforts to exercise jurisdiction were occasionally made, and the presence of the imperial Troops in the Colony was relied on to maintain this attitude and system . . . .

This inclined them to move into the forest away from any direct control and they relied on themselves and their own customs for the management of their own affairs, and preferred a life of seclusion . . . . Instead of a good understanding being arrived at, mistrust and ill feelings were engendered giving rise to threats and scares which have entailed a heavy expense on the Colony for some years past.[66]

The argument that the new policy of indirect rule would be cheaper no doubt carried considerable weight at the Colonial Office, where Treasury officials exercised great influence. At any rate, this "conciliatory policy" was approved, with the opinion being officially expressed that "the Indians should by all means be encouraged to feel themselves part of the colony."[67] The implementation of this new policy would not be without its own problems, however. To the extent the alcaldes became, and were seen to become, a part of the colonial system of government, their legitimacy as representatives of the indigenous people would tend to become eroded, as occurred throughout Spanish America. Indeed, the phenomenon of role conflict experienced by such "middlemen" is widespread in colonial polities and administrative systems.

It remains to be seen by what means and procedures the revised policy was implemented. Following Spanish customs and practices, alcaldes, and in some cases constables, were to be elected by the inhabitants of each village annually on 8 December, a traditional fiesta day, subject to the approval of the district magistrate who would ensure that they received their staffs of office and their stipends. In the event that one alcalde was succeeding another, the new alcalde was to receive the staff from his predecessor on the first day of the ensuing year, as an emblem of his due appointment and authority. The stipends of alcaldes and constables were to be $5 and $2 a month, respectively, or, in the case of more important villages or meritorious services, up to $10 and $5. (Fowler calculated that the saving effected by staffing 25 villages in this way, rather than by expanding the district police force, would be almost $500 a year,[68] a considerable sum.) According to a Colonial Office circular, the "alcaldes are not to be appointed under the Alcalde Act but are recognized officers of the Executive Government and the position of the district magistrate towards them is that of an agent of the Government, to whom an alcalde, as a subordinate officer, was to refer."[69] Since the alcaldes were defined as officers of the government, though elected by the villagers, they could be dismissed by the government on the recommendation of the district magistrate, presumably on such grounds as misconduct. One anomaly arising from this situation was resolved in 1886 by a single section Act which provided that no person was deemed to be disqualified from the office of alcalde by reason of his being an alien.[70] This was consonant with the terms of the 1884 circular which regarded the alcalde as an executive officer, from which status aliens were usually barred.

The Colonial Office circular gave no indication of the classes of case, civil or criminal, which could be heard by alcaldes, except to say that any "serious case" should be reported to the district magistrate for him to deal with. Jurisdiction may be assumed to have covered, and be limited to, all the minor civil and criminal matters defined in the 1858 Act, with the acquiescence of the district magistrate.[71] According to a law passed in 1871, presumably still extant, the alcaldes were bound to act as census enumerators in their respective districts.[72] Another duty expected of the alcaldes, as in the Spanish system, was to organize *fajina* labour. Each male inhabitant was expected to give twelve days' labour per annum (or to pay fifty cents for each nine-hour day he failed to work) towards the upkeep of public buildings, roads, and bridges. This was meant to be an obligation on the Indians "for the privilege of making their milpas on crown lands",[73] but it was not taken very seriously. The acting Commissioner of Cayo district reported on Benque Viejo and Succotz: "The Alcaldes elected by the people do not enforce the fagina [sic] labour but generally make excuses for their non-performance, and it is in their interest to do so, as it must be a recognized fact that the enforcing of such labour would make them unpopular among the people."[74] This suggests that the fact that alcaldes were elected, and not appointed by the colonial authorities, was important to the villagers who retained some control over their representatives. In any case, it is doubtful how much practical power and influence the alcaldes really possessed, except in their ability to allot lands and settle disputes.

In the late nineteenth century, alcaldes were elected in the various villages (though by what customary procedure is unknown), and the results were announced in the *Government Gazette* by the Colonial Secretary, saying that the Governor had been pleased to approve or confirm the following elections. I found no instance of an election being disapproved, and only two cases where the alcalde was appointed rather than elected, namely in the Mestizo communities of San Pedro, Ambergris Cay in 1884, and Rancho Dolores, Orange Walk, in 1892.[75] Of the twenty-seven villages in which elections were recorded between 1885 and 1893,[76] fourteen were Maya communities, or villages that included a high proportion of Maya in their population. The remainder were Mestizo or Garifuna communities. Nine of the Maya communities were in the western district of Cayo, three were in the north (Corozal and Orange Walk), and two were in the south (Toledo).

It is hard to see any regular pattern among the names of the first and second alcaldes elected in these villages. In some cases individuals held office for many years in succession (Felipe Tun, for example, was the first alcalde of San Antonio, Cayo, every year between 1885 and 1893, and Juan Pedro Chi was his second alcalde from 1885 through 1891). Asunción Ek, who was a leader of the group of Chichanhá Maya that migrated south in the 1850s and settled in the Yalbac Hills, was still the first alcalde of San Pedro in 1889.[77] In other cases there was almost a regular annual turnover with new people in both offices (in Chorro, thirteen men shared the two offices over eight years). There were only eight instances of a second alcalde becoming a first alcalde, sometimes as a result of the death of the latter, but more often succeeding to the higher post after several years out of office. There is no known case of a man, having once been first alcalde, being elected as a second alcalde. This hierarchy of offices is much simpler than the political-religious hierarchy of traditional Maya communities (Nash 1970: 177; Farriss 1984: 234, 344-345). However, it appears to be the case, first, that it is not unusual, though far from common, for a second alcalde to succeed to the top position, and, second, that once a man has been first alcalde he would not take the lower office.

Another element of the alcalde system that synthesizes traditional and new elements is the symbols of office. It is not clear when the colonial authorities began to give the alcaldes staffs of office, but this is an old Spanish custom. The staff, of hard ziricote with a handsome silver head, was similar to those given by the Dutch to Indian "Captains" in Guiana, a practice that was continued there by the British (Menezes 1977: 118). At the time of the 1858 Act, it was mentioned that they were to receive only a "Commission" and that, by designating the place where the alcalde was to exercise his jurisdiction as a "Court," the office would gain dignity and respect.[78] The purpose of giving the alcaldes a staff of office, and also a flag, was to support their authority, and to tie it symbolically to the British colonial regime,[79] in a manner that was compatible with the Spanish colonial tradition to which the Maya were accustomed.

At the end of the nineteenth century some disputes surfaced concerning the colony's boundaries and the jurisdiction over alcaldes of the more remote Maya villages. In 1882 General Santiago Pech of Icaiché stated that "he had Alcaldes, appointed by him, stationed at Hololtonich, San José and San Pedro, and had always understood that his jurisdiction extended to those places."[80] Pech's successor, General Gabriel Tamay, continued to intervene in these villages, presumably because he refused to recognize the boundary the British were trying to draw through the forest, thus dividing Maya from Maya in an arbitrary manner. In 1886 Governor Goldsworthy asked Tamay to order the alcalde of Kaxiluinic, who considered his village to be in Mexican territory, to stop interfering with the British party which was surveying the western boundary.[81] When the acting Commissioner of Cayo visited Kaxiluinic in 1895, describing it as "a very dirty Indian village ... claimed by the Ycaiche Indians," he said that the alcalde kept close links with General Tamay. He also reported that the alcalde of San José had complained that Tamay was threatening them and "were in dread lest the soldiers would return," coming via Kaxiluinic. Tamay claimed jurisdiction over San José, and would apparently take whatever he required from

149

the villagers without giving payment. Failing to be reassured "that there was nothing to fear from the Ycaiche Indians as long as the British flag floated over their heads," they expressed the feeling that "they were not protected...and they did not wish to remain at San José." Asked if they would like to join Yalbac, San Pedro, and Santa Teresa "and make a town like Benque Viejo, the site of the proposed town to be selected by the Alcaldes," they readily agreed.[82] Nothing came of this proposal, however, and San José remained a village until 1936, when the people were removed by the Belize Estate and Produce Company, on whose lands it was situated (Thompson 1939: 4). Throughout the period under discussion the British tried to impose their control in a largely unexplored region of over 1,000 square kilometers in which the Maya were migrating back and forth over an ill-defined boundary. Finding themselves unable to police the Maya effectively by direct means, the British changed their policy to one of indirect rule, incorporating the alcaldes into their system of government. The alcaldes maintained a degree of autonomy in their villages, and the practice of elections was important in ensuring some community control, but the British eventually succeeded in enforcing a *pax Britannica* in the colony.

The alcalde system has continued to the present day. The "Alcaldes Ordinance" of 1913 amended Cap. 110 of the Consolidated Laws (1886), to the effect that any fines inflicted by the alcalde should be transmitted to his District Commissioner "to the credit of the village over which such Alcalde has jurisdiction" to be expended by the alcalde, with the approval of the District Commissioner, in village improvements.[83] In 1924, another ordinance amended the alcalde system and defined the manner of cases and penalties that came within the alcalde's jurisdiction.[84] An order-in-council made in 1939 implied that the Alcalde Jurisdiction Ordinance had not been applied, as it ordered that "the said ordinance *shall be put in force* in the districts and places described hereunder,"[85] almost all of which had at some time elected their alcaldes. This suggests that the alcaldes exercised their judicial function on a largely customary, traditional basis until the Alcalde Jurisdiction Ordinance was put in force in 1939. Shortly after, their jurisdiction was again modified,[86] but no indication was given of the actual law to be applied by alcaldes, which presumably remained customary to the communities themselves.

In 1952, almost a century after the first Alcalde Act, changes were made in the alcalde system, as part of a general revision of the colonial judicial structure. The 1952 ordinance defined Alcalde jurisdiction as part of the system of Inferior Courts and specified that the "civil jurisdiction of the court shall be exercised in accordance with the common law of the colony" and the "criminal jurisdiction of the court shall be exercised in accordance with the criminal law and practice of the colony."[87] While this shows that the alcaldes had become completely incorporated within the colonial judicial structure, it does imply by the phrase "common law of the colony" that the native customs, prevalent among the rural populations to whom the alcalde courts apply, are to be considered in civil cases, even if displaced in criminal matters by the criminal code and statutes. Today, alcalde courts continue to exercise both civil and criminal jurisdiction in accordance with the common law and criminal law and practice of Belize. The alcalde and his deputy are appointed by the Governor, who may remove them from office at any time. In addition to his judicial functions, the alcalde may be assigned various administrative duties.[88]

An examination of current regulations and procedures regarding alcaldes is beyond the scope of this paper, but it is important to understand not only that the alcalde remains an important official in local government, but also that Maya traditions have had a persistent influence on the definition and practice of this institution.

VI

When the British consolidated their Central American colony of Belize in the second half of the nineteenth century they were faced with the problem of incorporating the indigenous Maya into the colonial society. The policies they devised, more pragmatic than principled, were adapted from time to time according to what was practicable in the administration of a remote and generally unsurveyed frontier region. The British authorities attempted in the 1860s and 1870s to control the Maya directly, through a system of police and appointed alcaldes, and to confine them to rented land or reserves on Crown land. When this attempt proved impracticable, the colonial administration in the 1880s shifted its policy to one of indirect rule, through elected alcaldes, and largely abandoned the idea of granting reserves to the Indians.

The evolution of this Indian policy was, in part, influenced by general financial and humanitarian considerations then prevalent in the Colonial Office, but the tiny, poor settlement of Belize was not given much attention by the chief policy makers in London. More important in the evolution of this local policy were local considerations, namely the changes occurring in the colonial political economy and, in particular, the role of the Maya themselves. The decline in the mahogany trade and the beginnings of plantation agriculture caused the colonists to change their view of the Maya, from a threat to the timber reserves to a potential labour force. But when the hopes for plantation agriculture faded, the colonial authorities were more inclined to leave the Maya to get on with their traditional agriculture. This coincided with the abandonment of the Indian reserve policy and the shift toward indirect rule.

The role of the Maya in shaping British policy is important, though hard to assess. First, their military activities in the late 1860s had an impact on the colony's politics and resulted in a major constitutional change. The expense of administering the colony increased as a result of having to pay for military expeditions and garrisons against the Maya, at a time when the economy was severely depressed. Whereas the landowners resisted the taxation of land and favoured an increase on import duties, the merchants preferred the opposite. These conflicting interests produced a stalemate in the Legislative Assembly, which failed to authorize the raising of sufficient revenue. Unable to agree among themselves, but pressed by the need to raise additional revenue, the members of the Legislative Assembly "committed political suicide" (Gibbs 1883: 152), surrendering the privilege of self-government in return for greater security against the persistent Maya threat. The Assembly having abolished itself, the Crown Colony constitution was inaugurated in April 1871 (Bolland 1977: 191-192; Clegern 1967: 50-51).

Second, the Maya had an effect on the development of local government in the colony, not only by provoking the need to create rural administration in the 1850s, but also, specifically, through the institution of alcalde. Both the pre-Columbian *batab* and the Spanish colonial alcalde were military heads as well as judicial officers at the village level. That this dual function persisted in Belize is indicated by the action of alcaldes in the Yalbac Hills villages in 1866, and also by the fact that several alcaldes in Belize, such as Asunción Ek, were often referred to as *comandante* or *capitán*, in accordance with the hierarchy of Maya political-military organization. When the British authorities defined the duties of alcaldes within their colonial judicial system, this military function was, of course, excluded, though the alcaldes retained something of the role of constable as well as magistrate. What is perhaps even more important is that, by adopting the policy of indirect rule and accepting the procedure by which the villages elected their own alcaldes, the British conceded a degree of community control over people whom they themselves thought of as executive officers of government. This was a significant concession in a colonial polity, where control over the native population was a primary concern. Moreover, they also conceded that the alcaldes were to apply a combination of customary Maya law and statutory British colonial law. The laws that the alcaldes were to apply were left so unspecific that, although their jurisdiction was subject to the supervision of District Magistrates (later, commissioners), the alcaldes seem to have had considerable autonomy, at least in minor matters.

The dialectic of British colonization and Maya resistance in Belize resulted in the evolution of institutions and practices in the later nineteenth century that simultaneously incorporated the Maya into the colonial society while enabling them to retain a degree of integrity and autonomy. Whether the alcaldes have retained much of their Maya tradition in the twentieth century,[89] or whether they have become just an unusual, rather alien anomaly in an essentially Anglo-Saxon system of local government (Dobson 1973: 291-92; Grant 1967), is beyond the scope of this ethnohistorical paper. The study of the status, role, and function of present-day alcaldes requires a contemporary ethnography, but this analysis of the alcaldes in the late nineteenth century should contribute to our understanding of the peculiar institution and the place of the Maya in present-day Belize.

Notes

Research for this paper was carried out primarily during the summer of 1986 in the Public Records Office, London. I extend my gratitude to the John Ben Snow Memorial Trust, whose generous grant to the Native American Studies Program at Colgate University made this research possible. Previous research on which this paper is based was conducted at the Public Records Office and the British Library, and at the Belize Archives, supported by the Institute of Social and Economic Research, University of the West Indies, and by grants from the Research Council of Colgate University.

I have benefited from the advice of Grant Jones, Assad Shoman, and Gary Urton, who criticized an earlier version of this paper. I thank them for their comments and absolve them from any responsibility for the final product.

01. Acting Superintendent Price to Governor Darling, 1 July 1861, CO 123/105.

02. Captain Charles Mitchell to Governor Sir William Grey, 15 February 1877, CO 123/160.

03. Superintendent William Stevenson to Percy Doyle, 16 October 1856, CO 123/93.

04. 21 Vic. c. 13, 1858, CO 125/1.

05. Address by Superintendent Frederick Seymour, 21 January 1858, Votes of the Second Legislative Assembly, CO 126/3.

06. Letter from Henry John Bull, 1 April 1858, CO 123/96.

07. Ibid.

08. Ibid.

09. Ibid.

10. 21 Vic. c. 13, 1858, S 5, CO 125/1.

11. Ibid., S 5.

12. Letter from Bull, 1 April 1858, CO 123/96.

13. 21 Vic. c. 13, 1858, S 6, CO 125/1.

14. Ibid., S 7.

15. Ibid., S 8.

16. Ibid., S 9.

17. Ibid., S 10.

18. Ibid., S 14.

19. Ibid., S 15.

20. Ibid., S 11-13.

21. Ibid., S 16-17.

22. Ibid., S 18.

23. Ibid., S 19.

24. Seymour to Darling, 3 May 1858, CO 123/96.

25. Price to Darling, 3 May 1860, CO 123/101.

26. Ibid.

27. Ibid.

28. Ibid.

29. Edward L. Rhys to Seymour, 3 Nov. 1862, BA, R. 78.

30. Seymour to Governor Eyre, 13 July 1863, BA, R. 81.

31. Lt. Governor John G. Austin, 28 February 1867, BA, R. 96.

32. Lt. Governor James R. Longden to Governor Sir John P. Grant, 6 March 1868, BA, R. 98 and CO 123/133, emphasis in original.

33. Census of 1871, enclosed in Robert Harley to Grant, 20 May 1872, CO 123/148.

34. Austin to Eyre, 26 May 1864, BA, R. 81.

35. See "Map of British Honduras" in Sampson 1929 (CO 854/73).

36. Lt. Governor William W. Cairns to Governor Rushworth, 14 December 1872, CO 123/150.

37. Ordinance No. 35, 1872, "to regulate the management and sale of the Crown Lands," CO 125/3.

38. Cairns to Rushworth, 14 December 1872, CO 123/150.

39. Edmunds to Samuel Cockburn, 31 May 1867, BA, R. 96.

40. Lt. Governor Sir Frederick P. Barlee to Governor Sir A. Musgrave, 1 August 1879, CO 123/163.

41. Ibid.

42. Ibid.

43. *Colonial Guardian*, 22 July 1882.

44. Barlee to Sir Michael E. Hicks Beach, 8 March 1880, CO 123/165.

45. Henry Fowler to Lord Derby, 27 May 1884, CO 123/172. Incidentally, he reported that the imposition of rents for house plots in Stann Creek in 1878 "caused serious disturbances" because the Garifuna "do not know why they are to pay rent as Stann Creek is their place, that long ago the land was given to them and they settled the place."

46. Ibid.

47. William Miller's Report on Indian Reservation, enclosed in Governor Hubert Jerningham to Lord Knutsford, 28 September 1888, CO 123/190.

48. Robert W. Pickwood's report, 16 February 1889, enclosed in Governor Roger Goldsworthy to Knutsford, 26 February 1889, CO 123/192.

49. Report from Ernest McDonald, 12 October 1895, enclosed in E.B. Sweet-Escott to Joseph Chamberlain, 5 November 1895, CO 123/215.

50. Ibid.

51. Sweet-Escott to Chamberlain, 5 November 1895, CO 123/215.

52. Report from Frederic Keyt, enclosed in Governor David Wilson to Chamberlain, 19 April 1897, CO 123/223.

53. Ibid.

54. Wilson to Chamberlain, 23 December 1897, CO 123/226.

55. Act. Governor P.C. Cork to A. Lyttelton, 8 August 1904, CO 123/247.

56. Ibid.

57. Ibid., minutes attached.

58. Barlee to Musgrave, 1 August 1879, CO 123/163.

59. Barlee to Hicks Beach, 8 March 1880, CO 123/165.

60. Report by Alvan Millson, 7 December 1883, CO 123/172.

61. Ibid.

62. Fowler to Derby, 24 January 1884, CO 123/172.

63. Ibid.

64. Ibid.

65. Fowler to Knutsford, 27 April 1887, CO 123/183.

66. Ibid.

67. Ibid., CO minutes attached.

68. Fowler to Derby, 24 January 1884, CO 123/172.

69. Circular 7/1884, in Bristowe 1892:135.

70. Ordinance No. 8, 1886, CO 125/5.

71. The Alcalde Act of 1858 was consolidated in 1886, Cap. 110 of Consolidated Laws 1886.

72. Ordinance No. 7, 1871, CO 125/3.

73. Report by McDonald, 12 October 1895, enclosed in Sweet-Escott to Chamberlain, 5 November 1895, CO 123/215.

74. Ibid.

75. *Government Gazettes*, 17 May 1884, CO 127/5; 9 April 1892, CO 127/7.

76. The announcement for 1887 was not found.

77. *Government Gazette*, 23 March 1889, CO 127/6.

78. Letter from Bull, 1 April 1858, CO 123/96.

79. Fowler to Derby, 24 January 1884, CO 123/172.

80. Memorandum, 13 October 1882, BA, R. 93.

81. Goldsworthy to General Gabriel Tamay, 6 January 1886, BA, R. 121.

82. Report by McDonald, enclosed in Sweet-Escott to Chamberlain, 30 October 1895, CO 123/215.

83. Ordinance No. 33, 25 September 1913, CO 125/10.

84. Ordinance to amend the Alcalde Jurisdiction Ordinance, Cap. 174 of the Consolidated Laws, 1924, CO 125/15.

85. S.R. & O. 14, 25 January 1939, S. 2.

86. Ordinance No. 24, 1939.

87. Ordinance No. 18, 1952, Appendix C (Inferior Courts), Part VI, Alcalde Jurisdiction, CO 125/17.

88. *The Laws of Belize* (1980 revised edition) Cap. 77, Part VI, Alcalde Jurisdiction.

89. Some present-day alcaldes are still concerned with the question of access to land, as were their ancestors in pre-Columbian Maya society. Over 70,000 acres of Toledo District is "reserved for occupation by Indians," on payment of an annual occupancy fee. Alcaldes are responsible for ensuring that persons who occupy such land are present on the appointed days to pay the District Commissioner, they decide disputes between occupiers regarding the boundaries of their holdings, and they are responsible for maintaining the boundaries of the whole Reserve. (*The Laws of Belize*, 1980 revised edition, Cap. 147, "Toledo Indian Reserve Rules").

Part 3

Labour Control, Resistance and the Labour Movement since Emancipation

6. Labour Control and Resistance in Belize in the Century after 1838

I

If we avoid the simple antinomy of slavery and freedom we are better able to view the mid-nineteenth century as a period of transition from one system of domination to another, each involving distinct forms of labour control and patterns of labour resistance. While it is incontrovertible that the abolition of slavery in 1834 and of the apprenticeship system in 1838 changed the prevailing forms of domination in the British West Indies, we should distinguish between the ideological claims made about the new system and its reality. Given the fact that a variety of forms of coercion persisted on a large scale throughout the West Indies long after 1838, we cannot agree that real freedom, or human emancipation, was achieved at that date. Just as we have learned to identify and distinguish between varieties of legal bondage, so, too, we must learn to identify and distinguish between forms of coercion that exist in societies in which labour is legally free (Bolland 1981).

This perspective stresses the continuities between slavery and the period after emancipation, especially with regard to the coercion of labour, rather than conceiving of a sharp break between slavery and freedom. From this perspective, then, we should expect, rather than be surprised by, continuities in protests by labourers against their continuing oppression. As the former masters sought to develop new forms of coercion, the former slaves sought new means of freedom. While the goals of each party in the social dialectic remained essentially the same, their tactics changed after 1838. The labourers' legal status was newly defined after 1838, but they continued to struggle to make their freedom a reality.

One of the ideological claims made about the nineteenth century is that, with the termination of apprenticeship, labour power suddenly was freed as a commodity. The fact is, however, that labourers, like land, were not freed from

159

the very real constraints of persistent power structures. In the British West Indies, as elsewhere, the control of labour and the control of land were two dialectically related aspects of a changing but persistent structure of colonial domination, both before and after 1838. The control of each aspect was a means for the further control of the other. Thus, the efforts of the masters to continue to limit access to land was a way of keeping the working people dependent, while their success in controlling their labourers by a variety of other means enhanced their ability to maintain monopolistic claims to the land. Such monopolistic control of land and labour was primarily a function of social and political factors—in brief, the distribution of social power—rather than of simple population density, as some have maintained (Green 1984; Bolland 1984). This becomes especially clear when we examine the decline of this system of domination. To the extent that the relations of labourers and capitalists changed, and they began to change in many parts of the Caribbean in the 1930s, they did so as a consequence of a shift in the distribution of power, not as a result of any change in population densities. A century after the legal abolition of slavery a wave of labour unrest ushered in the modern era of class struggle in the Caribbean and the dialectics of labour control and resistance changed their form yet again.

What follows is an account of the system of labour control in Belize after 1838, and of the resistance of labourers to that control, a resistance that culminated in widespread unrest in the 1930s and subsequent changes in labour laws, relations, and institutions. This particular case, which, though unique, is comparable in many ways to other parts of the Caribbean, illustrates and reinforces the importance of examining continuities in systems of domination, even when we are studying changes in the forms of labour control and resistance to control. The account shows that, just as the negation of slavery made way for a new form of domination, so, too, the system of labour control after 1838 generated social conditions that led to its eventual transformation.

II

In Belize, which had been a British colony in all but name since the seventeenth century, a handful of the self-styled "Principal Inhabitants" monopolized the land, labour, and commerce of the settlement. Until the 1830s, this white settler oligarchy also controlled the institutions of the settlement's government and administration, to a degree that was unusual among British colonies (Bolland 1977). A brief summary of the nature and extent of this oligarchy's power is necessary in order to appreciate the continuities that existed in structures of domination before and after 1838.

At the end of the eighteenth century, when Britain still acknowledged

Spanish sovereignty over Belize, the "Principal Inhabitants" of the settlement passed a series of resolutions, known as "location laws", by which they allocated vast tracts of land to themselves and treated such land as freehold private property. A shift from logwood to mahogany cutting at this time encouraged the concentration of landownership and the evolution of a settler oligarchy.[1] Within months of the passage of the location laws in 1787, the Superintendent reported that 12 settlers held four-fifths of the available land under the 1786 treaty, or about 2,000 square miles. The other great concentration of property was in slaves. In 1790, the 20 largest "estates" possessed a total of 1,085 slaves, or about half of all the slaves in the settlement. The same large land and slave owners used their connections with London merchants to develop the import trade, so vital since the local cultivation of provisions was prohibited, and consequently they controlled retailing. They also controlled taxation and fixed the price of logwood and mahogany.

From this economic basis the wealthy settlers controlled the political, legal and administrative system of the settlement in the form of the Public Meeting and the Magistracy. The oligarchy succeeded in challenging the Crown's representative when they got Superintendent Despard suspended in 1789, and Superintendent Arthur was only partially successful when he attacked what he called the "monopoly on the part of the monied cutters" in 1817. He proclaimed that all unclaimed land was henceforth Crown land to be granted only by the Crown's representative, but the existing monopoly of landownership was unchanged. Arthur complained about his position that "The Office is, and ever has been, so very undefined as to deprive the Representative of the Crown of the Authority necessary for the administration of Public Business".[2] Although the Superintendent took the authority to appoint Magistrates in 1832, the oligarchy continued to make and execute laws and to administer the public business of the settlement in their private interests, and until 1854 the constitutional anomalies of Belize remained unresolved.

The mahogany trade had its ups and downs, of course, but the greatest boom, between 1835 and 1847, coincided with the period of emancipation. Not surprisingly, the masters at this time sought to ensure that all their slaves, along with most of the free population, remained a dependent labour force. We will see, shortly, to what extent they succeeded. Here it is necessary to say that this boom contributed to the greatest depression in the mahogany trade, a depression that resulted in a major realignment of the economic and political power structure of the settlement, though no significant gains accrued to working people. After a peak in 1846 of almost 14 million feet of mahogany exported, exports fell to about 5 1/2 million feet in 1859 and less than 3 million feet in 1870, the lowest recorded annual figure since the beginning of the century. The high demand of the 1840s resulted in the cutting of all easily accessible trees, even young trees, and a serious depletion of timber resources. As the cutters moved further into the interior in search of mahogany, the cost of production rose. Although mahogany and logwood continued to account for over 80 per cent of the total value of exports, the price of these goods was so low that the economy was in a permanent state of depression after the 1850s.

One major result of this prolonged depression was the increasing consolidation of capital and the intensification of metropolitan ownership. The failure of some of the mahogany cutters resulted in their assets, chiefly land, being put up for auction, mortgaged, or taken over by creditors. In order to facilitate this, and to increase the confidence of potential British investors, a formal constitution, allowing for an assembly of 18 members elected on a limited franchise, was adopted in 1854 and, in the following year, the Laws in Force Act declared the validity of existing laws, including the old location laws that were the basis of land ownership. The Honduras Land Titles Acts, passed between 1858 and 1861, allowed land in Belize to be sold even if a legal title to the land could not be proved. The law, one of the most important in the country's history, was drafted by a conveyancer hired by the British Honduras Company, registered in 1859. This company originated in one of the old settler families, that of James Hyde, whose surviving relative, James Bartlett Hyde, entered into partnership with John Hodge, a London merchant, and transferred their lands to the company. The British Honduras Company not only survived the prolonged depression in the mahogany trade; it was also able to purchase more land from those firms, like Young, Toledo & Company, that were forced into bankruptcy. In 1875, the British Honduras Company changed its name to the Belize Estate and Produce Company, a metropolitan-based business that owned about half of all the privately owned land in the colony and has been the chief single force in Belize's political economy for over a century (Bolland and Shoman 1977: 77-83).

This concentration and centralization of capital in the hands of metropolitan companies, and of one in particular, has meant that the pattern of land use and the direction of the colony's economy were largely determined in the companies' boardrooms. But it has also meant the almost complete eclipse of the old settler elite as a major class within the colony's social structure and as the major political force in its power structure. "British Honduras" was declared a colony in 1862 and in 1871 the Legislative Assembly abolished itself and the British government established Crown Colony rule. Although unofficial members of the Legislative Council were in the majority after 1892, this hardly diminished the power of the Governor who nominated them, and the elective principle was not reintroduced until 1936. One of the people consistently nominated was the manager of the Belize Estate and Produce Company, thereby ensuring that private company's persistent influence on the colony's public affairs.

What this brief summary shows is that, despite a change in the mid-nineteenth century from a white settler oligarchy to a more metropolitan-dominated political economy, the vast majority of people in Belize continued to be the victims of a system of domination whose purpose was to keep them poor, dependent, and powerless. It remains to be shown how this system maintained itself, that is, by what means the former slaves of Belize were kept under tight control.

III

The former slaves of Belize were subjected to a variety of coercive means of labour control that kept them dependent on wage labour and disciplined them as a work force. Among the means of labour control used in Belize were the monopolization of land ownership, which inhibited the development of an independent peasantry, a system of labour contracts, a combination of advance and truck systems to induce indebtedness, the use of magistrates and police as agents of labour discipline, and the increasing use of schools and churches, in the hands of missionaries, to internalize the virtues of humble work, social order and decorum, and obedience to authority.

We have seen already that the concentration of land ownership was one of the chief characteristics of the political economy of Belize since the late eighteenth century. Land was intentionally kept from the former slaves after 1838 in order to keep these people dependent on the landowners. Until 1838, the land claimed by the settlers had been acquired gratuitiously, first under their own location laws and then, after 1817, by Crown grant. In this way a handful of the settlers had gained control over almost all the accessible and utilizable land of Belize. Shortly after emancipation the Colonial Office instructed the Superintendent that Crown land should henceforth be sold, as the gratuitous granting of land would "discourage labour for wages".[3] This strategy to keep Crown land away from the former slaves was successful, as no such land was sold in the period up to 1855[4] and, by 1868, the total amount of Crown land sold was said to be "utterly insignificant".[5]

The price of £1 per acre demanded for Crown land, though low in comparison with other places in the West Indies, was unattractive in Belize where such land was in wild and unexplored areas that were remote from the only market in Belize Town. When private land changed hands, it was sold by the smaller settlers to the bigger, thereby contributing to the concentration of land ownership. As a consequence, the freed slaves, denied access to private land and offered only the virtually useless Crown lands, remained landless. Though they had become legally free in 1838, and possessed in theory the freedom to choose whether or not to continue working for their former masters in the forests, their inability to acquire land severely curtailed their options and ensured their continued dependence upon the mahogany lords at a time when the latter were eager to retain their labour force.

163

By 1838 the masters already had experience in controlling free labourers and this experience helped them retain their former slaves during the great mahogany boom at that time. In 1832 there were as many "free people of colour" as slaves in the population and many of them worked alongside slaves, in similar conditions, in the mahogany gangs. Free labourers were hired by contracts for six and, more often, 12 months. These contracts were enforced by constables and the courts. In February 1838, the clerk of the courts reported that "where the Servant has failed in his Contract, the Master has had the power to bring him up at once on Warrant, and have him summarily punished by Imprisonment and Public Whipping".[6] This contract system was an effective mechanism of labour control even before it was incorporated into the laws in 1846. As amended in the 1850s, these labour laws allowed the apprehension of a worker by the employer or his agent, without warrant, and the forcible removal of the worker to his place of work. Workers who failed to perform according to the contract were treated as criminals and often given imprisonment with hard labour for three months. Astonishingly, this was still true a century after emancipation.

At the centre of the system of labour control was a combination of advance and truck systems that induced indebtedness. Labourers were given advances on their wages when they signed contracts at the beginning of the season, around Christmas time. Ostensibly, the advances were intended to enable the labourer to purchase supplies prior to going to the forests for the season, but the money was generally spent in "keeping Christmas" with his family and friends in Belize Town. The result was that labourers had to purchase their supplies on credit and at exorbitant prices from the employers' truck shops at the camps in the forest. Often, the balance of the wages a worker received was insufficient to meet his expenses and he would end his season in debt to his employer. To work off his debt, the labourer would have to sign another contract with that employer the next season, with the result that the advance and truck systems effectively bound the labourers to their employers in a form of debt servitude.

Fifty years after emancipation was supposed to have been achieved, the Colony's handbook reported:

> It is well known that a system has prevailed in the colony unchecked ... of labourers being kept in debt by their employers for the purpose of receiving a continuance of their labour, as such labourers consider themselves bound to serve until such debt is extinguished. Advantage has been taken ... to keep them in debt by either supplying them with goods or drink for the purpose, and they thus become virtually enslaved for life (Bristowe and Wright 1888: 199).

Though the custom of giving advances declined as the supply of labourers came to exceed the demand, the truck system, and even the partial payment of workers in rations and commissary tickets, was still widespread in the mahogany camps in the 1930s.

The District Magistrates enforced this system of labour control. Much of their time and effort seems to have been taken up with enforcing the Masters and Servants Acts, in a way that favoured the employers and served as a means of disciplining and intimidating the labourers. The Corozal magistrate, for example, reported that, in 1869, *all* of the 286 cases decided by him under the colony's labour laws were against employees: 245 were punished for "absenting themselves from work without leave", 30 for "insolence and disobedience", six for "assaults on bookkeepers", and five for "entering into second contracts before the expiry of the period of former ones".[7] Such infringements of the labour laws were commonly punished with three months' imprisonment with hard labour. In 1868 and 1869, only one of the 147 labourers brought to court by their employers in Belize Town was freed without punishment, whereas only one of the ten employers brought to court was convicted, and he was given a two dollar fine.[8]

This policing system appears to have been a practical and effective means of enforcing labour discipline, long after the labourers were declared legally free. The Magistrates' records show, nevertheless, the extent of persistent unrest among the workers and of continuing labour problems for the employers, as indicated by the high frequency of absenteeism, "neglect of work", and disobedience. The discontent was sometimes expressed in the form of group action, as in the case of a strike by 31 sugar workers in 1869. They tried to improve their situation by withdrawing their labour at a critical moment of the production process, but their appeal to a magistrate backfired, as his report shows:

> The defendants were put by the Manager of Regalia Estate to cut canes by day work, which they did not like, wishing to work by task, but which the Manager would not consent to, as they hurried through their work and did not cut the canes properly. The defendants then left off working at 10 o'c in the morning and came down to Allpines to ask me to compel the Manager to give them task work .... I think their principal reason for striking was to try and frighten the Manager into what they wanted. This happened during crop and the Mill had to be stopped for the day. They were by my advice arrested and tried and I ordered each of them to pay their employers the sum of $2.50 and the costs of $1.50 which they consented to do, and the Manager agreed to stop it out of their wages.[9]

The issue here appears to have been primarily one of control over the work situation, the workers preferring the more autonomous task work and the manager insisting on his right to control their labour. After this experience in court, these workers would be unlikely to appeal to the magistrates again. Since workers on that estate received only about $7.00 per month, half in cash and half in goods, their effort to improve their work situation proved costly.

Presumably, most dissatisfaction among the workers did not develop into such militant action as this strike. One of the reasons for the absence of greater militancy on the part of the workers was the influence of missionaries, through their churches and schools. The missionaries, whether deliberately or not—and there is evidence from various parts of the West Indies to show that they were often self-conscious about it—were agents of social control.[10] Baptist and Methodist missionaries first appeared in Belize in the 1820s, competing with the already established Anglican church. Though a thorough study of the impact of these missionaries has yet to be done, their influence was widespread by 1838, through churches and schools. In 1836, the Public Meeting voted to support a school that would provide "moral and religious Instruction" to the apprentices,[11] perhaps in response to the urging of Lord Glenelg who had pointed out "the important interest which the Proprietors of Land in Honduras have in the religious Instruction of the Labouring Population, and the diffusion among them of those principles which afford the best Security for good order, and the right discharge of every social duty".[12] The missionaries not only preached the virtues of social duty and the principles of hard work and orderly conduct; they also educated children by means of rote learning and authoritarian relationships, backed by corporal punishment. Such an educational system, which has been persistent in Belize, would tend to guarantee, even if it was not actually calculated to induce, passivity and obedience, rather than a critical intellect and a sense of self-worth and autonomy, among its victims. More positively, the churches frequently offered a valuable sense of community and a meaningful status to their members which was otherwise denied by, and was a kind of compensation for, their lowly secular status. In various ways, then, the missionaries and their successors in the churches and schools of Belize have played an important long-term role in buttressing the authority system of the colony and maintaining the "good behavior" of its working people.

The system of labour control that has been briefly described here was a major component of the total situation of the working people of Belize after 1838, and, combined with the chronic economic depression that transpired after the mid-century, was responsible for terrible conditions among the labourers well into the twentieth century. It was not until the workers themselves took events into their own hands that these oppressive labour laws and conditions were ameliorated in the 1940s.

IV

After 1838, as before, Belizean workers resisted labour coercion and expressed their dissatisfaction in various ways. The magistrates' records are full of convictions for absenteeism, disobedience, assaults on bookkeepers, and breaking contracts, and, as we have seen, there were sometimes strikes. Occasionally, there were also demonstrations and riots, as in 1894 when mahogany workers returned to town from the camps to find that a currency devaluation had severely reduced their wages. Their employers would not raise their wages, so a deputation, led by John Alexander Tom, went to the governor. When the governor refused to do anything, the workers rioted and looted stores. After British troops landed to quell the disturbances, the employers conceded to an increase in wages. Another riot occurred in 1919, when demobilized Belizean soldiers who had returned from the Great War in Europe attacked business establishments in protest against racist treatment. The most extensive, organized, and effective disturbances occurred in the mid-1930s, however, when Belize was shattered by economic depression and a hurricane, the brunt of which was felt by the working people.

Forest produce in 1930 accounted for 85 per cent of exports by value and most labourers sought employment in that sector. But the number of contracts signed under the Labour Ordinance fell quickly: 1927 - 1,103; 1928 - 968; 1929- 832; 1930 - 629. *The Colonial Report for 1931* stated that "contracts for the purchase of mahogany and chicle, which form the mainstay of the Colony, practically ceased altogether, thereby throwing a large number of the wood-cutters and chiclegatherers out of work" (1933: 13-14). The colonial administration was organizing relief work by June 1931, but for only about 150 of the unemployed. Despite these problems, and the poor quality of rations and absence of medical attention in the forest camps, Governor Burdon still regarded labour conditions as "generally satisfactory" in July 1931.[13] This persistent official optimism was swiftly shattered by the great hurricane that demolished the town of Belize on 10 September 1931, killing over a thousand people and destroying at least three quarters of the housing. After this natural catastrophe, the economy continued to decline. The total value of imports and exports in 1933 was $2,729,000, or little more than a quarter of what it had been in 1929, namely $9,934,000.

There can be no doubt that these economic conditions, aggravated by the disastrous hurricane, were responsible for severe hardship among the working class in Belize. Whether we evaluate conditions by the purchasing power of wages, food and nutrition, housing standards, or health, it is fair to say that the effects of the depression and hurricane simply made a chronically bad situation even worse. Even after trade revived between 1934 and 1936, the conditions experienced by labourers and their families remained bad. For example, a

Committee on Nutrition reported in 1937 that malnutrition and cases of ill health due to disorders of nutrition were increasing and laid the blame upon poverty and the truck system which was still prevalent in the 1930s. Workers in the mahogany camps were given rations that were less than the rations said to be given to slaves in the early nineteenth century. The average diet of a mahogany worker per week was stated by the Committee to be seven quarts of "inferior" flour, one packet of baking powder, two quarts of beans, one packet of tea, one pound of salt, four pounds of pork, and two pounds of sugar, with few fresh vegetables (Cheverton and Smart 1937: 19-21). The Committee referred to common abuses of the truck system by "unscrupulous employers", including draft bills that had to be exchanged at the commissaries before any actual cash was handed over, and recommended that the "truck system should either be abolished or strictly controlled" (Cheverton and Smart 1937: 45). Major Orde Browne in 1939 referred to the ration system as "archaic" and a "relic of slave days". He acknowledged that the truck system was "open to abuse" and said that "complaints of undue profit and unfair exploitation are frequently made" (Orde Browne 1939: 195-6).

In brief, the labour conditions of forest and agricultural workers, and the living conditions of their families, were similar in the 1930s to what they had been in the nineteenth century: the dependency upon rations, the inferior food, the low wages, the absence of medical attention and the prevalence of medical problems associated with malnutrition, and the poor and unsanitary accommodations, constituted a terrible set of living and working conditions. The condition of labourers and their families remained so bad for a century because they had no legal recourse. The law governing labour contracts in the 1930s, which had been passed in 1883, was a revision of the Master and Servants Acts of 1846. It made a breach of contract by the labourer a criminal offence, punishable by 28 days imprisonment with hard labour. Despite the deteriorating conditions in the early 1930s, Governor Burdon advised against bills that could have improved the labourers' situation. He rejected proposals to legalize trade unions and rejected proposed legislation to apply a minimum wage and for sickness insurance. The governing officials only changed their tune after the labourers of Belize had forcefully demonstrated their discontent and their determination in a series of meetings, demonstrations, strikes, petitions, and riots in 1934 and 1935.

In 1933 the economy was shattered and some 2,000 people were unemployed.[14] On 14 February 1934, some of the unemployed people formed themselves into the "Unemployed Brigade" and marched around town carrying placards and chanting slogans. They petitioned the Governor for relief. On 16 March 1934, Antonio Soberanis Gomez, a barber by trade, denounced the Unemployed Brigade's leaders and turned the people in a more militant direction. Soon, between 600 and 800 people were meeting twice a week to cheer

Soberanis' attacks on the Governor and his officials, the rich merchants, and the Belize Estate and Produce Company. The bi-weekly meetings lasted four or five hours and, according to the Superintendent of Police, "the more violent the language used from the rostrum the more the crowd enjoyed it."[15] Soberanis, called the "Moses of British Honduras", created and led the Labourers and Unemployed Association. While the labourers made specific demands for relief and a minimum wage, these demands were couched in broad moral and political terms that began to define and develop a new nationalistic and democratic political culture in Belize. Before the end of 1934 Soberanis had organized a strike in Stann Creek and was arrested in connection with a major riot in Belize City. The colonial authorities' response to these labour disturbances, which were soon to occur throughout the West Indies, was to victimize the leaders but they also moved slowly toward concessions and improvements in the labourers' working and living conditions. By 1939 such investigators and officials as Major Orde Browne and Governor Burns acknowledged that Belizean workers had legitimate grievances and they proposed legal remedies.

Major Orde Browne recommended the repeal of the penal clauses of the 1883 Masters and Servants Ordinance. This "exceptional and peculiar legislation", he said, was "a cause of resentment on the part of the labourer" (Orde Brown 1939: 198). The law (Section 40 of Chapter 104 of the Consolidated Laws of British Honduras) defined a considerable list of offences on the part of the labourer and, most provocatively, authorized his arrest by his employer for trial before a District Commissioner. Governor Burns, too, criticized the penal sanctions and debt practices enshrined in the colony's labour laws. When he opened the Legislative Council's sessions in 1939, he indicated that he would not tolerate opposition to proposed labour reforms, including a minimum wage bill, a workers' compensation for injury bill, a new Masters and Servants Ordinance, and a Trade Unions bill. Trade unions were legalized in March 1941, after the Colonial Development and Welfare Fund had made this a condition of the Colony receiving funds. That bill was of limited value, however, because the recognition of unions by employers was not made compulsory and the penal clauses of the Masters and Servants Ordinance rendered it ineffectual.

When the new governor, Sir John Hunter, introduced the bill to repeal the penal clauses from the 1883 Ordinance and the Fraudulent Labourers Ordinance of 1918, it was defeated by the employers among the unofficial members in August 1941. Reintroduced as the Employers and Workers Bill it was passed on 27 April 1943, despite continued opposition by employers who wanted to retain penal sanctions as a means of labour control. By removing breach of labour contract from the criminal code, this legislation enabled the infant trade unions of Belize to pursue the struggle for improving labour conditions. The fact that Antonio Soberanis was the Secretary of the Workers and Tradesmen Union in

1940 shows there were links between the Labourers and Unemployed Association of 1934-35 and the trade unions of the early 1940s. The General Workers Union, registered in 1943, quickly grew into a nationwide organization and provided crucial support for the nationalist movement that took off with the formation of the People's United Party in 1950.

It should be stressed that the legislation of 1941-3 did not conclude the labour struggle—far from it. A wartime law, the Essential Worker Ordinance of 1943, forbidding strikes in the mahogany industry, which was still the colony's chief industry, was not amended until 1953, following years of protest by the GWU, and the Belize Estate and Produce Company continued to deny union officials access to the camps. Nevertheless, 110 years after the British Parliament passed the act to abolish slavery throughout the colonies, this legislation marked a turning point in the organization of labour and in the relations of workers and employers. The dialectics of labour control and resistance after emancipation climaxed in the disturbances of the 1930s and gave rise to a new era of labour struggles in Belize.

Notes

01. Logwood grows in clumps near the coast, is a small tree and was exported in small, easily manageable chunks. Mahogany is a huge tree that grows sparsely inland and was exported in long trunks. Consequently, the shift to mahogany extraction required more land and labour, so only the wealthier and more powerful settlers succeeded in making this transition.

02. Superintendent George Arthur to Earl Bathurst, 31 July 1819, CO 123/28.

03. Lord Normanby to Superintendent Macdonald, 22 April 1839, BA 15.

04. Superintendent Stevenson to Governor Barkly, 30 July 1855, BA 48.

05. Governor Longden to Governor Grant, 6 March 1868, BA 98.

06. James Walker to Macdonald, 12 Feb. 1838, CO 123/52.

07. Edwin Adolphus to Longden, 15 Jan. 1870, BA 92.

08. Police Magistrate Cockburn to Longden, 24 Feb. 1870, BA 106.

09. Magistrate Hamilton to Longden, 17 Feb. 1870, BA 106.

10. In 1835 the Reverend John Sterling argued that the Churches and their schools could play an important role in the West Indies in keeping the ex-slaves as dependent and orderly labourers:

> There are now more or less directly under the Imperial Government in the different colonies about 770,000 persons who have been released from Slavery by the Emancipation Act, and are now in a state of rapid transition to entire freedom. The Peace and Prosperity of the Empire at large may be not remotely influenced by their moral condition.... For although the Negroes are now under a system of limited control which secures to a certain extent their orderly and industrious conduct, in the short space of five years from the 1st of next August, their performance of the functions of a labouring class in a civilized community will depend entirely on

the power over their minds of the same prudential and moral motives which govern more or less the mass of the people here. If they are not so disposed as to fulfill these functions, property will perish in the colonies for lack of human impulsion.... There has been since the 1st of August a great increase of the desire for knowledge... its certain result where the minds of the people are at all in movement will be a consciousness of their own independent value as rational beings without reference to the purposes for which they may be profitable to others. (Quoted in Gordon 1968:   59-60).

11. Minutes of Public Meeting, 4 July 1836, CO 123/48.

12. Lord Glenelg to Cockburn, 25 Nov. 1835, CO 123/48.

13. Governor Burdon to S.S., 23 July 1931, BA 158.

14. According to the 1931 census, there were about 17,000 "gainfully occupied" persons in the population, including self-employed, of whom 4,566 were male labourers. Most of the unemployed in 1933 were in this category, so it is reasonable to suppose that about a third of the male labourers were then out of work.

15. Minute paper 1666-34, 29 Nov. 1934, BA.

An earlier version of this paper was presented at a symposium at the Centre for Caribbean Studies, University of Warwick, in 1984.

7. The Labour Movement and the Genesis of Modern Politics in Belize

I

Labourers in Belize, as elsewhere in the Caribbean, have persistently struggled against the various systems of control that have been imposed upon them. The revolts and desertions that punctuated the era of slavery gave way after 1838 to spontaneous strikes and absenteeism in an economy that was largely stagnant after about 1850. Disturbances occurred periodically, such as the riots of 1894 and 1919, but the turning point, in Belize as elsewhere, came in the 1930s. As Arthur Lewis noted in 1939, it was not until then that there was "anything that could be called a movement" (Lewis 1977: 18) among the working people of the West Indies. A number of common factors, including wage cuts, unemployment, and increased taxation, a drift of the unemployed to the towns, and a rising political consciousness, provoked the emergence of trade unions and political organizations throughout the British West Indies in that decade of depression. Accounts of this developing labour movement, which formed the basis of nationalist movements and modern politics in the 1940s and 1950s, have ignored the similar developments that occurred in Belize, though the demonstrations, strikes, and riots began in Belize a year before those in St. Kitts that are generally held to have started the widespread disturbances (Hart n.d.; Macmillan 1935).

The Great Depression, and a devastating hurricane that destroyed Belize Town on 10 September 1931, shattered the economy of Belize and made still worse the chronically poor living conditions of the majority of the people. Governors and employers, who had resisted progressive labour legislation, were forced to give way before the increasing determination and organization of the working class. Beginning with the Labourers and Unemployed Association of 1934-36, and continuing with the British Honduras Workers and Tradesmen Union of 1939-43, in both of which Antonio Soberanis Gomez played a key role, the labouring poor of Belize organized and pressed for improvements in their working and living conditions. In so doing they became increasingly conscious and active politically. Their labour organizations, culminating in the General Workers Union (registered under the new trade unions law in 1943), and radical nationalist agitation during World War II, presaged and prepared for the nationalist movement of the 1950s. While most of the respectable middle-class members of the Legislative Council seemed eager to behave like British parliamentarians, crucial support for the young and more radical members of the Belize City Council in the devaluation crisis of 1950 came from the members and leaders of the General Workers Union (GWU).

The importance of the labour protests and organizations of the 1930s and 1940s in the emergence of modern Belizean politics has not been adequately recognized or documented.[1] The fact that the People's United Party (PUP) sprang from the devaluation crisis, and that the PUP had close links with the GWU, has been generally recognized, but it is often held that it was the devaluation of the dollar and not the labour movement that gave rise to modern politics in Belize. Grant, for example, asserts, "The political calm remained generally unruffled throughout the first fifty years of the twentieth century and in particular during the 1930s when the West Indian colonies were engulfed in disturbances and riots" (1976: 61). He relegates the 1930s protests to insignificance and concludes that it was only with "the British government's decision to devalue the Belizean dollar that Belize was rudely awakened from its apparent slumber" (1976: 61).[2] Shoman (1973) and Ashdown (1978) have begun to revise this view, but the former has not documented the 1930s events and the latter, who describes them in detail, characterizes them as "still-born" and fails to examine their connections with the later nationalist movement.

This paper aims to give the labour protests and organizations before 1950 their due. Belize, far from slumbering through the 1930s and 1940s, was actually one of the first of the West Indian colonies to participate in the widespread labour unrest that, when organized, provided the mass political base for a generation of middle class leaders. I will describe the early labour protests and organizations of Belize and will show that there were important links between them and the PUP in the early 1950s. First, however, it is necessary to provide the economic and political context of these events.

II

The economy of Belize, since the origins of the British settlement in the seventeenth century, consisted of the extraction of a limited natural resource, namely timber.

Logwood and mahogany provided successively the staple exports of Belize and its economic *raison d'être*. This monocrop economy suffered, not only from the usual susceptibility to fluctuations in demand and prices, but also from the fact that heightened demand led to a more rapid depletion of limited accessible resources and hence to increasing costs. The techniques and technology of timber extraction, which depended upon human and animal power to cut and haul the huge trees to river banks whence they could be floated to a boom near the coast, remained essentially unchanged until the 1920s when the introduction of caterpillar tractors and log wagons permitted logging operations in more remote areas. But it was not until the 1930s that the construction of roads and the use of great trucking camions signalled the end of dependence on animal haulage and water transport, while the use of mechanical saws replaced axes and two-handled saws. Since no attempt was made to conserve or replace forest resources, it appeared that the colony's timber would soon be exhausted. At the same time, the mechanization of felling and hauling meant that more timber could be extracted with a smaller labour force. By the time legislation was introduced in the 1940s to protect labourers from exploitation and to enforce some measures of forest management, the mahogany trade was in its final decline. The export of other forest products, including particularly cedar and chicle (extracted from the sapodilla tree to make chewing gum), declined at the same time.

Forest products in the 1920s accounted for about 85 per cent of exports by value (they continued to predominate until about 1958) and most labourers sought employment in that sector. The forestry and mercantile interests had long dominated the colony and had used their dominance to suppress agriculture and hold back expenditure on the development of communications and social services. Under a variety of constitutional forms the "forestocracy" continued to exercise power and control the colony's land and labour. One company in particular, the Belize Estate and Produce Company, which owned over a million acres or about a fifth of the entire colony, was for a century the biggest landowner and employer. The structure of this economy, and the political processes associated with it, left Belize and its working people especially vulnerable to the effects of the Great Depression.

The *Colonial Report for 1932* stated that the total volume of exports was less than half those of 1931, which were themselves half those of 1930. "Mahogany cutting was entirely stopped" and there was "no market for the Colony's staple products, mahogany and chicle, and unemployment was more severe than in 1931" (1933: 12, 31). The export of products, such as coconuts, also declined. By June, 1931, the colonial administration was organizing relief work, but for only about 150 of the unemployed. Despite these grave problems the Governor complacently reported labour conditions as "generally satisfactory" in July 1931.[3] This blind official optimism was shattered by the great hurricane that killed over a thousand of the 16,000 inhabitants and demolished at least three-quarters of the buildings of Belize Town.

The economic and social conditions of the depression, aggravated by the disastrous hurricane, were responsible for severe hardship among the working people of Belize. As the economy continued to decline after the hurricane, conditions worsened and people became increasingly desperate. Forest workers were paid pitiful wages, supplemented by inferior rations from truck shops; they lacked medical attention and lived in unsanitary accommodations in the camps. Bad as the living and working conditions were in the camps, however, the brunt of the poverty was often borne by women, children and old people who, separated from the working men by six-month logging seasons, had little security of income. They suffered in Belize Town from poor diet and, particularly after the hurricane, from overcrowded housing.

Yet such conditions in themselves seem to lead as often to fatalism as to activity, so what can account for the politicization of the people in Belize in the 1930s? Judging by the nature of their demands and protests, they seemed to hold the colonial administration increasingly responsible for their situation. On two previous occasions, remembered by many people in the 1930s, there were serious popular protests in Belize Town in which people openly criticized the colonial system of government. The first of these occurred in December 1894 when forest workers rioted over a currency devaluation that effectively reduced their wages. The second was a more serious outburst, starting on 22 July 1919, among demobilized soldiers of the British West Indian regiment who objected to racist treatment and the injustices of British colonial domination. Both disturbances suggest that something more than persistent poverty provoked people into protesting against the colonial government.

The same was true in the 1930s when the government began to take some responsibility for relief for the unemployed and hungry and for reconstruction of hurricane damage. There was considerable dissatisfaction with the way the government responded to the crisis after the hurricane. Faced with the huge task of feeding and housing thousands of people while starting to clear up the mess, avoid epidemics, and begin reconstruction, government opened soup kitchens, established a temporary camp at the airport and kept open public buildings to shelter the homeless each night. People made their own shacks from the wreckage, called "dog-sit-downs," while government constructed a series of barracks of single rooms for which a weekly rent of 75 cents was charged. It probably seemed insensitive, if not exorbitant, to charge about a day's pay to the needy in such a situation.

Three months after the hurricane, the Acting Governor was still trying to raise a reconstruction loan in England.[4] The British government would guarantee such a loan only if reserve powers were restored to the Governor. The unofficial members of the Legislative Council passed a resolution to the effect that they agreed to the constitutional change only to secure the needed financial aid and that they realized it was against the people's wishes. What seemed to the British government to be an opportunity to impose Treasury control on its colony, probably seemed to Belizeans uncomfortably like kicking a man when he was down. There can be no doubt that the callous attachment of this condition to the Hurricane Loan, and the inordinate delay in obtaining the loan, fostered resentment against the British officials. This resentment smouldered through the 1930s and 1940s and exploded when the Governor used his reserve powers to impose devaluation in 1949.

III

When a group calling itself the "Unemployed Brigade" marched through Belize Town on 14 February 1934 it started a broad movement that had a lasting effect on Belizean politics. In the depths of the depression and two and a half years after the hurricane had destroyed the town, unemployment and poverty remained widespread and housing was deplorable. Though the people were desperate, the demonstration was orderly. In answer to their appeal, Governor Kittermaster promised immediate outdoor relief for the hungry, told the unemployed to register at the Belize Town Board offices, and said that the Hurricane Loan Board would not foreclose on debtors.[5] The Governor's relief measures, redolent of the nineteenth century, proved woefully inadequate and provoked further resentment. A daily ration of a pound of badly cooked rice and three ounces of local sugar issued at the prison gate was started on 21 February and people were allowed to break rocks in the Public Works Department yard for five cents each day to "keep them from starving".[6] The usually pro-Government *Clarion* called the proferred relief "degrading and humiliating."[7]

The complete inadequacy of the Governor's response can be gauged by the fact that 1,100 men and 300 women registered as unemployed as soon as the list was opened and this was recognized by the Governor to be a "large proportion" in a town of 16,000 people.[8] "By this time," according to the Police Superintendent's report, "the masses of the unemployed had become restless"[9] and were dissatisfied with the leaders of the Unemployed Brigade. At a meeting held in the Battlefield, an open square in front of the Court House, on 16 March 1934, a new leader emerged. Antonio Soberanis Gomez (1897-1975), a barber who had travelled in Central America and the U.S.A.,[10] denounced the Unemployed Brigade's leaders and took over the movement.

Soberanis held meetings in the Battlefield two or three times a week, with between six and eight hundred people attending. He was joined by a group of colleagues that included Benjamin Reneau, John Lahoodie and James Barnett. Though the Governor first referred to Soberanis as a "man of no importance," the organization that Soberanis created and led, called the Labourers and Unemployed Association, soon became a major political force in Belize. It was reported that Soberanis "always said he was forming a labour union,"[11] but

176

unions could not be legally registered at the time. His association, though not quite a union, was nevertheless far more political than the numerous Friendly Societies that existed to provide mutual aid and support for their members. Though the LUA organized food and medical care from time to time, its chief orientation from its inception was political in so far as it used such techniques as petitions, demonstrations, pickets, strikes, and boycotts to pressure the employers, merchants, and colonial officials into making concessions in favour of working people. Increasingly, Soberanis' attacks on the Governor and various colonial officials, which were said "to please the people immensely,"[12] became an attack on colonial government itself. According to the Police Superintendent, "the more violent the language used from the rostrum the more the crowd enjoyed it." Soberanis was called the "Moses of British Honduras who had been sent by God to lead the people to better things."[13]

In April Soberanis was convicted of threatening the Police Superintendent and cautioned. Undeterred, he organized a petition signed by several hundred people, demanding that the Government find work for the unemployed at a minimum wage of $1.50 per day. He led a procession of about 500 people around the town and the crowd waited outside the Court House while their leader presented the petition to the Governor. Soberanis called for "British Honduras for British Honduraneans.... We are a new People, ... we are only asking for our rights. Justice to all men.... British Honduras has been sleeping for over a century, not dead, only sleeping.... Today British Honduras is walking around."[14] While the specific demands were for relief work and a minimum wage, these demands were couched in broad moral and political terms that began to define and develop a new nationalistic and democratic political culture.

Kittermaster replied that wages were governed by the world market price. A minimum wage of $1.50 a day, he said, would force enterprises to close for lack of profit, so "It is better to get work steadily at 50 or 75 cents a day all the year." This was an astonishing recommendation in a situation where hundreds of Belizeans could obtain no work at all and where most labourers had never had contracts that lasted all year. The Governor said he could do no more about the unemployed: "It is only by asking for charity from England that there will be enough money this year to pay for services such as schools and hospitals. England herself has 4,000,000 unemployed and yet she is generously helping us here in our difficulties."[15] Soberanis rejected this argument and pointed out that many officials drew large salaries while 50 cents per day is considered "sufficient for the poor man and his family." He also rejected English charity: "What we are receiving from England is only what belongs to us.... We will not throw up the sponge, but continue to agitate for our rights."[16] Soberanis and the LUA continued to agitate and developed new and successful tactics in the next few months.

Kittermaster obtained only $2,000 to provide relief work building the Northern Highway. Eighteen men were sent up every week on a rotation basis, each given ten days work; for each 8 hour day they received 60 cents, mostly in the form of credit for provisions at local stores. Since about 1,500 men were registered for work this was a woefully inadequate response. In August, it was reported that "unemployment will get worse shortly. The Belize Estate and Produce Company are practically closing down," and the Chairman of the Belize Town Board observed that there was "considerable want and even distress," especially hungry children, among the unemployed.[17] Soberanis and the LUA responded to this urgent need by pressuring local merchants and tradesmen to donate to the poor. When some merchants refused (these were among the largest: Harley, Brodie, and Melhado), the LUA organized a boycott. During the 10th of September celebrations, with the town full of unemployed, Soberanis led a march of about 3,000 people that culminated in a huge picnic for the poor. The Police Superintendent commented, "This procession and feed added greatly to the prestige of Soberanis and he was referred to as a 'Moses' more than ever."[18]

Encouraged by his success and widespread support, Soberanis broadened his attack and became increasingly militant. He demanded that Denbigh Phillips, a notoriously severe magistrate, should be removed from the bench, and that C. S. Brown, the manager of the Belize Estate and Produce Company and a member of the Legislative Council, should not be allowed to live in Government House. Soberanis frequently held meetings in Stann Creek (now Dangriga), which was then the second largest town with a population of about 3,000. On 27 September he organized a strike there among the stevedores who loaded grapefruit, and achieved another encouraging victory when their pay was raised from 8 cents to 25 cents per hour.

On 29 September, Soberanis, back in Belize Town, reiterated his demands concerning Phillips and Brown and announced that on Monday, 1 October, the LUA would picket the big stores and organize a strike at the Belize Estate and Produce Company sawmill. The police arrived at the sawmill before Soberanis and 200 of his followers, so the mill started as usual at 7:00 a.m. When all seemed quiet the police dispersed, but by 8:45 some 500 people, "armed with sticks," succeeded in closing the mill. When the police returned this crowd split and went to different parts of the town. One group broke down the gates of the Public Works Department and told the director he should pay his labourers more; another group closed the office of Mr. Esquivel, a coconut exporter; another stopped the dredger working at Fort George; and another closed Harley's lumber yard. In the Police Superintedent's words, "it was not a case of workmen striking for more pay but a case of unemployed men forcing employed men to strike for more pay."[19]

About 300 men and women, armed with sticks, went to the Belize Town

Board. When Matthews tried to arrest a man for threatening the Deputy Chairman of the Board, a struggle ensued. Eight men and one woman were arrested and, when the crowd increased to about 1,500, the police, in two ranks, pushed it back down Queen Street. Several constables were assaulted, shots were heard and one of the crowd was wounded.[20] At 10:50 a.m., with the situation threatening to get out of control, the Acting Governor ordered the police to halt and return to their station while he talked with the crowd's leaders. (It is not clear who these leaders were. None of the LUA leaders were named, nor were any of them among those arrested during the riot.) At noon Soberanis arrived at the Police Station in a "very truculent" mood, and demanded bail for all those arrested. At 5:00 p.m. he bailed out 16 of the 17 persons who had been jailed, but he was promptly arrested himself and charged with threatening Mr. Phillips on 29 September. As this news spread, the crowd at the Station increased to 2,000. Several efforts to release Soberanis on bail were refused, and he remained in custody. Heavy rain dispersed the crowd, a planned meeting at the Battlefield was abandoned, and the night passed peacefully.

On 2 October, Soberanis was charged in court and refused bail. About 500 people abused the magistrates and 1,000 gathered in Market Square. Some, it was said, "were inclined to be disorderly...it was women who were the most virulent," but no one was armed.[21] At 8:00 a.m. on 3 October, about 150 men who were assigned jobs refused to work for 60 cents per day and, demanding $1.00, they dispersed. On the following day a "large gang of men" failed to stop others from working for 60 cents per day.[22] The crisis was over, and the British cruiser that the Acting Governor had inquired about was not needed. The sawmill remained closed until 18 October and the people obtained a promise of $3,000 for immediate outdoor relief. Meanwhile, 26 of the 32 persons who were prosecuted for participating in the riot were sentenced, receiving between three days and one year of hard labour. The jurors having failed to agree, Soberanis was released on bail on 6 November and his freedom was celebrated by a big rally. In January 1935, Soberanis was acquitted of the charge of threatening Phillips who, it transpired, had threatened to horsewhip him. Soberanis continued to lead the LUA but the movement was weakened when Lahoodie and Reneau split away and formed the British Honduras Unemployed Association.

Shortly after the peak of the disturbances in October 1934, a new Governor, Alan Burns, arrived. While he viewed Soberanis as a professional agitator who should be locked up, Burns was shocked by the people's condition and he made a major effort during his six years in Belize to bring relief. In March 1935, the Senior Medical Officer reported that the people, especially the children, were dangerously undernourished and hence susceptible to disease. Burns commented that the unemployment situation was still acute, that those who were employed were receiving lower wages and that when their contracts ended in June these wages could not tide them over the season. He considered "the situation is most serious and that it will shortly become desperate . . . . The people have behaved, in the circumstances, with admirable restraint, but their temper is rising and matters must come to a head within a few months unless something is done."[23] Since Soberanis continued to hold mass meetings and his speeches became increasingly "offensive and inflammatory,"[24] Burns prepared legislation to help control the situation, namely a law to prohibit processions without police permission, one to give the Governor emergency powers to maintain order, and a seditious conspiracy bill.

In May 1935 Soberanis helped organize a strike among railway workers in Stann Creek, whose wage of 65 cents per day was below the rate for Government workers elsewhere, which ranged between 75 cents and $1.00. Soberanis had made several visits to the Stann Creek and Toledo Districts, "holding meetings and preaching discontent," in the words of Superintendent Matthews.[25] On 20 May, following a meeting in Stann Creek Town, a crowd of about 300 unemployed stopped the railway workers at Havana Bridge and told them to strike for $1.00 per day. The workers went home and made no attempt to go to work the next morning. That afternoon four railway employees who tried to pass the bridge were beaten by pickets and the police could not make arrests because of "the very threatening attitude" of a crowd of about 400 people. Later the crowd dispersed peacefully and the District Commissioner spoke with the local leaders, Abraham Dolmo and Zacharias Flores, Soberanis having left by boat. That night police reinforcements arrived from Belize Town "to crush the disorders without bloodshed." One woman and five men were convicted of impeding passage and disorderly conduct and were fined. None of the strikers was re-employed and those workers who were hired received the usual 65 cents per day. Burns felt that "in consequence Soberanis has suffered in repute as a leader."[26] Burns claimed that Soberanis' support and influence in general was waning as a result of the colonial development grants that employed people in road work and thus changed people's attitude to the government, but he still kept the police "constantly on the alert in case of a possible sudden outbreak."[27] By July, Soberanis himself acknowledged that the LUA was declining. He blamed Lahoodie and Reneau for splitting the organization, and suggested "that they must have been paid to do so."[28]

When Burns refused to allow Soberanis or any member of the LUA to Government House on the anniversary of emancipation, Soberanis responded in a rather quieter manner than usual. The LUA, he stated, was "organized to agitate for a living wage and justice for the Workers of British Honduras," and he insisted that they had the right to try to better their situation. He claimed that, by organizing a band of 22 nurses, they helped and cheered up the workers and unemployed and that the LUA's community work had benefited hundreds of people.[29]

For months the government had been planning to change the law so that "Soberanis could be successfully prosecuted for sedition."[30] Shortly after the seditious conspiracy ordinance was passed on 24 October 1935, Soberanis was charged for using "abusive and seditious language" at a public meeting in Corozal, though this meeting was held on 1 October, the first anniversary of the riot, *before* the amendment was passed.[31] Burns was determined to put Soberanis behind bars, but without provoking further disturbances. He instructed E. A. Grant, the magistrate of Orange Walk, to try Soberanis in Corozal because the Corozal magistrate was "suffering from cold feet." He added that "One of my reasons for sending Grant to try 'Tony' was that he was a black man. I did not want the trial to be a black v. white affair."[32] He wanted Soberanis "put away for a good long sentence." The trial was, as anticipated, a tense affair. People in Corozal and nearby Indian villages contributed over $200 to Soberanis' assistance and, because of "a state of civil commotion which threatens the public safety," meetings were prohibited in the District. Soberanis was fined $85 (or four and a half months hard labour), plus $30 costs, for using insulting words concerning various people. In January 1936, Soberanis was acquitted by the Supreme Court on the charge of attempting to "bring His Majesty into hatred, ridicule or contempt," but the Corozal conviction, along with the split in his organization, the muzzling effects of the new laws, the Governor's efforts to expand relief work,[33] and an improvement in the economy in 1935 and 1936, combined to spell the decline of his influence and of the LUA. The LUA continued to hold meetings and processions in 1936, but much of Soberanis' effort consisted of attacking Lahoodie's BHUA.

After the persistent agitation and tension of 1934-35, during which Soberanis and his LUA made a mark on Belizean history, there was a distinct lull in the labour movement, but Soberanis and his associates did not disappear and, with another slump in the economy in 1938 and 1939, labour militancy reappeared. Before examining these later events, however, let us first assess the importance of the LUA. Ashdown has correctly stated that Soberanis' movement was of "greater historical importance than the earlier disturbances" because "Soberanis had a definite political purpose" (1978: 67). Soberanis linked the concerns of his followers, which were chiefly with wages, prices, employment, food, health and housing, with an attack on the colonial administration and the merchant elite, whom he characterized as incompetent and overpaid, ruthless and callous in their relations with workers and the poor, and as the cause of much of the poverty and injustice experienced by most Belizeans. Soberanis, who organized the working people who were unrepresented in the Legislative Council, developed a variety of techniques to help the voiceless be heard, namely petitions, processions, boycotts, strikes, mass meetings, as well as mutual aid efforts. Though the core of these activities was in Belize Town, where a third of the colony's population was concentrated,

Soberanis was active in the districts from north to south, among the Maya Indians around Corozal and the Garifuna in Stann Creek. He initiated a national movement, in which labour issues and interests were in the forefront of a critique of colonial government, and a developing national working-class consciousness, thereby presaging the labour and national movements elsewhere in the British West Indies. When Ashdown says that Soberanis' "mantle was not to be taken up again until the coming of the People's Committee and the revitalization of the General Workers' Union in 1950" (1978: 68), he ignores many connections and continuities in these political developments during the late 1930s and 1940s.

IV

The constitution that was passed in April 1935 readmitted the elective principle for the first time since 1871, though with the high property and income qualifications demanded by the unofficial majority. In 1922 Hon. E.F.L. Wood, M.P., had recommended a reduction of the official majority and the inclusion of elected members in the Council (Wood 1922), but it was not until the Governor was granted reserve powers in 1932 that the elective element was readmitted in Belize. From 1936 to 1954 the Council consisted of the Governor and 5 (later 3) other officials, 2 (later 4) nominated unofficial members, and 5 (later 6) elected members. Voters had to be 21 years old (30 years for women, until 1950) and receive an income of $300 per annum, or own real property worth $500 or be a householder paying rent of $97 per annum. Candidates were required to have real property valued at $500 or an annual income of $1,000. In 1945 (after Jamaica had achieved universal adult suffrage) the entire registered electorate of Belize numbered 822. The working people could not vote, but could support opposition to the "establishment" candidates. Some of the Creole and Mestizo elite resented the control of land, commerce and government by a coterie of expatriates and developed a liberal "Natives First" orientation. With support from working people, who had neither votes nor candidates of their own, these early "nationalists," like Arthur Balderamos, a black lawyer, Robert S. Turton, a chicle millionaire, and L.P. Ayuso, a local businessman, were elected to the Legislative Council, defeating two Englishmen and a lawyer from Guiana.

Never having been allowed to represent itself, the working class of Belize was used to looking to members of the elite to represent it. The 1936 constitution encouraged this, with the result that much of the political activity of the working people and the LUA in 1936 was focused on supporting the "people's men" in the elections. Endorsed by the LUA and a middle-class Citizens' Political Party, these men became the chief "parliamentary opposition" after

182

1936. As working-class agitation continued, all six seats on the Belize Town Board, which was elected with a broader franchise, went to middle-class Creoles who appeared sympathetic to labour in 1939.

Though the LUA disappeared, Soberanis and several of his associates continued to agitate and organize in the late 1930s. At a Battlefield meeting attended by about 500 people on 20 June 1938, Soberanis, along with James Barnett alias Bangula (who had helped in the Stann Creek strike in 1935), John Neal, and Thomas Sabal (a Garifuna from Stann Creek), complained about wages and rations and demanded that Governor Burns must go. Soberanis, speaking in Spanish and English, said he had collected $40 from people in Stann Creek to register a union but when he asked for donations people began to leave. He chastised them and said they needed more loyalty, like the Jamaicans who had demanded Bustamante's release, if they were to get what they wanted.[34]

Later that year, Burns reported that unemployment was much worse and that he needed to provide work for more men so as to prevent disorder. On 19 November over 600 men gathered to apply for work at the Public Works Department where only 200 could be hired. One man was arrested for assaulting the clerk, but danger of serious trouble was "averted by a promise to the men that more would be taken on in a few days."[35] Burns organized a series of road works, reclamation and drainage projects, as relief schemes for the unemployed. Under the *quincena* system gangs of labourers were hired for two-week periods so that, by rotation, all the unemployed were given a chance of intermittent work. At any one time there were about 600 men so employed, but Burns, concerned that about 1,000 fewer men would be hired in the mahogany industry in 1939, proposed opening a quarry at Gracy Rock to provide work for 300 men and stone for the Belize-Cayo road. The development of better communications in Belize through road construction was clearly of secondary importance to Burns, whose primary concern was to avoid trouble in the streets. "This year there appears to be very little money and crowds of unemployed men are in the streets. The local agitators have not missed the opportunity to stir up trouble."[36] While it seems that the Governor's strategy was largely successful, as further widespread disorders were avoided, it was not because Soberanis and his colleagues had retired. In fact, their continued agitation was clearly a factor in pushing Burns and the Colonial Office to expand the relief schemes.

The economy deteriorated in 1939 and Burns had to lay off half of the men working on the Northern Highway, leaving 847 men in Belize Town seeking work.[37] In March, the following telegram was sent from a public meeting to the Secretary of State for the Colonies:

Suffering and uneasiness acute Belize. Due to unemployment. Developing into dangerous situation. Cannot continue without disastrous results.

Government approached and admits situation grave but unable to help. Wholesale laying off by Government on public works not understood by the masses. Population pray for immediate intervention.[38]

Burns attempted to belittle this by saying that the chairman of the meeting, L.D. Kemp, was "trying to make capital out of the situation."[39] Kemp, an associate of Soberanis and cousin of Lahoodie, was a journalist who, under the *nom de plume* of "Prince Dee" had for years attacked the colonial administration and supported Soberanis in the *Belize Independent*.[40] He continued to be politically active and influential in the 1940s.

Shortly after this meeting a crowd became disorderly, when only 75 men were engaged for road work out of 591 applicants, and was ejected from the Public Works Department by the police.[41] The number of unemployed men registered in Belize Town alone rose from 1,200 in April to 1,953 in August.[42] Once again, public anxiety and the prospect of unrest were relieved by announcements of continuing relief work, though everyone knew this was only a palliative in a sick economy.

Early in 1939, Soberanis and R.T. Meighan, a former member of the Belize Town Board, founded the British Honduras Workers and Tradesmen Union (BHWTU),[43] the first organization to be called a union in Belize, though it could not be legally registered as such at that time. In July 1939 the BHWTU supported a strike of about 170 Garifuna road workers near Stann Creek. While Meighan had the title of President of the BHWTU in 1939, Soberanis held that office from 6 March 1941, when he was reported as saying that "Trade Unionism is...the only medium by which the working class can get a square deal."[44] The BHWTU was said to have branches in Stann Creek, Corozal and San Ignacio, that is, in the south, north and west of Belize. Later that year Soberanis petitioned the Commissioner of Cayo District to do something about the awful living and working conditions of Maya labourers at Baking Pot,[45] but in 1942, discouraged by trying to organize people under wartime conditions when they "could not give vent to their feelings,"[46] he went to Panama where he stayed for six years.

In a confidential report written after the visit of the Moyne Commission in 1938, Burns attributed most agitation and discontent to "colour feeling... fomented by a small group, of whom the principal is R.S. Turton."[47] He named four "professional agitators" (Soberanis, Adderley, Kemp, and Balderamos) but devoted three quarters of his report to Turton, whom he accused of financing the agitators "in order to discredit and embarrass the administration and its officers. The agitation appears to be on behalf of the working class: actually it is in the interests of the worst type of capitalist."[48] Whatever may be the truth of Burns' assertion, it cannot apply to Soberanis who was always desperately poor and whose efforts over eight years to create a union were independent of Turton and

184

were certainly inspired by working class interests. Perhaps the organizations formed by Lahoodie and Reneau (British Honduras Unemployed Association) and by Kemp (British Honduras Federation of Workers Protection Association), neither of which functioned as unions, were supported by Turton. Kemp was said to live rent-free in one of Turton's houses.[49] A radical nationalist group, first called the British Honduras Independent Labour Party, then the People's Republican Party, and finally the People's Nationalist Committee, was formed in 1940, and may have been supported by Turton. The radical nationalists' pro-American and anti-British stance (which became confused when the U.S. joined Britain in the war) reflected the interests of Turton, who sold chicle to Wrigley's of Chicago.

Among the leaders of this group were John Lahoodie and Gabriel Adderley, alias Nehi, who had formerly been with Soberanis in the LUA, but the chief figure was Joseph Campbell, known as the "Lion of Judah". Born in 1901, of a Jamaican father and Belizean mother, Campbell had worked for many years for United Fruit in Honduras. He daily attacked the British and predicted their coming defeat as just punishment for all the "dirt the English had done".[50] At their meetings the nationalists demanded the expulsion of all white men, the creation of a local republic in union with the U.S.A., and the substitution of the national flag of "Belize Honduras" for the Union Jack. They were often attacked at these meetings by loyalists, who called themselves the "Unconquerables". Campbell was repeatedly imprisoned and the Governor tried to deport him in July 1941. On 5 September, with Campbell already in jail, Lahoodie and Adderley were held in a special detention camp in Corozal. The Governor indicated that he was avoiding a trial and holding the prisoners far from Belize Town in order to keep trouble from spreading.[51] While Kemp protested his cousin's detention, the 72 year-old Lahoodie refused to appeal, saying "He has asserted his desire to be rid of the British administration of this Colony and would have no truck with it."[52] By 14 February 1942 the Governor felt confident enough to release Lahoodie and Adderley, subject to certain restrictions. Lahoodie and Adderley went to live in Guatemala but Campbell was active again in 1948.

In the meantime, mass meetings were held in various parts of the colony in 1941 to demand adult suffrage and the right to elect the government. A broad spectrum of Belizean politicians took part in these meetings, including elected middle-class members of the Legislative Council and the Belize Town Board, like Arthur Balderamos and E.S. Usher, as well as radicals and trade unionists, such as L.D. Kemp and R.T. Meighan.[53] Though the Governor himself felt that the Council was "undemocratic if not oligarchic,"[54] the Colonial Office decided that Belize, unlike Jamaica, was too backward and so made only minor constitutional changes in 1945. These constitutional issues did not go away, however, and became a primary part of the PUP platform in the early 1950s.

Another link between many of these labour and political activities in the

1930s and 1940s was provided by Garveyism. The "official" flag and colours of the LUA were the red and green of Garvey's Universal Negro Improvement Association (UNIA) and several leading figures in Soberanis' organization were members of the Belize branch of UNIA that was founded in 1920. Kemp was a Garveyite, as was Calvert Staine, who was a Vice President of the Belize UNIA and later Chairman of the Belize Town Board and a member of the Legislative Council. When the parent UNIA split in 1929 over the disposal of the estate of Isiah Morter, a wealthy Belizean benefactor, there was a split in the local branch that was not healed by Garvey's visit to Belize in February of that year.[55] Cain, Kemp, and Staine remained loyal to Garvey but in February 1941, Lionel Francis, the Trinidadian President of the rival UNIA Inc., came to administer the Morter estate and decided to settle in Belize. In 1942 he won a seat on the Belize Town Board as leader of the "People's Group," displacing Staine in the process. Francis and his group controlled the Belize City Council (as it became in 1943) until 1947. An Edinburgh-educated physician, he was seen as a "respectable" spokesman of Creole Belizeans and, as President of the British Honduras Trades and Labour Union, he attended the Caribbean Labour Congress in Jamaica in August 1947.

Staine, who was nominated to the Legislative Council by Governor Hunter in 1942, joined with R.T. Meighan (they were both members of a Creole middle-class group called the Progressive Party) to support the Employers and Workers bill in 1943. Though trade unions were legalized in 1941, it was only when the Employers and Workers Bill was passed on 27 April, 1943, that breach of labour contract was removed from the criminal code and the infant trade unions of Belize could pursue the struggle for improving labour conditions. The bill had been previously defeated by the employers among the unofficial members in August 1941, so it was the efforts of men like Staine and Meighan that made the crucial difference in 1943.

After the passage of the Employers and Workers Bill the first trade union, the BHWTU, was registered in May 1943, its name soon to be changed to the General Workers Union.[56] Though strikes in the mahogany industry were forbidden by a war-time essential services law that was not amended until 1953, and the Belize Estate and Produce Company refused to allow union officials to visit the lumber camps, the GWU quickly expanded into a nation-wide organization. Beginning with about 350 members in the forest industry and on the waterfront, this union engaged a militant struggle to improve labour conditions and wages. For just a few years in the middle of the war the unemployment problem in Belize was in remission, partly because of a revived demand for mahogany but largely because about 900 men were recruited into a Forestry Unit to work in Scotland (Ford 1985) and even more went to work in Panama. In early 1944 over 400 of the men who had gone to Scotland and about 1,000 of the labourers from Panama returned to Belize. Although by June some of these were recruited to work in the U.S., the problem of re-absorbing all of these workers remained acute. In this context, a successful unionized strike of stevedores in July 1944 and the election of a radical, Clifford E. Betson, to the presidency of the GWU were responsible for the rapid growth of that union.

By the late 1940s the GWU claimed a membership of over 3,000. Based in Belize City, with branches in the districts and in remote chicle and mahogany camps, this organization, more than any other, helped to raise the political consciousness of the working people of Belize in the 1940s. The wretched conditions in which these people lived and worked were translated, through protracted struggles with the Belize Estate and Produce Company and the colonial government, into a protest against colonialism itself. The part played by the BHWTU-GWU, in the eleven years of their existence prior to 1950, in establishing a basis in both consciousness and organization for the nationalist movement and the PUP, can hardly be exaggerated.

An example of the GWU's growing power and influence in this period is the strike against the Belize Estate and Produce Company at the sawmill in Belize City in 1947. The sawmill hands had been negotiating for a raise since 3 January when Betson, the GWU President, urged them to unite: "The inertia of B.H. workmen in respect of their rights must disappear and there must be an end to the exploitation of workers."[57] By early February some 300 men were on strike and Betson told them, "we are dealing with a company who are in a position to pay what we ask of them. . . . It is only right that we should share some of the profits of our land." This nationalist note was echoed by the GWU treasurer, who said, "a meeting of this kind stretches into the life and economy of British Honduras. You men are here to decide whether you shall live as slaves or as freemen in your homeland."[58] For twenty days the employer ignored GWU's demand for a raise from $1.25 to $2.00, and when he eventually offered a 10 per cent increase the men refused it. Farmers from Santana, Salt Creek and other villages on the Northern Highway, many of whom were unemployed persons from Belize Town who were settled there in the mid-1930s, offered free food for the strikers. In early March an arbitration board awarded the sawmill men $1.90 a day, which was a major victory for the workers and their union.[59]

The success of this strike in early 1947 led to others at the Corozal sugar factory and on the Belize waterfront where 45 longshoremen walked off the job in a wildcat strike. It was in the context of this labour agitation that George C. Price and some other middle-class alumni of St. John's College, members of a Jesuit Christian Social Action Group, got their feet on the bottom of the political ladder. Price, who was R.S. Turton's secretary, had failed to get elected to the Belize City Council in 1943 but in November 1947 he succeeded. Price, along with John Smith, Herbert Fuller and Karl Wade (and the editors of the *Belize Billboard*, Philip Goldson and Leigh Richardson) belonged to the "Natives First" Independent Group. These middle class Catholic nationalists succeeded in ending the domination of the Belize City Council by Lionel Francis' People's Group, by linking Belize's social and economic troubles to the wider colonial context. However, when Betson, in his New Year Message to the GWU in 1948, called for a "united labour front, the election of representatives of labour," and the introduction of Socialism to Belize, the *Belize Billboard* editors, though they published Betson's message, dissociated themselves from its "dangerous tendency."[60]

Soberanis returned to Belize in 1948 and joined "Kid" Broaster and L.D. Kemp in the Open Forum[61] in a further public challenge to British colonialism. Their meetings were characterized by pro-Americanism, complete with renditions of the "Stars and Stripes" and "God Bless America", and a rather equivocal attitude toward the Guatemalan territorial claim. While their goal was political independence, they argued that "The Guatemalan stand opens the gateway for natives to have legal rights to self-determination" (Soberanis and Kemp 1949: 10). The Open Forum group sharply distinguished itself from the Legislative Councillors who expressed loyalty to the British Crown and who, like the lawyer Harrison Courtenay, favoured the proposed West Indian Federation. Soberanis and Kemp saw advantages for Belize, especially in labour opportunities, in a closer association with the Central American republics.

Belize in the 1940s, far from slumbering, was in a political ferment. Among the chief issues that agitated Belizeans, including universal suffrage and constitutional reform, West Indian Federation, import controls and immigration, and the Guatemalan claim, was the widespread economic distress and unemployment that followed the return of almost two thousand labourers from abroad and the renewed depression in the chicle and mahogany industries.[62] Of the many groups and organizations involved in politics after the war, including the People's Group, the "Natives First" Independent Group, the Christian Social Action Group, and the Open Forum, the only mass organization involved in political issues was the GWU, that sprang from the LUA and BHWTU. The intense labour and political activity of the union prepared the ground for the middle-class politicians who seized the opportunity provided by devaluation at the end of 1949. The independence movement in general, and the PUP in particular, grew out of the labour movement that had been developing for sixteen years before devaluation.

The People's Committee, formed in response to the devaluation of the dollar on 31 December 1949, included people of diverse social backgrounds and political opinions who united over the issue of devaluation because it dramatically brought together economic and labour problems with concerns about colonial control and constitutional reform. Devaluation produced an immediate fall in the people's purchasing power and standard of living whilst protecting the interests of the Belize Estate and Produce Company and others who traded in the sterling area. Serious as the economic effects of devaluation were, the event was politically explosive because it came after repeated assurances by the British Government (which had devalued the pound in September) that the BH dollar would remain at parity with the U.S. dollar, and it was enforced against the majority of the Legislative Council who could claim at least to be the elected representatives of Belize. The Governor passed devaluation on the instructions of the Colonial Office, by the use of the reserve powers that were incorporated in the constitution in 1932. There could hardly have been a more perfect issue for the incipient nationalist movement to exploit.

On the night that the dollar was devalued, the Open Forum held a protest meeting at the Battlefield and John Smith and George Price were among the guest speakers.[63] When the People's Committee (PC) was formed, with Smith as Chairman and Price as Secretary, one of the members was Clifford Betson. Within a month the PC and the GWU were holding joint meetings, discussing issues ranging from devaluation to labour legislation and from federation to constitutional reform. Many of the labour and political pioneers of the 1930s and 1940s were active in the months following devaluation, often at meetings organized by the PC and GWU. In early February, the Open Forum and the PC were said to have "amalgamated and started a vigorous campaign by means of public meetings, processions through Belize, and petitions"[64] but soon the "old hands of the Open Forum," namely Broaster and Soberanis, split from the PC.[65] In November Soberanis and Meighan contested the Belize City Council elections as Independents. They lost and the PUP won five of the nine seats.[66] Soberanis wrote later that he and Kemp decided to hand everything over to Price in 1950, "to carry on the same fight for independence."[67] In 1951, Joseph Campbell was reported to have said at a meeting at the Battlefield that "the PUP have some educated young men to lead them, and he is very glad that at last some young fellows have come along to form this movement."[68] While Soberanis, Meighan, and Campbell no longer had the influence or following they once had, it is important to note these continuities between the early political agitation in Belize and the PC and PUP in 1950 and 1951.

Above all, the links between the GWU and the PC were important in the rapid rise of the nationalist movement after 1950. Without the support of the GWU, the only extant mass organization of the working people with branches nationwide, the early success of the PUP would have been unthinkable. The President and General Secretary of the GWU were national figures before 1950. Henry A. Middleton, the Secretary, had been an organizer since 1939 when he was the representative of forest workers on the BHFWPA.[69] Despite the PC's dependence on the experience and organization of the GWU's leaders, the middle-class members of the PC, all of whom were St. John's College alumni and members of the Christian Social Action Group, took over the leadership of the union at its Annual Meeting on 28 April 1950. Nicholas Pollard, President of the weak Mercantile Clerks Union, became President of the GWU, John

Smith Vice-President, and George Price and Philip Goldson members of the Executive Council. Betson fought the takeover in vain. After seven years as a militant and pioneering union chief, he was given the dubious honorific title of "Patriarch of the Union." Middleton remained as General Secretary, and in April, 1951, he apparently objected to the further consolidation of PUP control over the union, when Price was made Vice President, Goldson became Assistant Secretary, and Richardson joined the Executive Committee. Shortly after, Middleton was dismissed by the PUP officials, and when Kemp claimed in the *Daily Clarion* that this was a conspiracy to get rid of black officials who were not Catholic, he, too, was expelled from the GWU by the new committee. Betson, who had been made a life-member of the Executive Council in 1950, attended no Council meetings after June 1951.[70]

The PUP and GWU had become essentially identical and were entirely dominated by former members of the Christian Social Action Group. It is hard not to conclude that this group deliberately set about to take over the union for its own political purposes. The labour movement declined in the 1950s as it became increasingly dependent upon the politicians. The middle-class leadership of the PUP was successful in achieving constitutional decolonization, but at the expense of an authentic and autonomous working-class voice in the nationalist movement.

V

The labour movement in the British West Indies in the 1930s produced modern trade unions and nationalist movements that have led, in most cases, to universal adult suffrage and independence. Belize was no exception to this pattern; indeed, the movement may even be said to have started in Belize in 1934. As in the rest of the West Indies, the working people of Belize, beginning to act as a class for the first time in the 1930s and 1940s, unwittingly served as the vehicle for the relatively weak but intensely manipulative middle classes in their rise to political power.[71] When, in 1954, twenty years after the beginning of the labour movement in Belize, universal adult suffrage was attained, it was the middle-class leaders of the PUP who reaped the benefits of the labour struggle and the GWU's organization.

The explanation of these events in Belize is broadly parallel to that of the similar events elsewhere in the British West Indies, with some variations. Conditions of the working people everywhere were terrible—low wages, intermittent employment and spreading unemployment, atrocious housing, hunger and bad health, poor education or none at all, and an absence of the civil rights of suffrage and union organization. Immediate concerns about jobs, food, and housing quickly grew into demands for rights and social justice, and thence into nationalist demands for self-government and independence. The reaction of the colonial administration in Belize was similar to that of such administrations elsewhere, in part because they all followed broadly defined Colonial Office policy, but also because similar structurally defined conditions limited their options. One of the chief functions of the colonial state was to maintain the property of capitalists (whose leading members were invariably nominated to the Legislative Council in Belize), and, as part of that function, to ensure the supply of a cheap labour force. When this could no longer be provided by the immigration and coercion of slaves, the colonial judicial and police system enforced labour laws that made breaches of labour contract by the workers a criminal offense. It was this system that, in the 1930s crisis, was challenged by the working people.

The colonial administration responded to this challenge essentially in three ways. First, by police action, with surveillance, intimidation, force and legal action. When the laws were seen to be inadequate, new ones were quickly passed in order to detain, punish, and isolate the more radical elements and to divide the movement. Second, by making concessions, largely in the form of providing (or sometimes just promising) relief to assuage a proportion of the working people. This began early in Belize and was developed as a deliberate response to the labour movement by Governor Burns in 1935. This strategy, like that of repression, was later used in response to labour rebellions throughout the British West Indies,[72] and became part of the Colonial Development and Welfare program (which was always more welfare than development).[73] This policy was still prevalent in 1949 when the Governor wrote, "Very early launching of relief scheme is necessary owing to the serious position in the Belize and Cayo districts particularly, where I am advised riots might break out if quick action is not taken."[74] Third, the formation of a Labour Department in 1939, ostensibly "to assist and guide the labouring classes in the formation of trade unions along the right lines,"[75] retarded the development of autonomous trade unions by usurping union functions. "The Labour Department was the institutionalization of the colonial approach to trade unionism" (Hamill 1978: 12; see also Ashdown 1979), namely, to paternalistically organize labour and encourage "responsible" labour leaders in order to control the labour movement. The British Trades Union Congress, especially under Sir Walter Citrine who was a member of the Moyne Commission, worked closely with the labour advisors of the Colonial Office and the various Labour Departments in the colonies to propagate "responsible" trade unionism by stressing "the separation between industrial disputes and militant political action" (Craig 1977: 79).

Even when the Colonial Office and its local representatives identified their immediate task as restoring order and quashing rebellion, they retained their role of maintaining a suitable supply of cheap labour for local capitalism. But it was in this regard that the colonial administration became entangled in contradictions. When, for example, Garifuna road workers demanded a raise in July 1939, it was acknowledged by the Acting Governor that "Any increase in the rate of wages paid by Government would of course create difficulties for other employers of labour in the locality."[76] Yet, at the same time, the administration was forced by the workers, who "bitterly resented"[77] the miserable wages paid by the Government, to concede wage increases from time to time. Moreover, as relief work began, with the collapse of the mahogany and chicle industries, to be reconceived less as a temporary palliative and more as a permanent necessity, Government itself became the largest single employer of labour in the colony.[78] That was surely the central contradiction: the colonial state was forced, by the bankruptcy of the very capitalist economy it was there to serve, to substitute a long-term relief work economy. Such welfare became a permanent means of social control because of the inadequacies of the economy, but this only served to raise working people's demands on the government whose economic role was increasingly transparent.

A casual labour market, in which seasonal low paid work and frequent unemployment were the norm, was always a structural condition of the Belizean economy, with resultant insecurity and persistent poverty for the working people. When this economy collapsed in the 1930s the colonial government itself became the chief employer of labour, not simply the means of ensuring its supply to local capitalists. The expanding economic role of the government, and its inability to meet the people's demands in this context, sowed the seeds of nationalism within the labour movement in the 1930s and 1940s and thereby fueled the anti-colonial and independence movement that followed.

Notes

01. Dobson 1973 makes no mention of labour protests and organizations prior to the GWU in her discussion of the development of trade unions and her discussion of politics in the two decades prior to 1950 is almost entirely limited to the Legislative Council and constitutional changes.

02. Grant gets the name of Soberanis' first organization wrong and is incorrect when he says that the agitation "never spread beyond Belize City;" (p. 67).

03. Gov. Sir John Burdon to Secretary of State (S.S.), 23 July 1931, BA 158.

04. Act. Gov. H.G. Pilling to S.S., 12 Nov. 1931 and 3 Dec. 1931, BA 158.

05. *Clarion*, 22 Feb. 1934, 165.

06. Police Superintendent P.E. Matthews report to the Governor, 27 Nov. 1934, CO 123/346/35524 and BA, SP25.

07. *Clarion*, 15 March 1934, 232.

08. Gov. Sir Harold Kittermaster, to S.S., 7 March 1934, CO 123/346/35524.

09. Matthews, op. cit.

10. See the autobiographical letter, A. Soberanis to Vernon Leslie, 10 July 1973, BA, SP 27. Soberanis' father, Canuto Soberanis, came to Belize from Yucatán in 1894 and

lived in San Antonio, Orange Walk. His mother, Dominga Gomez was born in Corozal. Antonio, the eldest of seven children, was born on 17 January 1897. He attended R.C. Primary School in Belize Town until 1912, went to Honduras and all the other Central American countries and the U.S.A. Soberanis was a member of the Volunteers Guard in World War I and served in the Cayo expedition in 1914. See also "Oral History: The L. and U.A.," National Studies 2:3 (1974), 3-10.

11. Matthews, op. cit.

12. Ibid.

13. Ibid.

14. "Memorial in regard to conditions in the Colony," Soberanis to Kittermaster, 17 May 1934, BA, MP 700-34.

15. Kittermaster to Soberanis, 18 May 1934, BA, MP 700-34.

16. Soberanis to Kittermaster, 21 May 1934, BA, MP 700-34.

17. See reports enclosed in Acting Gov. Hunter to S.S., 14 Aug. 1934, CO 123/346/35524.

18. Matthews, op. cit.

19. Ibid.

20. Absolom Pollard recovered from his wound and it was never discovered who shot him. The police contended that it was a member of the crowd but it was widely believed that Corporal Building was responsible.

21. Matthews, op. cit.

22. Ibid.

23. Gov. A.C. Burns to S.S., 31 March 1935, CO 123/352/66554.

24. Burns to S.S., 26 July 1935, CO 123/353/66571.

25. Matthews report, 12 June 1935, included in Burns to S.S., 13 June 1935, CO 123/353/66568.

26. Burns to S.S., 13 June 1935, CO 123/353/66568.

27. Burns to S.S., 23 May 1935, CO 123/353/66571

28. Serg. A.B. Clarke's report, 20 July 1935, CO 123/353/66571

29. Soberanis to Burns, 23 Sept. 1935, CO 123/353/66571.

30. Att. Gen. S.A. McKinistry to Burns, 22 July 1935, CO 123/353/66571.

31. Burns to S.S., 30 Oct. 1935, CO 123/353/66571.

32. Burns to Beckett, 15 Nov. 1935, CO 123/354/66648. A Colonial Office official approved of Burns' action: "The Governor took the right line in putting Mr. Grant on to try Tony, so as to avoid any suspicion of colour clash;" Rootham's minute, 13 Dec. 1935, CO 123/354/66648.

33. The amount spent on outdoor relief, distributed largely in Belize Town, had increased rapidly from $2,600 in 1931 to about $10,000 in 1935 and 1936 (Cheverton and Smart 1937:47).

34. Corpl. Cornelius A. Building to Supt. of Police, 21 June 1938, CO 123/367/66648

35. Burns to S.S., 22 Nov. 1938, CO 123/366/66553.

36. Ibid.

37. Burns to S.S., 5 Jan. 1939, CO 123/373/66553

38. Burns to S.S., 13 March 1939, CO 123/373/66553.

39. Ibid.

40. This paper was owned by a black radical, Herbert Hill Cain. Kemp's column, called "The Garvey Eye," was viewed with suspicion by the colonial administration.

41. Burns to S.S., 24 March 1939, CO 123/373/66553.

42. Act. Gov. Johnston to S.S., 10 Aug. 1939, CO 123/373/66553.

43. This was not related to the British Honduras Federation of Workers Protection Association, which Kemp formed earlier in 1939, and which was still functioning in 1941, though not really as a union. The newly created Labour Department reported that the BHFWPA "could not qualify as a trade union" and that it often "proved of considerable assistance to the Department in relief work and other matters" (Labour Department Report, 1940).

44. *Belize Independent*, 26 March 1941.

45. Soberanis to S.J. Hudson, 3 June 1940, BA, SP 25.

46. Soberanis to Leslie, 10 July 1973, BA, SP 27.

47. Burns to S.S., 28 Dec. 1938, CO 123/376/66824.

48. Ibid.

49. Ibid.

50. Gov. J. A. Hunter to Lord Moyne, 24 Oct. 1941, BA 174.

51. Hunter to Viscount Cranbourne, 5 March 1942, BA 174.

52. Ibid.

53. *Belize Independent*, 27 Aug. 1941.

54. Hunter to Stanley, 8 Feb. 1943, CO 123/380.

55. Garvey had previously visited Belize in 1910 and 1921. (This account of Garvey and the UNIA in Belize is indebted to Ashdown 1981.)

56. Annual Report of the Labour Department, 1943.

57. *Belize Billboard*, 12 Jan. 1947.

58. *Belize Billboard*, 2 Feb. 1947.

59. *Belize Billboard*, 9 March 1947.

60. *Belize Billboard*, 3 Jan. 1948.

61. Joseph Campbell was probably one of this group. It was later reported that he had "preached anti-British propaganda" in 1948 (Gov. R.H. Garvey to S.S., 5 Sept. 1951, CO 537/7375).

62. 1,166 people were registered as unemployed in Belize City in October 1949 and the situation was expected to get worse; Bradley's report, 31 Oct. 1949, CO 123/401/66985. By March 1950 there were 2,415 unemployed; Garvey's report, 30 Sept. 1950, CO 123/406/66985.

63. Since much of the story of the development of nationalist politics between 1950 and 1954 has already been told it will not be repeated here; see Shoman 1973 and Grant 1976: Chap. 4.

64. Garvey to S.S., 26 Feb. 1950, CO 537/6132.

65. Garvey to S.S., 29 March 1950, CO 537/6132.

66. Garvey to S.S., 25 Nov. 1950, CO 123/403/66152/2.

67. Soberanis to Leslie, 10 July 1973, BA, SP 27.

68. C.M. Flores police report, 14 Aug. 1951, CO 123/403/66512/6.

69. *Daily Clarion*, 25 May 1939. He was a delegate at meetings of the Caribbean Labour Congress and the Free World Labour Conference in London in 1949; Garvey to S.S., 20 Jan. 1950, CO 537/6132.

70. GWU newsletter, 25 April 1952, CO 1031/784.

71. For a monumental study of the Jamaican case, in which this argument is made, see Post 1978 and 1981.

72. A Colonial Office official advocated the use of relief work in Jamaica in December 1938 as an "insurance against disorder"; quoted in Post 1978:438.

73. The general case about welfare as a means of social control appears in Piven and Cloward 1971.

74. Garvey to S.S., 26 Aug. 1949, CO 123/394/66620/5

75. Labour Department Report, 1939. The Governor recognized that the sole Labour Officer was "not qualified to assist and guide the labouring class in the formation of Trade Unions, or to speak with any authority on questions of labour legislation;" Hunter to S.S., 5 Aug. 1940, CO 123/379/66807

76. Act. Gov. Johnston to S.S., 22 Aug. 1939, CO 123/377/66853.

77. Burns to S.S., 3 Jan. 1939, CO 123/373/66553.

78. "The Public Works Department employs the largest labour force in the Colony... (exclusive of relief work)," namely 1,284 workers compared to 1,091 employed by the Belize Estate and Produce Company; Garvey's report on Economic Development and Employment, 30 Sept. 1950, CO 123/ 406/66985.

An earlier version of this paper was presented at a symposium at the Centre for Caribbean Studies, University of Warwick, and at the Ninth Annual Conference of the Society for Caribbean Studies, 1985.

Part 4

Decolonization and Nationhood

8. Ethnicity, Pluralism and Politics in Belize

Introduction: Ethinicity and Pluralism

Ethnicity, like "race," class, and gender, is a social construction, a set of ideas or ideology about people's identities and relations. It is an aspect of culture that is created, challenged and redefined by people even while it constrains them. In fact, those ideas that constrain people the most, such as ideas about "race" and gender, are generally those that appear to be "natural" and hence irrevocable. Ideologies about "races," which are conceived in biogenetic terms, are part of a contested social process of identifying "cultures" and drawing boundaries between "ethnic groups." Not only are cultures defined partly in racial terms, therefore, but "racial groups" also claim more or less exclusive ownership of cultures. It follows that if one or more of these groups tries to establish its political dominance in a culturally heterogeneous society, they will engage in an ideological struggle with others over the "national culture." This struggle, which may involve a group claiming historical priority or numerical predominance, is premised on the assumption that "culture" and "race" are inextricably and inevitably linked, and are immutable, rather than socially constructed, variable and historically changing. Whatever form of cultural nationalism emerges from the anti-colonial and post-colonial periods, therefore, is the consequence of the outcome of this cultural and political struggle, the parameters of which are culturally defined and contested in racial, religious, linguistic, class, and gender terms.

Individuals define themselves and their social identities in constrained circumstances and largely in terms which are handed down to them, but individuals also become "tokens" of racial, ethnic, and class types, thus participating in the shaping of group identities and contests for national identity. Who is defined as a "National Hero," and who is an "immigrant"? What meaning is attached to the identity of "Creole" in terms of citizenship in the new nation-state?[1] In what ways is the culture of the nation contested and negotiated around concepts of the "Indigenous," the "Creole," and the "Alien"?

How are myths about a people's origin and claims about their contribution used to negotiate the definition of a group and its "place" in the nation? How is this cultural struggle related to the control of resources, the production and distribution of the material bases of social life, the economy and class structure? How is the ideological struggle affected by the use or threat of force? How does this dynamic process of cultural contestation, this "politics of cultural struggle" (Williams 1991), shape and invent the "tradition" of the new nation? What aspects of a "given" tradition, in the sense of objectified culture, will be selected as symbols to be used in the struggle against an old, or to establish a new, cultural hegemony? How will this selection affect the continuing creation of ethnic groups, and their relations and realignments, as well as the place of people who are more ambiguously identified outside these groups? How are the relations of the new state with other states affected by, and how do they affect, this struggle about national identity and culture? These questions suggest that what comes to be defined as the national identity, culture and tradition, far from being predetermined by supposedly primordial identities, is actually the outcome of a complex and multi-layered political and ideological struggle.

People who struggle to shape their social identities, and to have them accepted by others, do so in the concentric contexts of their family, community, state, region, and the world, so trends of nationalism, class, gender and racial consciousness in other places affect the terms and outcome of their struggle. The removal of colonial hegemony in any one place occurs while nationalist and pan-national movements are taking place elsewhere, and while a new imperial hegemony or "world order" seeks to replace the old. In the cases of Belize and Guyana, for example, these "external" factors, including the imperial succession from Britain to the United States, the politics of the Cold War, the emergence of Pan-African and Black Power movements, and the territorial claims of neighbouring states, influence the "internal" struggles in these societies (Bolland 1997).

Ethnicity is part of a social process, along with class and gender, in the construction of social and collective identities. The central components of ethnicity are "ideas of inheritance, ancestry and descent, place or territory of origin, and the sharing of kinship, any one or combination of which may be invoked as a claim according to context and calculation of advantages" (Tambiah 1989: 335). Consequently, the social meaning of ethnic identities, far from being fixed, varies according to the historical social context in which they occur and is the continually shifting outcome of competing claims. In the Caribbean, a historical preoccupation with the idea of "race" has left its powerful mark in the prevailing conceptions of ethnicity, not only in the sense that racial or somatic traits are generally considered an aspect of ethnic identity, but also in the widespread assumption that ethnic identity is an ascribed characteristic, a matter of common descent linked with "race." Categories of ancestors and their descendants are often labelled interchangeably as "ethnic groups, races, nations, peoples, or castes" (Williams 1991: 168).

Ethnicity is both an ideological idiom and a structural principle, a way of describing and ordering social relations. Ethnicity is simultaneously the way we identify ourselves and the way we distinguish ourselves from others, according to particular contexts. The ways in which people identify themselves and others in terms of "race" and ethnicity, therefore, are profoundly affected by their positions and relations in the economy and power structure, the class and gender system, of their society, which is linked to the relations that the society has with others. This is especially evident in colonial societies where several racially and ethnically distinguished groups have such distinct economic functions that they are bound together as a society only by the political hegemony of the colonial power. Nevertheless, the colonial hegemony, which influenced the ways people think of themselves and others, and even how such concepts as "race", ethnicity and gender are constructed, was itself contested. During the colonial period, when the imperial country exercised a monopoly of power over all the ethnic groups within the colony, and greatly influenced how such groups were defined, these groups often coexisted with little interaction, each with its own set of social institutions, in a segmentary social structure.

This is essentially M.G. Smith's model of a "plural society," derived from the work of J.S. Furnivall on colonial Southeast Asia, which he applies to "Caribbean Creole societies" (Smith 1991). Furnivall argued that, within the colonial polity, the various racial and ethnic groups occupied distinct economic niches that were related through the market system. Socially, each group holds by its own religion, its own culture and language, its own ideas and ways...[It is] a plural society...different sections of the community living side by side, but separately, within the same political unit (Furnivall 1948: 34).

Smith, in applying this idea to the British Caribbean, argues that it is only the exercise of colonial power that holds the plural society together: "Given the fundamental differences of belief, value, and organization that connote pluralism, the monopoly of power by one cultural section is the essential precondition for the maintenance of the total society in its current form" (Smith 1965: 86).[2]

Smith subsequently distinguished between cultural pluralism and a plural society. Whereas cultural pluralism was simply "the condition of institutional and cultural diversity within a given population," plural societies are "those culturally split societies governed by dominant demographic minorities whose peculiar social structures and political conditions set them apart" (Smith 1984: 29). In a plural society the culturally diverse groups act in the public domain as corporations:

Plural societies are constituted and distinguished by corporate divisions that differ culturally, and...these may be aligned in differing ways to create hierarchic, segmented or complex pluralities.... In short, while the coexistence of culturally distinct aggregates is sufficient and necessary to constitute pluralism, to constitute a plural society such divisions must also operate as corporations, *de jure* or *de facto*, within the public domain (Smith 1984: 32).

What distinguishes a plural society from a society exhibiting cultural pluralism, therefore, is the existence of discrete cultural and social segments that engage in political divisions and conflicts. According to Smith, the relations between these social segments, which are distinguished in terms of status as well as culture,

are *ipso facto* political relations.... Moreover, since sectional norms, interests, and institutions are sharply divergent and often conflict, the balance of sectional forces will regulate the course of political development (Smith 1965: 320).

In an essay published in 1991,[3] Smith reiterated the need to distinguish not only between culturally homogeneous and heterogeneous societies, but also between

those that institutionalize cultural pluralism as social or structural pluralism by segmental or differential incorporation in the public domain, and those that do not. This typology rests on two sets of conditions, namely, on the cultural similarity or diversity of members of a common society, and on the modes of their incorporation (Smith 1991: 10).

Smith creates three classes of "Caribbean Creole societies," as distinct from the Hispanic societies consisting of Cuba, the Dominican Republic, and Puerto Rico. The first class consists of the "miniscule units," generally the "dependencies of dependencies," such as Carriacou and Providencia, some of which contain people of a single racial stock, while others include both blacks and whites....Whether of common race or not, some of these small communities are socially homogeneous while others are not, though notably less split and less hierarchic than the larger, better known Caribbean societies (Smith 1991: 11).

The second class is of "modally biracial and *de facto* hierarchic pluralities of greater population and size, which may or may not contain two or three social sections" (Smith 1991: 12), such as Barbados, Haiti, Martinique, Guadeloupe and Jamaica. Societies in the third class, called "modally segmental pluralities," contain "three or more racial stocks, cultures and languages, incorporated as equivalent segments, though now *de facto* dominated by the Creole group or one of its sections" (Smith 1991: 12). The "Creole segments" of these segmental societies are "hierarchic like the biracial Creole societies" (Smith 1991: 12). Smith places Belize, Trinidad, Guyana and Suriname in this third category.

Smith states that his goal is to see whether his analyses of "the social compositions and plural structures" of six selected case studies—Haiti, Suriname, Grenada, Guyana, Jamaica, and Trinidad—"provide a fuller and more detailed understanding of their recent political and ideological developments" (Smith 1991: 5) than alternative theories. However, Smith leaps directly from his outline of types of *plural* society to his case studies without articulating a *theory* of plural societies. Theories must explain a relationship between variables, and Smith's typology of Creole Caribbean societies is not a theory because it does not posit an explanation of the political and ideological developments in terms of factors independent of these developments. On the contrary, his evidence for the classification of these plural societies is inseparable from the developments themselves, so his argument is circular: these are plural societies because the cultural groups compete politically, and the cultural groups compete politically because these are plural societies.

For the plural society analysis to succeed as a theory it must be able to *explain* why cultural groups "operate as corporations"—thereby constituting a plural society—in some instances and not others. Such an explanation cannot depend simply on the existence of such segments, but must refer to the influence of other factors which would, or would not, induce them to interact in this particular way. If Smith's real purpose is actually to test his plural society "theory", or to evaluate it in relation to alternative theories, then the appropriate method would be to select examples that really *test* it, in the sense of exploring the limits and exposing the weaknesses of the theory. However, Smith appears more concerned with defending his analysis from his critics, so his examples are selected to show how well they can fit his model. Having identified Belize as a "modally segmented plurality," he says nothing more about it and discusses only the other three examples of this type, namely Guyana, Suriname, and Trinidad. The study of Belize, then, may expose the limitations of Smith's approach. We need to be able to explain why some societies, such as Guyana, have, in Smith's terms, institutionalized cultural pluralism as structural pluralism in the public domain, while others, such as Belize, have not (Bolland 1997). We must conclude that *cultural pluralism does not necessarily result in corresponding political divisions and conflicts*, hence, in order to understand why these divisions and conflicts occur in some cases and not others, we need to examine the specific economic and political circumstances in which these groups come to be formed and to interact. The explanation of the differences in these societies, then, lies not in the assumed *a priori* existence of such groups, but in the dialectical interrelation between such groups-in-formation and other factors in the wider context within which they emerged. This essay will show how Belize became a "culturally pluralist" society, but not, or at least not yet, a "plural society" in M.G. Smith's sense.

Cultural Diversity and Ethnicity in Belize

One of the most striking features of Belize is its cultural diversity (Bolland 1986: 39-68). More than 250,000 people live in a country that is slightly larger than El Salvador or about twice the size of Jamaica. The majority of Belizeans are descendants of immigrants who came from various parts of the world in the last two centuries. The demographic history of the colony of Belize may be divided into three periods: first, from the initial British settlement in the mid-seventeenth century to the middle of the nineteenth century; second, from the mid-nineteenth to the mid-twentieth century; and third, from the mid-twentieth century to the present.

The British settlement at Belize began in the seventeenth century when the indigenous Maya population already had been considerably reduced by epidemics spreading from Spanish incursions (Bolland 1994). The British colonists' economy was based on the export of logwood until about 1770 and then increasingly on mahogany. This economic shift had three important social consequences, as a result of the fact that logwood was a small tree that grew in clusters near the coast and was shipped in small chunks, whereas mahogany was a huge tree that grew sparsely in the interior and was shipped in giant squared logs. First, the search for mahogany led the colonists ever deeper into the interior, to the north, south, and west, though the logging camps were generally temporary and the chief settlement remained at the mouth of the Belize River, down which many of the logs were floated. The Maya resisted this expansion but in the early nineteenth century they withdrew further into the interior to avoid the British camps (Bolland 1977a, 1977b: 14-24). Second, the British settlers, who first cut and shipped logwood by themselves or with a few slaves, needed more labour to extract mahogany, so they imported hundreds more slaves in the late eighteenth and early nineteenth centuries. These were acquired largely in West Indian slave markets and were African or of African descent. By the early nineteenth century there were almost 3,000 slaves in Belize, amounting to about three quarters of the population. When slavery was finally ended in 1838, over 90 percent of the population of the British settlement was of African or part-African descent (Bolland 1973, 1977b: 49-105). Third, the shift from the small-scale operation of cutting and shipping logwood to the large scale of mahogany extraction led to a concentration of property, essentially in slaves and land claims, in the hands of a tiny minority of chiefly British origin. Calling themselves the "Principal Inhabitants," they controlled the settlement, which was a colony in all but name, in their own interests (Bolland 1977b: 25-48, 156-73).

During this period, between the mid-seventeenth and the mid-nineteenth centuries, the core of Belize's Creole culture was established, centred around Belize Town (Bolland 1987a). There was considerable African influence in this emerging culture, but the British colonizers continually repressed African cultures and dominated the formal institutions—legal, administrative, political, economic, religious, and educational. By the early nineteenth century the Garifuna, who are descendants of Carib people of the Lesser Antilles and Africans who had escaped from slavery, had settled along the coast in southern Belize. The Garifuna, after resisting British and French colonialism, were transported from St. Vincent across the Caribbean to the Bay Islands in the Gulf of Honduras and in the early 1800s established villages along the mainland coast (Gonzalez 1988). By the 1840s, Dangriga, called Stann Creek by the British, was a flourishing Garifuna community. The Garifuna lived chiefly by fishing and growing fruits and vegetables, some of which they traded in Belize Town, but the British treated them as squatters and a source of wage labour for the mahogany gangs (Bolland 1977b: 132-5). After the abolition of slavery the power of the settler oligarchy declined, but the British maintained power through metropolitan-based companies and the formalization of colonial institutions, and cultural hegemony was increasingly effected through churches, schools and legal institutions. In the 1850s Britain explicitly asserted its sovereignty over the colony and approved the first official constitution in 1854 (Bolland 1977b: 174-93).

The second period of the colony's demographic history began during the Caste War in the Yucatán peninsula, a devastating struggle that halved the population of the area between 1847 and 1855. Thousands of Maya and Mestizo refugees fled to Belize and many settled. They established towns and villages in the north and west where they quickly became the overwhelming majority of the population. They brought Maya traditions of *milpa* farming and also developed the first sugar plantations of the colony (Bolland 1974, 1977a, 1977b: 125-32). The 1861 census recorded over 25,000 people in Belize, 57 percent of whom were born outside the colony. This census, though not accurate, suggests a population composition in proportions similar to those today, with the two largest ethnic groups, namely the Mestizo and the Creole, together accounting for between two thirds and three quarters of the total, but neither constituting a majority. While some Mestizos prospered as farmers and traders, most remained poor and they were treated by the British as aliens, defined by their race, language, and religion as "Spanish," and stereotyped through a long history of colonial rivalry and prejudice. By 1857 the northern town of Corozal, which was only six years old, had 4,500 inhabitants, predominantly Mestizo, and was second only to Belize Town which then had 7,000 inhabitants, chiefly Creole.

The Maya refugees were even less fortunate in their relations with the British. By 1862 about 1,000 Maya had established several villages, clustered around their centre in San Pedro, in the remote area of the Yalbac Hills in the west. When one group attacked a mahogany camp and demanded ransom for their prisoners and rent for their land, the British retaliated. The Maya routed the British detachment sent to San Pedro in 1866 but the next year the British sent a larger force and destroyed the Maya villages, provision stores and crops. Skirmishing continued in the west and north of Belize until the Maya leader, Marcos Canul, was killed during an attack on Orange Walk Town in 1872. After this the British saw the Maya settlers less as a threat than as a potential source of cheap labour for their early plantation economy, along with hundreds of imported Chinese and Indian labourers, while they viewed the Creoles as unsuited to agricultural tasks (Bolland 1974, 1977a, 1977b: 136-55).

Landownership continued to be highly concentrated, with ownership shifting from old settler families to British-based companies. Only a few years after the largest landowners had obtained firm and formal titles to their vast estates (Bolland and Shoman 1977: 72-7) the Crown Lands Ordinance of 1872 created a system of reservations for the Maya and Garifuna settlers while denying them titles to such land. By the Alcalde Jurisdiction Act, 1858, a system of indirect rule was established, by which Maya and Garifuna people could seek permits to use land through the *alcaldes* in their villages. The office of *alcalde*, which was adopted from the Spanish system of local government, was left deliberately vague and indeterminate in order that real authority remained in the colonial power structure. Despite the Maya's efforts to resist colonization, they became increasingly incorporated into the colony as a defeated, dispossessed, and dependent people (Bolland 1977a, 1987b).

Groups of Mopan and Kekchi Maya who fled from forced labour in Guatemala and came to Belize in the 1880s and 1890s found themselves in similar conditions to the other Maya. They settled in the south, chiefly in a cluster of villages around San Antonio in Toledo District, in a remote and quite isolated part of the country. There they maintained a strong sense of identity and more of their traditions, for example in language, dress, and religion, and were less integrated into the colony than the other Maya who earlier had settled in the north and west. In different times and places and in different ways, then, the Maya who returned to Belize in the nineteenth century became incorporated into the colony as poor and powerless people, but most remained quite isolated from the Creoles and Garifuna.

By the end of the nineteenth century the pattern of settlement that has persisted in the twentieth century was essentially in place: Protestants, largely of African descent, who spoke English or Creole, lived in and near Belize Town; the Roman Catholic Mestizos and Maya, who spoke Spanish, were settled chiefly in the north and west; the Mopan and Kekchi Maya lived in the southern interior and the largely Catholic Garifuna, who spoke their own language and often Spanish or English as well, lived on the southern coast. Along with the very small but powerful group of settlers of British origin, and small groups of (East) Indians who lived in villages in the far north and south, these added up to about 37,000 people at the turn of the century. This population continued to grow slowly, without marked changes in its composition, until by 1946 there were 59,220 people (West Indian Census: 1948).

The third period, from the mid-twentieth century to the present, is characterized by an accelerated rate of population growth, resulting largely from natural increase because the infant mortality rate has declined dramatically while the birth rate remains high. The average annual rate of population increase was just over 3 percent between 1946 and 1960, when the population reached 90,505. The rate of increase slowed, partly because of emigration, but the population continued to grow, to 119,645 in 1970, then 145,353 in 1980, and 184,722 in 1991 and 232,111 in 2000. The ethnic composition of this population, which was fairly stable in the first half of last century, has changed recently. As in the nineteenth century, this change was caused chiefly by migration patterns, but with a difference: not only have thousands of immigrants settled in Belize, but also thousands of Belizeans have emigrated. The perception and evaluation of these changes has recently become an emotional issue in Belize, particularly among Creoles who, after several decades as the largest single ethnic group, are once again outnumbered by the Mestizos. These changes, and the increasing politicization of ethnicity in Belize, are the result of economic changes within the country, and also of changes in neighbouring countries and in Belize's relations with Britain and the United States.

The timber trade declined in the 1850s and 1860s and never fully recovered. Though the export of chicle produced a brief boom for some people, and many Maya, Mestizo, and Garifuna people engaged in small farming, the colonial economy essentially stagnated while the population grew. Several plantation crops were tried but until the 1950s none succeeded. Few of the urban-based Creoles were attracted to agriculture and most people in the town of Belize were very poor, especially after the onset of the Great Depression and a catastrophic hurricane that virtually destroyed the town in 1931. The decline in the economy and the disastrous hurricane intensified the endemic poverty, and led to widespread unemployment and increasing social dislocation. People responded. A series of demonstrations and strikes and the formation of the Labourers and Unemployed Association (LUA) in 1934 led in five years to the first trade union. In the 1940s this organization, the General Workers Union, brought together thousands of working people in different parts of the country and provided the crucial base for the rapid development of the People's United Party after 1950 (Bolland 1988a).

The economic crisis of the 1930s was only temporarily relieved during World War II when several thousand Belizeans obtained work abroad. The economically active population grew rapidly from about 20,000 people in 1946, to 27,000 in 1960, 33,000 in 1970, and over 46,000 in 1980, amounting to an increase from 55 to 65 percent of the population over 15 years old. Much of this increase is accounted for by the rapid rise of economically active women, especially in the expanding clerical, sales, and service sectors. Meanwhile, the production of sugar and citrus expanded in the 1950s, and the value of sugar and citrus exports has exceeded that of forest products since 1959. Despite these developments, and a growth in fishing and tourism, the Belizean economy has not kept pace with the growth in the labour force. Unemployment, officially estimated to account for 14.3 percent of the labour force in 1980, has increased subsequently with the crisis in the sugar industry and spreading recession (Bolland 1986: 69-102).

The unemployment problem is especially acute in Belize City and Dangriga, where Creole and Garifuna people are concentrated. Nationwide, over 40 percent of young people, aged 15 to 24 years, remain out of work after leaving school, many of them never having experienced a regular job. In Belize City, where the rates are even higher, such a lack of prospects resulted in dramatic increases in gangs, crime, and drugs, and also emigration. As economic and cultural ties with Britain weakened, even before independence, most Belizean emigrants go to the United States, primarily to cities such as New York, Los Angeles, Chicago, Miami, and New Orleans. Of an estimated 70,000 Belizeans now living abroad, the vast majority are Creole or Garifuna, aged between 20 and 34 years. They contribute millions of dollars in remittances to families back home, but this emigration has reduced the Creole and Garifuna communities of Belize substantially.

Meanwhile, the number of immigrants in Belize has increased. The proportion of the population that was foreign-born increased from 8 percent in 1960 to 11 percent in 1980, due to an influx of thousands of people from Mexico and Central America, including several thousand German-speaking Mennonites who began coming to Belize in 1958. In the 1980s, in particular, there has been a major influx of immigrants from Central America, many of them refugees from wars in Guatemala and El Salvador, amounting to somewhere between 25,000 and 31,000 persons. Settling mostly in Cayo and Toledo, the western and southern districts, and as poorly-paid workers on banana plantations in Stann Creek District, they are visible in most of the country, including the sidewalks and markets of the towns where some are vendors. Many Belizeans, particularly among the Creoles of Belize City, refer to these people as "aliens" or "Spanish" and view them as something of a scapegoat for the nation's problems.

The net result of these patterns of emigration and immigration is a change in the proportions of the ethnic groups in Belize. While such shifts are not new in the country's demographic history, some feel that a "traditional balance" in favour of the Creoles, which for them, at least, had defined Belizean society, is somehow being subverted as recent migration patterns are producing an "imbalance." The censuses, which define "ethnic groups" in such a way as to reinforce an orthodoxy that they are absolute and largely hereditary categories, show that despite some changes in proportions there is actually considerable continuity in settlement patterns. In the northern districts of Corozal and Orange Walk, Mestizos constitute 74 and 72 percent of the population, respectively, whereas in Belize District 68 percent of the population is Creole. Garifuna people are still concentrated in Stann Creek District, and Mopan and Kekchi Maya are largely in Toledo District. While some towns, such as San Ignacio in Cayo District, are more diverse, other towns and villages have a very distinct ethnic character. Creoles and Garifuna are still the most urbanized ethnic groups, accounting for 44 and 11 percent, respectively, of the 88,069 people classified as urban residents, while half of the remaining 98,653 people, the rural population, are Mestizo (see Table 4). If these demographic trends continue, even if at a slower rate, then Belize will become less of an Afro-Caribbean and more of a Central American nation within the next generation.

However, it is an oversimplification to think of these "ethnic groups" as static, fixed identities, as the censuses imply, because the historical forces, particularly economic and political forces, which have been the source of a dynamic process of ethnic group formation and redefinition will surely continue in future. Most ethnic groups in Belize today, including the three that are the most numerous—the Mestizo, Creole, and Garifuna—are themselves the results of considerable mixtures over several centuries and they are continuing to change. There is intermarriage between members of these groups, as there is also between Mopan and Kekchi Maya, and the East Indians and other Belizeans. Moreover, recent Central American immigrants are not culturally identical to Belizean Mestizos, and many young Belizean Creoles are increasingly influenced by African American and Afro-Caribbean cultures. Not only is Belize a complex and changing multi-ethnic mosaic, but many individual Belizeans, perhaps even a majority, are in many respects multi-cultural. What, then, does "ethnicity" mean in Belize?

Several features, most notably "race," language, and religion, are seen as socially significant markers of ethnic categorization in Belize, as elsewhere, and they are often used as a shorthand for identifying groups, such as "Spanish" and "Creole." Yet, while the census categories and data contribute towards a kind of orthodoxy and rigidity, they also reveal considerable overlap and relativity among these categories. The racial concept of Creole, for example, refers to a spectrum of African and European ancestry in which a variety of physical features, including hair texture and facial features as well as shade of skin, coexist in prolific mixtures, but Creole is also the language which is spoken by many Belizeans who are not of African and European descent. While Belize's official language and the language of instruction in schools is English, most people speak Belizean Creole. As a result of their education and experience many people can shift their speech according to the social context between Creole and standard English, but increasingly with an American accent and idiom. Spanish is the first language for at least a third of the people, while for others it is

Garifuna, German, or a Maya language, and almost two-thirds of the population is bilingual or multilingual.

Religion, also, defines and overlaps "ethnic groups." The English influence on the Creoles was Protestant and the earliest churches were Anglican, Methodist, and Baptist, but their combined adherents now constitute less than 20 percent of the population. After the first modern Catholic church was established in 1851, following the influx of refugees from the north, it succeeded in converting many Creoles and Garifuna, chiefly because of its extensive influence through schools. Catholicism, consequently, unites over 60 percent of Belizeans, from different backgrounds and parts of the country, in one church. While the established Protestant denominations have declined, new fundamentalist and evangelical ones, such as the Pentacostal and Seventh-Day Adventist churches, are growing rapidly, and many of their converts are among former Catholics, of all ethnic groups. Moreover, many Garifuna and Maya people maintain traditional beliefs and rituals alongside their Christian practices, a fact that the census does not acknowledge.

Some scholars have simplified the pluralism of Belize by describing it as divided essentially into two cultural "complexes" or segments. M.G. Smith, for example, writes of the "cleavage" between the "Negro-white Creole and the Spanish-Indian Mestizo" segments which are distinguished "culturally, linguistically, and by race" (Smith 1965: 310). C.H. Grant distinguishes between what he calls the "Creole and Mestizo complexes," the former including whites, Creoles, and Garifuna, and the latter consisting of Spanish, Mestizo, and Maya (Grant 1976: 8). Others, myself included, have argued that this two-segment model is an oversimplification that ignores the dynamics of Belizean culture history and obscures the complexity of the social structure (Bolland 1986: 39-68, 1988b: 191-206, 1991).

A survey of secondary school students found eight different permutations of Creole identity, and people of Mestizo ancestry who no longer spoke Spanish in the home or who spoke Spanish but identified themselves as Maya. Self-identification revealed much more complex categories than those of the census and some ambivalence about the use of ethnic categories.

> Not all individuals of multiple ancestries felt comfortable identifying with a particular ethnic group; in the words of one Belizean youth, many Belizeans were "all mix up." A small, but significant number of people eschewed potentially divisive ethnic categories and referred to themselves simply as "Belizeans." Ethnicity competed with other identities, such as those based on status, occupation, and political affiliation, for primacy in social interaction. Belizean society was as divided by class differences as it was by race, language, religion, and ethnicity (Rutheiser 1993: 204).

Many Belizeans not only practice or participate in more than one cultural tradition but are also coming to share an overarching national identity as they interact with people of different ethnic groups. Though Belizean nationalism remains relatively weak, increasing national consciousness contributes to changing social identities and redefining ethnic boundaries.

Most important, political party affiliation constitutes an identity that often cross-cuts rather than reinforces ethnic identity because party politics is not organized along ethnic lines. Party politics in Belize, from its origins between the 1930s and 1950s, has cut across ethnic group boundaries. The pioneering labour and nationalist leader, Antonio Soberanis Gomez, whose mother was from Corozal and father an immigrant from Mexico, created Belize's first labour organizations. He organized Creole workers in Belize Town and Garifuna workers in Stann Creek. When on trial in Corozal he received donations from the Maya in neighbouring villages and he later spoke up for Maya workers at Baking Pot in the west. His British Honduras Workers and Tradesmen Union had branches in Stann Creek, Corozal, and San Ignacio, that is, in the south, north, and west, in addition to its base in Belize Town. Its successor, the General Workers' Union (GWU), which was led by Clifford E. Betson until 1950, had over 3,000 members and branches in every district, including the remote mahogany and chicle camps. The union's strikes and struggles helped develop an embryonic class and national consciousness on pan-Belizean lines and provided the essential organizational basis for the group of young nationalists who created the People's United Party (PUP) in 1950 (Bolland 1988a). Soberanis and Betson were pushed aside by these new politicians, however, and both died in 1975 with their pioneering role unacknowledged.

Politics In Belize

Until 1954 electoral politics was restricted to less than 2 percent of the population by a narrow franchise, based on a combination of property or income and literacy qualifications. A handful of proto-nationalists who articulated a "Natives First" campaign were elected to the Legislative Council after 1939 but the Belize Town Board (later the City Council), which was elected on a broader franchise, provided a greater opportunity for aspiring politicians to establish a popular base. Most candidates were from the educated middle classes, particularly alumni of St. John's College, the elite Jesuit secondary school in Belize City, who formed the Christian Social Action Group (CSAG) and started a weekly newspaper, the *Belize Billboard*, in 1946. One of the four St. John's alumni who was elected to the City Council in 1947 was George Cadle Price, a Creole Catholic who later became leader of the PUP and Belize's first Prime Minister.

211

The devaluation of the British Honduras dollar on 31 December 1949 brought labour and nationalist forces together around a clear issue. On the one hand, the educated middle classes, whose representatives in the Legislative Council had been overruled by the Governor's reserve powers, wanted a more representative form of government, such as was then being introduced in Jamaica. On the other hand, the working people of Belize, already suffering from widespread unemployment and poverty, experienced an immediate fall in their purchasing power when devaluation caused a rise in the price of imported U.S. goods, including food. In October 1949 there were 1,166 people registered as unemployed in Belize City and they increased to 2,415 by March 1950. On the night that devaluation was declared, Betson of the GWU and members of the CSAG formed the People's Committee (PC) and joint meetings were organized in the new year (Shoman 1973; Bolland 1988a).

The Belizean independence movement emerged initially, therefore, as a coalition between a broadly based trade union and a group of educated middle-class Catholics. On 28 April 1950, however, the latter took over the former. Betson was made the honorary "Patriarch" of the GWU and the CSAG used the union as a basis for the political party, the PUP, that they formed upon dissolving the PC on 29 September 1950. Subsequently, a series of rivalries and splits between the politicians badly divided and weakened the labour movement with the result that constitutional rather than labour issues came to predominate in Belizean politics (Bolland 1986: 103-24, 1988a).

From its inception, and using its union base, the PUP sought support from all Belizeans, regardless of their class, region, religion, language, or "race". Its leaders recognized that their best hope of challenging the colonial government lay in mobilizing all Belizeans in the struggle. In the first election based on universal adult suffrage, on 28 April 1954, almost 70 percent of the electorate voted and the PUP won 66.3 percent of the votes and 8 of the 9 elected seats in the new Legislative Assembly. The opposition, led by Anglophile professional and middle-class members of the old Council and supported by the colonial administration, calling themselves the National Party (NP), were soundly beaten. The PUP, following the Jesuit-inspired CSAG which had close ties with the credit union movement, advocated "distributive justice" through "cooperativism" and "wise capitalism," in a context of "national unity."

The PUP, espousing a centrist Christian Democratic ideology, has won all general elections in Belize except those in 1984 and 1993. A typical populist party, the PUP's policies and strategies have traditionaly been defined by a small elite, dominated by George Price, with little real participation from the membership. Political struggles within as well as between parties are highly personalized and there are frequent factional struggles, often resulting in splits and new, fragile alliances. This emphasis on personalities, associated with struggles over loyalty and patronage, inevitably means that ethnic identities and allegiances are part of the political idiom and currency, but it is striking that ethnicity has never dominated party politics in Belize as it has in Guyana and Trinidad and Tobago (Bolland 1991, 1997).

After a split in the PUP in 1956, Philip Goldson formed the Honduran Independence Party (HIP) but was defeated in the 1957 elections when the PUP won 59 percent of the vote and all nine elected seats. In 1958 the HIP joined with the NP to form the National Independence Party (NIP) to oppose what they defined as Price's Central American orientation. Price opposed the inclusion of Belize in the West Indies Federation because it would have led to immigration from the islands and his opponents charged him with wanting to "latinize" Belize. Guatemala's irredentist claim to Belize came to be a major issue in Belize's politics and threatened to reduce party allegiances to pro-Price or anti-Guatemala reactions. However, neither party could win with the support of only one ethnic group and so long as the NIP appeared to be a "Creole party" supported by black, English-speaking Protestants it could not win against the broader base of the PUP. The colonial administration's attempt to discredit Price, when the Governor accused him of preparing to sell Belize to Guatemala and removed him from the Executive Council, backfired because it made Price the focus of attention and colonialism the central issue. In November 1958 the PUP won 29 of the 33 seats in seven municipal elections and Price became the mayor of Belize City, the centre of the Creole community.

In the 1960s Price came to accept the British process of constitutional decolonization and the British came to accept George Price as the national leader. The PUP's aspirations towards independence became more respectable and the party consolidated its central position, winning all 18 seats in 1961, 16 in 1965, and 17 in 1969, with Price becoming the Premier in a ministerial system of government in 1964. It was not until the 1970s that the PUP lost some of its popular support and a more united and broadly based opposition emerged. In September 1973 the NIP merged with the People's Development Movement (PDM) and the Liberal Party into the United Democratic Party (UDP), which won 38 percent of the vote and 6 seats in the 1974 election, while the PUP's support fell to 51.3 percent of the votes. The UDP received support in Dangriga and in Toledo District but in Belize City it obtained only 48.8 percent of the vote to the PUP's 50.2 percent. While Price continued to lead the PUP, the UDP changed its leaders several times. Dean Lindo, who had led the PDM, replaced Goldson in 1974 but was himself replaced when he lost the election and his own seat in 1979. The new leader, Dr. Theodore Aranda, a Garifuna, was in turn challenged by the UDP's Belize City elite who replaced him in 1983 with Manuel Esquivel, a physics teacher and former mayor of Belize City (Shoman 1987). The disgruntled Aranda formed a Christian Democratic Party (CDP), but it won neither of the seats it contested in 1984 and then merged with the PUP in 1988.

213

The PUP won the 1979 election with 51.8 percent of the vote to the UDP's 46.8 percent but it was losing support, especially among young people who perceived its leaders as aging and lackluster. Belize achieved independence on 21 September 1981, but the continued presence of British military forces, made necessary by Guatemala's irredentist claims, was a painful reminder of the new nation's dependence and of the old fears of "latinization." The economic crisis of the early 1980s further eroded PUP support and the old populist coalition became deeply divided, with left and right wings attacking each other at the party convention in 1983. After the Belize City Council elections in December 1983, when the UDP won all 9 seats by a massive majority, Price reshuffled his cabinet but he continued to rely on his loyalists and changed too little, too late. In the first election under the Independence Constitution, with the number of seats increased to 28, each division representing between 2,000 and 3,000 electors, on 14 December 1984, 75 percent of the electorate voted. The PUP received a crushing defeat, holding only 6 seats with 43.3 percent of the vote to 53.3 percent for the UDP (Shoman 1987).

Esquivel's leadership of the UDP was strengthened when he became Prime Minister, while Price, who lost his seat in 1984, had to allow Florencio Marin, head of the PUP's northern caucus, to become official leader of the opposition in the House of Representatives. Price maintained his leadership of the party, however, while members of the right and left wings left the PUP and Said Musa became the new party chairman. In 1989 the PUP fought back, and, using the slogan "Belizeans First," accused the UDP of pandering to foreign speculators. On 4 September 1989, 72 percent of the 82,556 registered voters actually voted, giving the PUP a slender victory as they won 50.3 percent of the votes and 15 seats to the UDP's 48.4 percent and 13 seats. In December one UDP member switched parties so the PUP's majority in the House grew to four. Price regained the role of Prime Minister and Said Musa, as Minister of Foreign Affairs, Economic Development, and Education, increased his stature as Price's possible successor.

Price called an early election in 1993, anticipating victory and a further five years in office. However, the Guatemalan issue suddenly became central once again. Diplomatic relations had been established between the two countries for the first time in 1991 and the issue, long defined as the "Anglo-Guatemala dispute," seemed about to be settled. Early in 1992, when Esquivel and his former minister of foreign affairs and deputy leader, Dean Barrow, supported the PUP's proposals for settling the dispute, hard-line members of the UDP split and formed the National Alliance for Belizean Rights (NABR), reflecting the persistent Hispanophobia among many traditional UDP supporters. On 13 May 1993 the British government announced that its 1,500 troops would be reduced and eventually withdrawn because of public spending cuts and because they were no longer required. Two weeks later, Jorge Serrano, the Guatemalan President who had negotiated the new relationship with Belize, imposed a dictatorship and a week later was overthrown. As anxieties about Guatemala increased, the UDP patched up its differences with the NABR and made Belizean security, the British withdrawal, and the PUP's relations with Guatemala a major election issue. Esquivel argued that Belize, with a Defence Force of approximately 700, needs a continuing defence commitment from Britain and that Price had not tried hard enough to secure one. The fear that some 3,000 jobs, many held by Creoles, and as much as 5 percent of the GDP would be lost with the British withdrawal also became an issue. Moreover, the UDP accused the PUP of registering hundreds of Central American migrants to vote, thereby reinforcing the old fears of a "Spanish takeover."

On 30 June 1993 the PUP won about 1,700 more of the 70,000 votes cast but the UDP won 16 of the 29 seats, the number of representatives having been increased to avoid the possibility of a tied House. The election was so close that if a handful of votes had gone the other way in several close constituencies the PUP would have won the majority. Instead, Esquivel became Prime Minister for the second time. In October 1996, Price stepped down as the PUP leader. In the ensuing election at a party convention in November 1996, Said Musa won 358 (or 63 percent) of the votes, while Florencio Marin received 214 (37 percent). This was a victory for the leader who is more likely to extend his appeal beyond a parochial base. Musa, a successful lawyer, was born in San Ignacio, Cayo District in 1944, the son of an immigrant from Palestine and a Belizean mother. He joined the PUP in 1974, won his first election in 1979, and held several important ministerial posts in Price's governments, including Attorney General, Foreign Affairs, Economic Development, and Education, Sports and Culture.

The PUP swept the municipal elections in 1997 and on 27 August 1998 won a landslide victory in the general elections, taking 26 seats to the UDP's 3. In an extraordinarily high turnout, with over 90 percent of the 94,173 registered voters casting ballots, 50,330 (60.3 percent) voted for the PUP and 33,237 (39.2 percent) for the UDP. Esquivel, the incumbent Prime Minister, received only 43.6 percent of the vote and was defeated in his Belize City constituency - and then quit his party's leadership - but Musa won by the largest of margins, with 74.6 percent of the vote in another Belize City constituency, and became Belize's third Prime Minister. Price retained his seat in Belize City with 53.2 percent of the vote. The landslide, which may be attributed in part to the electorate's disillusionment with the UDP government, reflected renewed hope in the revitalized PUP, which introduced several new candidates. Of the three seats won by the UDP, two were in Belize City and the other, which was won by just ten votes, was in the far west. The PUP's margin of victory was often very large, with eight of their candidates winning two-thirds or more of the votes in their constituencies, and was comprehensive around the country.

These results, like those in past elections, defy analysis in terms of simple ethnic politics, and they do not reveal any sharp regional or rural/urban differences. The PUP won 60.9 percent of the vote in Belize City and 61.8 percent in the rural constituencies of Belize District. The PUP share of the vote was also slightly above the national average in constituencies in the districts of Corozal (61.2 percent) and Toledo (61.3 percent), in the far north and far south of the country, respectively, and slightly below average in the other three districts, Orange Walk (59.0 percent), Cayo (54.2 percent) and Stann Creek (58.3 percent), but the PUP won in all regions and among all ethnic groups. On 5 March 2003 the PUP won 22 seats with 53.2 percent of the votes, and the UDP won the remaining 7 seats with 45.6 percent of the votes. The PUP won 6 of the 10 Belize City seats, where Musa won 76.6 percent of the votes cast in his constituency and Mark Espat won an astonishing 82.8 percent, and the other 16 seats are all around the country. The UDP, led by Dean Barrow, won 4 seats in Belize City and one each in Belize rural south, Corozal south west, and Cayo west. Although the PUP's share of the vote and the government's majority was reduced, this was an impressive and historic victory as it was the first time a party had won re-election since independence.

The elections in 1984, 1989, 1993, 1998 and 2003 show that Belizeans are committed to orderly democratic procedures, working within a two-party system based on the Westminster model. Though the PUP dominated politics until the 1970s, this was in part because the opposition parties were too narrowly based and disorganized. When the UDP got better organized under Esquivel's leadership it could seriously challenge Price and the PUP nationwide. Since 1996, however, the revitalized PUP, under Said Musa's leadership, has again dominated Belizean politics because it has succeeded in appealing to voters all over the country.

Ethnic identity and Political Allegiance

While ethnic identity certainly affects political allegiances in Belize it rarely seems to determine them and both major parties continue to draw their support from the various ethnic groups and regions of the country, as indeed they must if they are to win a majority of seats. The rapid shifts and swings in some voting patterns—in Belize City Council elections the PUP lost every seat to the UDP in 1983 and won them all in 1989—cannot be explained in terms of simple ethnic identity politics. Belize City, where three quarters of the people are Creole, has tended to dominate national politics for over half a century because of the concentration of the population, especially the more educated middle classes, and of the more liberal franchise there in the 1930s and 1940s. Though the leadership of both parties continues to be dominated by Belize City persons, both parties know that, with only 10 of the 29 representatives elected in the city, they cannot win if they lose the districts. The residential patterns of the population and the distribution of constituencies is such that, while individual politicians may be able to win in their constituencies by appealing to parochial ethnic allegiances, no party can win a national majority without forging broad coalitions across ethnic boundaries. Consequently, the political parties in Belize, instead of promoting ethnic sectarianism, provide contending allegiances that cut across racial and ethnic lines.

So long as racial and ethnic stereotyping and inter-group tensions exist, as they have long existed in Belize, there is a potential for conflict, but there is no history of violence between ethnic groups in Belize. Historically, residential separation and segmentation in the labour force during the period of colonial rule provoked little overt competition between ethnic groups and the political party system since 1950 has, for the most part, tended toward coalition building rather than hardening parochial allegiances. Some educators and politicians have deliberately sought to promote a multi-cultural, pluralistic vision of their nation, as a statement about "Culture and Sovereignty" in a school text commissioned by the Ministry of Education in 1983 suggests:

> Belize has its own rich culture which includes the heritage of the different ethnic groups of Belize.... For much of our history, the natural interaction of cultures which co-exist within one community was inhibited by the colonial policy of divide and rule, which ensured that our various cultures remained largely isolated from, and suspicious of each other, and that the colonizer's culture remained dominant. An essential part of the decolonization process must therefore be the elimination of all colonially inherited prejudices about each other's cultures.
>
> The historical origins of our people and the more recent influences upon our culture have produced diversity. Out of this diversity we must seek unity, while recognizing the value of our different customs and traditions (*A History of Belize: Nation in the Making* 1983: 73).

It would be naive, however, to portray Belize as a haven from strife and a model of ethnic harmony. Both before and since independence, several ethnically based associations have emerged, each seeking roots in their particular cultural traditions and promoting their particular interests. Among these are the United Black Association for Development (UBAD), the National Garifuna Council (NGC), and the Toledo Maya Cultural Council (TMCC).

An African-consciousness movement among Belizean Creoles dates, at least, from the riot in 1919 when ex-servicemen protested racial discrimination. One of them, Samuel A. Haynes, was a founder of the Belize branch of the Universal Negro Improvement Association (UNIA) in 1920 and became one of Marcus Garvey's principal lieutenants in the United States. Garvey himself visited Belize in 1921 and the influence of his philosophy was maintained by the Black Cross Nurses Association between 1920 and 1970 (Herrmann 1985: 39-46) as well as

217

the UNIA. Garveyism influenced some of the early labour and nationalist leaders, including Soberanis (Ashdown 1981), and its influence persisted into the 1960s when it was overtaken by the young Black Power movement called UBAD. The UBAD constitution, according to its founder and head, Evan X Hyde, was patterned on the UNIA constitution in 1969 (Hyde 1970: 8-13). UBAD started a breakfast program for needy children and a weekly newspaper, Amandala. Hyde still edits the paper and runs a radio station, KREM, which popularizes reggae and other Afro-Caribbean music. Along with other groups, such as Islam Nation Belize and the Rastafarians, UBAD reaches back to Garveyite Pan-African traditions and promotes a reevaluation of the African heritage.

Through the National Garifuna Council the Garinagu—their own name for themselves—promote their culture. November 19 is a national holiday commemorating their arrival in Belize with music, dancing, and other celebrations. Some are consciously reviving and teaching traditional crafts and customs, and putting them on videotape, and others advocate introducing their language into the schools. The popularity of punta rock music has recently boosted Garifuna culture nationwide[5]

Cultural revivalism is also stirring in Maya communities, often in response to Creole and Mestizo characterization of "Indian" culture as backward and primitive. The Yucatec, Mopan, and Kekchi Maya of Belize are culturally distinct, and the "emergence of a common identity as Mayan Belizeans has been slow and imperfect, and was more a product of colonial policy than of people recognizing their common heritage and roots" (Wilk 1986: 74). As the Kekchi Maya in Toledo District became increasingly exposed to missionaries, government officials, and wage labour, they reacted by trying to protect and even to extend their land rights and by emphasizing their distinctive cultural identity. In the early 1980s the TMCC emerged "as an ethnic-awareness group, composed of both conservative and progressive people concerned about economic, linguistic, and cultural issues, although motivated most urgently by the issue of land and the future of reservations" (Wilk 1991: 235).

The TMCC, which consists of representatives from several Mopan and Kekchi villages, uses Maya traditions and history to further their economic and political goals. In 1988, when the International Fund for Agricultural Development and US AID began a project in Toledo that would divide up Crown Land and, eventually, the reservations into 50-acre parcels on which Maya families would be resettled, the TMCC petitioned the government for a "Maya homeland" of half a million acres in southern Belize. The Maya farmers were in danger of becoming boxed in by large estates in foreign hands and, as they fail to compete with rich foreigners, they would lose their land. The demand for a homeland, made in direct response to this threat to their security, would replace the existing reservations with land under their own control and would allow each village to decide what mix it wanted of private and communal tenure. The TMCC not only emphasizes their descent from the ancient Maya, ruins of whose civilization continue to be found throughout the region, but also works at self-representations of Maya life in videotapes of dance and ritual performances, and promotes the use of Mopan and Kekchi languages in education and radio programming.

It remains to be seen whether these manifestations of cultural revivalism and ethnic mobilization will be incorporated into a progressive definition of a culturally pluralistic nation or whether they will degenerate into parochial allegiances, increasing tensions, political factionalism and conflict. These ethnic organizations resist what their members perceive as threats to themselves by drawing on symbols from their own traditions, including their traditions of resistance, but they have not become political parties competing for power in the public domain at the national level. Contrary to an assertion made at the First Annual Studies on Belize Conference that there is "an escalating ethnic war" in Belize (Topsey 1987: 1), these ethnic mobilizations do not constitute, nor need they lead to, an ethnic war. The politicization of ethnicity in Belize, which is generally in response to long established prejudices, stereotypes and discrimination, may increase tensions and even conflicts at the individual level but will not necessarily result in conflict and violence at the communal or national level. Much depends, of course, on the ways that politicians, educators, employers, and others deal with these issues.

One of the most disturbing developments in recent years has resulted from the export-oriented, low-wage employment strategy of development that has led to a Belizean, and largely unionized, labour force in the expanding banana industry being replaced by desperately poor and often undocumented workers from Guatemala, Honduras, and El Salvador. A courageous attempt to organize these workers in a trade union, Banderas Unidas, in 1995 was countered by a vicious response by employers and government. As Mark Moberg's ethnography of this situation shows, the constructions of ethnic identities in this context "acquire salience because of their relationship to class" (Moberg 1997: xxiv). The poverty, racism, and legal marginalization that these immigrants experience affect the ways that Belizeans perceive and evaluate them and themselves. Many Belizeans were shocked to see on television dozens of soldiers from the Belizean Defence Force, wearing battle fatigues and armed with automatic weapons, threatening the unarmed banana workers. But others probably agreed with the policeman who, during the strike in 1995, said, "Why don't we just kill all these Spanish and dig a big hole and put them in there?" (Moberg 1997: 172). It is well known that ethnicity may divide a working class and impede collective resistance, but we must also recognize that the ways that a labour force is recruited and treated is one of the chief ways that ethnic identities and relations are constructed. Employers in the banana industry have developed a "myth" that

Belizean Creoles and Garifuna, who pioneered the industry, are unsuited to farm work, and that the Central American immigrants are more suitable. As Creole and Garifuna emigration and Central American immigration are shifting the "ethnic balance," the country's historically peaceful interethnic relations are threatened by the strategy of development that emphasizes the production of agricultural exports with low-wage labour (Bolland and Moberg 1995). This pattern of development in Belize, like the introduction of Asian indentured workers into the Caribbean in the decades after Emancipation, is establishing a structure of ethnic segmentation in the labour force and a political legacy of conflict that is made to appear as if it is based on "primordial" cultural or racial divisions.

In short, Belize is a *pluralistic* but not, or not yet, a plural society, in M.G. Smith's terms. During the colonial period, one minority section dominated all others but with the decolonization process since the 1950s no single cultural section has taken the hegemonic place of the British, though the Creole and Mestizo groups may each fear that the other will do so. Ethnic groups in Belize do not organize or interact *qua* groups in the political system, nor are the political parties mobilized or oriented primarily on an ethnic basis. This is not to say that racial and ethnic issues are irrelevant in Belizean society and politics, for that has never been true (Bolland 1986, 1988b, 1991). In fact, one of the most important consequences of Guatemala's persistent claim to Belize has been the perpetuation of internal disunity and mutual suspicions, with Creole Belizeans, in particular, fearing recolonization. The Guatemalan threat encourages Creole Belizeans to continue to think of Spanish-speaking Maya and Mestizo Belizeans as the British thought of them, namely as representatives of an alien culture. Many Creoles feel that Belize is and should remain a predominantly English-speaking, Afro-Caribbean country and fear that the "latinization" of Belize will displace them. Meanwhile, many Maya and Mestizo Belizeans feel that the Creoles, who were favoured by the British in the civil service and the police force, tend to dominate the entire society unfairly.

Though an Anglophone bias in the institutional structure of Belize was inherited from the colonial era, it has not enabled the Creoles to attach their particular identity to the state in such a way as to achieve hegemony over other ethnic groups, particularly the Mestizos. This is partly due to the colonial legacy of racism which discriminates particularly against people of African descent—both Creoles and Garifuna—while relatively favouring those with lighter skins and straighter hair. A light-skinned, straight-haired Mestizo child who learns English and attends the prestigious St. John's College is more likely to rise into the Belizean elite than a dark-skinned Creole-speaking child of African descent. Though racial discrimination has no legal sanction, for so long as somatic distinctions continue to correlate with class positions most Creoles will find it harder to be upwardly mobile and will express the belief that the "Spanish" are overtaking them educationally and economically as well as numerically. While these historically-derived racial and ethnic tensions persist they will affect Belize's political life, but so long as they do not become institutionalized in the political party system Belize will continue to be culturally pluralistic without becoming a plural society.

The plural society model emphasizes the tendency of independence movements and nationalist politics in segmental multi-ethnic societies to degenerate into communal conflicts. Indeed, it is part of the conceptualization of a plural society that politics is organised on the basis of cultural segments which compete for power in the national arena. However, this study of Belize shows that political parties are not necessarily based on ethnicity, and that even when conflicts arise they do not do so simply because of the existence of racial and cultural diversity. It is not the simple fact of pluralism, but rather the particular socio-economic circumstances in which it exists that affects the degree of conflict emerging in the society. The intimate relations between class and ethnicity are tied, in particular, to the state of the economy.

"Ethnicity" is commonly seen in the Caribbean as a hereditary repository of physical and cultural characteristics. However, if ethnicity is understood more accurately to be a socially constructed *process*, rather than a heritable characteristic or a bundle of traits, we can better analyze its dialectical relationship to class. Ethnicity can be very effective as an idiom of political mobilization, but not as an alternative to class because it is not really apart from class. Bourgois, in his study of ethnicity in Central American banana plantations, concludes, "there is no either/or relationship between class and ethnicity; the two are part of the same process of struggle. Ethnicity is not a characteristic or even a social relationship; it is a dynamic, ongoing, historical confrontation," and "the ethnicity of any given worker is a product of the worker's previous employment history and participation in class struggle" (Bourgois 1989: 226). Hence, the variations in the conceptualization and politicization of ethnicity in Belize must be understood in relation to the dynamics of economic development and changing social structure, among other factors, in the specific history of the society.

The analytical distinction between the *plural* and the *pluralistic* society may be conceived in terms of ranked and unranked ethnic systems (Horowitz 1985: 22), in which the former consists of two or more hierarchically ordered ethnic groups in a caste-like configuration, while the latter consists of two or more ethnic groups which, though internally stratified, are in a parallel social order, each group having a legitimately recognized elite. Max Weber referred to the latter social order as ethnic coexistences:

> the caste structure transforms the horizontal and unconnected coexistences of ethnically segregated groups into a vertical social system of super—and

subordination.... In their consequences they differ precisely in this way: ethnic coexistences condition a mutual repulsion and disdain but allow each ethnic community to consider its own honor as the highest one; the caste structure brings about a social subordination and an acknowledgement of "more honor" in favor of the privileged caste and status groups. (Gerth and Mills 1958: 189)

The pluralistic society of Belize more closely resembles the unranked ethnic system in which "ethnic coexistence" has characterized the relations between ethnic groups through most of their history. Encapsulated within a colonial territory, these groups were subordinate to the British but remained virtually strangers in relation to each other and with decolonization no single group has attained a general hegemony over the others. In Guyana, by way of contrast, the vicious colonial heritage of racial and ethnic stereotypes and prejudices gave rise, under the stimulus of external prompting, to an intense and institutionalized form of racial politics in which each of the major groups struggles to attain predominance—and this racial mobilization creates a plural society (Bolland 1997). Of course, there is always a potential for a pluralistic society to become a plural society, which occurs if the politicization of ethnicity becomes institutionalized in the political party system, but the fact that this has not happened in Belize as it has in Guyana provides grounds for continuing optimism. Whereas the concentration of ethnic groups in certain communities in Belize promotes parochial loyalties at the local level, it may also deter extremism at the national level in the present electoral system. Ethnic loyalties may remain localized so long as no group is numerous or powerful enough to dominate the political centre. Political leaders in Belize, in order to extend their influence beyond their parochial base, need to broaden and hence to moderate their appeal. One reason why Price and Esquivel proved successful as party and national leaders is that they can move easily between the Creole and Mestizo sectors of the society. Political leaders with narrower bases, however locally powerful, such as Aranda and Marin, are less likely to succeed in this political system at the national level so long as they are perceived as too parochial by members of ethnic groups other than their own.

The political systems and parties are not only influenced by the cultural pluralism of these societies, but they also have an active effect on such pluralism. Whereas the ethnically defined political parties of Guyana tend to foster further conflict, the non-ethnically based parties of Belize tend to moderate such conflict. On the one hand, ethnically based parties seek to consolidate their support among populations that are ascriptively defined, thereby pulling apart from each other and fomenting antagonisms. On the other hand, in non-ethnic two-party systems, "competition makes the parties converge; they compete for undecided or shifting voters whose views lie between the positions of the two parties. This creates a pull toward moderation" (Horowitz 1985: 347). The two major parties in Belize, instead of promoting ethnic sectarianism, provide contending allegiances that often cut across racial and ethnic lines. Belizeans of different ethnic groups may share allegiance to the same political party, while people of the same ethnic group may belong to rival parties.

Ethnic identities are not primordial and immutable, as they are generally conceived, nor do such identities necessarily determine political allegiances and activities. Cultural pluralism varies in its political importance according to the degree to which parties are ethnically based. The latter is determined, not by the simple presence of cultural diversity, but by a complex of historically shaped factors, including the different patterns of colonization and decolonization, and various strategies of development, which occur in historically specific forms in each society, so we should expect that the relations between ethnicity and politics will vary a good deal from place to place and time to time.

Notes

1. See Judd 1989 and Maurer 1997.

2. We need not accept, as Smith appears to, that the existence of "fundamental differences" in some beliefs, values, and organizations necessarily precludes the sharing of some other beliefs, values, or organizations—unless, by definition, this is what is meant by "fundamental." Nor need we assume, as Smith appears to, that when a "monopoly of power" maintains such a segmented society "in its current form," it is impossible to conceive of or create an alternative basis for the coexistence of the different cultural sections. Smith, a Jamaican anthropologist who developed his 'plural society' model during the period of decolonization, appears to have been extremely pessimistic about the political consequences of the withdrawal of colonial power from the Caribbean.

3. It was originally written for the conference on "New Perspectives on Caribbean Studies: Towards the 21st Century," at Hunter College, New York, in 1984.

4. The patterns of migration have reversed the trend toward urbanization. Since the 1930s, the majority of Belizeans lived in Belize City and the six next largest towns (Dangriga, Orange Walk, Corozal, San Ignacio, Punta Gorda, and Benque Viejo). In 1991, only 47 percent of the population lived in the eight towns that now include the new capital, Belmopan.

5. A leader of this cultural revival, Joseph Palacio, a Garifuna anthropologist who heads the University of the West Indies' School of Continuing Studies in Belize City, has also been involved with the Caribbean Organization of Indigenous Peoples which brings together representatives from Belize, Dominica, Guyana, and St. Vincent.

Bibliographical References

ALLEN, CAPT. D. M., 1887. *Report of Indian Soldiery*. Belize: Government Press.

ARMSTRONG, JOHN, 1824. A Candid Examination of *"The Defense of the Settlers of Honduras..."*. London: Butterworth.

ASHCRAFT, NORMAN, 1973. *Colonialism and Underdevelopment: Processes of Political Economic Change in British Honduras*. New York: Teachers College Press.

ASHDOWN, PETER, 1978. "Antonio Soberanis and the Disturbances in Belize 1934-1937," *Caribbean Quarterly* 24:61-74.

——, 1979. "Control or Coercion: The Motive for Governments Nurture of Organized Labour," *Journal of Belizean Affairs* 9:36-43.

——, 1981. "Marcus Garvey, the UNIA and the Black Cause in British Honduras, 1914-1949," *Journal of Caribbean History* 15:41-55.

BANCROFT, H.H., 1883-87. *History of Central America*, 3 vols. San Francisco: History Company.

BASTIDE, ROGER, 1971. *African Civilisations in the New World*. Translated by Peter Green. New York: Harper.

BETTELHEIM, JUDITH, 1979. "Jamaican Jonkonnu and Related Caribbean Festivals." In *Africa and the Caribbean: The Legacies of a Link*, edited by Margaret E. Crahan and Franklin W. Knight. Baltimore and London: Johns Hopkins University Press.

BLASSINGAME, JOHN W., 1972. *The Slave Community: Plantation Life in the Antebellum South*. New York: Oxford University Press.

BOLLAND, O. NIGEL, 1973. "The Social Structure and Social Relations of the Settlement in the Bay of Honduras (Belize) in the 18th Century." *Journal of Caribbean History* 6:1-42.

——, 1974. "Maya Settlements in the Upper Belize River Valley and Yalbac Hills: An Ethnohistorical View," *Journal of Belizean Affairs* 3:3-23.

——, 1977a. *The Formation of a Colonial Society: Belize, from Conquest to Crown Colony*. Baltimore and London: Johns Hopkins University Press.

——, 1977b. "The Maya and the Colonization of Belize in the Nineteenth Century." In Grant D. Jones (ed.), *Anthropology and History in Yucatán*. Austin: University of Texas Press, pp.69-99.

——, 1981. "Systems of Domination after Slavery: The Control of Land and Labor in the British West Indies after 1838," *Comparative Studies in Society and History* 23:591-619.

——, 1984, "Reply to William A. Green's 'The Perils of Comparative History'", *Comparative Studies in Society and History* 26:120-125.

——,1986. *Belize: A New Nation in Central America*. Boulder and London: Westview Press.

——, 1987a. "African Continuities and Creole Culture in Belize Town in the Nineteenth Century." In Charles V. Carnegie (ed.), *Afro-Caribbean Villages in Historical Perspective*. Kingston: African-Caribbean Institute of Jamaica, pp.63-82.

– ——, 1987b. "Alcaldes and Reservations: British Policy Towards the Maya in Late Nineteenth Century Belize." *América Indígena* 47:33-76.

– ——, 1988a. "The Labour Movement and the Genesis of Modern Politics in Belize. "In Malcolm Cross and Gad Heuman (eds.), *Labour in the Caribbean: From Emancipation to Independence*. London: Macmillan Caribbean, pp.258-84.

——, 1988b. *Colonialism and Resistance in Belize: Essays in Historical Sociology*. Benque Viejo del Carmen: Cubola Productions.

——, 1991. "Society and Politics in Belize." In Colin Clarke (ed.), *Society and Politics in the Caribbean*. London: Macmillan, pp.78-109.

——, 1994. "Colonization and Slavery in Central America." In Paul E. Lovejoy and Nicholas Rogers (eds.), *Unfree Labour in the Development of the Atlantic World*. London: Frank Cass, pp.11-25.

——, 1997. "Pluralism and the Politicization of Ethnicity in Belize and Guyana." In O. Nigel Bolland, *Struggles for Freedom: Essays on Slavery, Colonialism and Culture in the Caribbean and Central America*. Belize City: Angelus Press, pp.259-313.

BOLLAND, O. NIGEL, and MARK MOBERG, 1995. "Development and National Identity: Creolization, Immigration, and Ethnic Conflict in Belize." *International Journal of Comparative Race and Ethnic Studies* 2:1-18.

BOLLAND, O. NIGEL, and SHOMAN, ASSAD, 1977. *Land in Belize, 1763-1871: The Origins of Land Tenure, Use and Distribution in a Dependent Economy*. Mona: Institute of Social and Economic Research, University of the West Indies.

BOURGOIS, PHILIPPE I., 1989. *Ethnicity at Work: Divided Labor on a Central American Banana Plantation*. Baltimore: The Johns Hopkins University Press.

BRATHWAITE, EDWARD, 1971. *The Development of Creole Society in Jamaica, 1770-1820*. Oxford: Clarendon Press.

BRISTOWE, LINDSAY W., 1892. *The Handbook of British Honduras*. Edinburgh and London: Blackwood.

BRISTOWE, LINDSAY W., and WRIGHT, PHILIP B., 1888. *The Handbook of British Honduras for 1888-89*. London: Blackwood.

BROCKMAN, THOMAS, 1979. "Language, Communication; and Ethnicity in British Honduras." In *Sociolinguistic Studies in Language Contact: Methods and Cases*, edited by William Francis Mackey and Jacob Ornstein. The Hague: Mouton.

BULLARD, WILLIAM R., JR., 1965. *Stratigraphic Excavations at San Estevan, Northern British Honduras*. Toronto: University of Toronto Press.

BURDON, SIR JOHN ALDER, 1935. *Archives of British Honduras*, 3 vols. London: Sifton Praed.

CAIGER, STEPHEN, 1951. *British Honduras, Past and Present*. London: George Allen and Unwin.

CALDERÓN QUIJANO, J. A., 1944. *Belize 1663(?)-1821: Historia de los Establecimientos Británicos del Río Valis hasta la Independencia de Hispanoamérica*. Sevilla: Victoria-Artes Gráficas.

CHAMBERLAIN, ROBERT S., 1948. *The Conquest and Colonization of Yucatán, 1517-1550*. Washington: Carnegie Institution.

CHEVERTON, R. L., and SMART, H. P., 1937. *Report of the Committee on Nutrition in the Colony of British Honduras*. Belize: Government Printer.

CLEGERN, WAYNE M., 1967. *British Honduras: Colonial Dead End, 1859-1900*. Baton Rouge: Louisiana State University Press.

COHN, BERNARD, 1981. "Anthropology and History in the 1980s: Toward a Rapprochement;" *Journal of Interdisciplinary History* 12:227-252.

THE COLONIAL REPORT FOR 1931, 1933, London: His Majesty's Stationery Office.

THE COLONIAL REPORT FOR 1932, 1933. London: His Majesty's Stationery Office.

CRAIG, ALAN K., 1969. "Logwood as a Factor in the Settlement of British Honduras;" *Caribbean Studies* 9:53-62.

CRAIG, SUSAN, 1977. "The Germs of an Idea." In *Labour in the West Indies* by Arthur Lewis. London: New Beacon Books.

CROSS, MALCOLM, 1971, "On Conflict, Race Relations, and the Theory of the Plural Society," *Race* 12:477-494.

——, 1978. "Colonialism and Ethnicity: A Theory and Comparative Case Study," *Ethnic and Racial Studies* 1:37-49.

CROWE, FREDERICK, 1850. *The Gospel in Central America, containing... a History of the Baptist Mission in British Honduras.* London: Charles Gilpin.

DAMPIER, WILLIAM, 1699. *Voyages and Descriptions*, rep. 1906. London: E. Grant Richards.

THE DEFENSE OF THE SETTLERS OF HONDURAS AGAINST THE UNJUST AND UNFOUNDED REPRESENTATIONS OF COLONEL GEORGE ARTHUR, 1824. Jamaica.

DOBSON, NARDA, 1973. *A History of Belize.* London: Longman Caribbean.

DUMOND. D. E., 1977. "Independent Maya of the Late Nineteenth Century: Chiefdoms and Power Politics." In *Anthropology and History in Yucatán*, edited by Grant D. Jones. Austin: University of Texas Press.

ESCURE, G. J., 1979. "Linguistic Variation and Ethnic Interaction in Belize: Creole/Carib." In *Language and Ethnic Relations*, edited by Howard Giles and Bernard Saint Jacques. Oxford: Pergamon Press.

ESCURE, GENEVIEVE, 1982. "Contrastive Patterns of Intragroup and Intergroup Interaction in the Creole Continuum of Belize"; *Language and Society* 11:239-264.

EVERITT, JOHN C., 1984. "The Recent Migrations of Belize, Central America;" *International Migration Review* 18:319-325.

FARRISS, NANCY M., 1984. *Maya Society Under Colonial Rule: The Collective Enterprise of Survival.* Princeton: Princeton University Press.

FORD, AMOS A., 1984. *Telling the Truth: The Life and Times of the British Honduras Forestry Unit in Scotland (1941-44).* London: Karia Press.

FOSTER, BYRON,1986. *Heart Drum: Spirit Possession in the Garifuna Communities of Belize.* Belize: Cubola Productions.

FOWLER, HENRY, 1879. *A Narrative of a Journey Across the Unexplored Portion of British Honduras with a Short Sketch of the History and Resources of the Colony.* Belize: Government Press.

FURNIVALL, J.S., 1948. *Colonial Policy and Practice: A Comparative Study of Burma and Netherlands India.* Cambridge: Cambridge University Press.

GERTH, H.H., and C. WRIGHT MILLS, 1958. *From Max Weber: Essays in Sociology.* New York: Free Press.

226

GIBBS, ARCHIBALD ROBERTSON, 1883. *British Honduras: An Historical and Descriptive Account of the Colony from its Settlement, 1670*. London: Sampson Low.

GONZALEZ, NANCIE L., 1988. *Sojourners of the Caribbean: Ethnogenesis and Ethnohistory of the Garifuna*. Chicago: University of Illinois Press.

GORDON, SHIRLEY C., 1968. *Reports and Repercussions in West Indian Education, 1835-1933*. London: Ginn.

GRANT, C.H., 1967. "Rural Local Government in Guyana and British Honduras," *Social and Economic Studies* 16:57-76.

——, 1976. *The Making of Modern Belize: Politics, Society and British Colonialism in Central America*. Cambridge: Cambridge University Press.

GREEN, WILLIAM A., 1984. "The Perils of Comparative History: Belize and the British Sugar Colonies after Slavery," *Comparative Studies in Society and History* 26:112-119.

——, 1986. "The Creolization of Caribbean History: The Emancipation Era and a Critique of Dialectical Analysis," *Journal of Imperial and Commonwealth History* 14:149-169.

GREGORY, JAMES R., 1976. "The Modification of an Interethnic Boundary in Belize," *American Ethnologist* 3:683-709.

GUTMAN, HERBERT G., 1976. *The Black Family in Slavery and Freedom, 1750-1925*. New York: Pantheon Books.

HADEL, RICHARD, 1973. "Anansi Stories and Their Uses," *National Studies* 1(1):4-10.

HAMILL, DON, 1978. "Colonialism and the Emergence of Trade Unions in Belize," *Journal of Belizean Affairs* 7:3-20.

HART, RICHARD, n.d. [c. 1984]. *Origin and Development of the Working Class in the English-speaking Caribbean Area-1897 to 1937*. London: Community Education Trust.

HELLINGER, MARLIS, 1975. "The Study of Creole Proverbs," *National Studies* 3(1):28-38.

HENDERSON, CAPT. G., 1809. *An Account of the British Settlement of Honduras*. London: C. and R. Baldwin.

HERRMANN, ELEANOR KROHN, 1985. *Origins of Tomorrow: A History of Belizean Nursing Education*. Belize: Ministry of Health.

A HISTORY OF BELIZE: NATION IN THE MAKING, 1983. Belize City: Sunshine Books.

THE HONDURAS ALMANACK, 1829. Belize.

——, 1830. Belize.

HOROWITZ, DONALD L., 1985. *Ethnic Groups in Conflict*. Berkeley: University of California Press.

HUMMEL, C., 1921. *Report on the Forests of British Honduras*. London: Crown Agents for the Colonies.

HUMPHREYS, R.A., 1961. *The Diplomatic History of British Honduras, 1638-1901*. London, New York and Toronto: Oxford University Press.

HYDE, EVAN X, 1970. *The Crowd Called UBAD: The Story of a People's Movement*. Belize City: Modern Printers.

JONES, GRANT D., 1969. "Los Cañeros: Sociopolitical Aspects of the History of Agriculture in the Corozal Region of British Honduras." Brandeis University, unpublished Ph.D. dissertation.

——, 1971. *The Politics of Agricultural Development in Northern British Honduras.* Winston-Salem: Wake Forest University.

——, 1977. Introduction and "Levels of Settlement Alliance Among the San Pedro Maya of Western Belize and Eastern Petén, 1857-1936." In *Anthropology and History in Yucatán*, edited by Grant D. Jones. Austin: University of Texas Press.

——, 1984. "Maya-Spanish Relations in Sixteenth Century Belize," *BELCAST Journal of Belizean Affairs* 1:28-40.

JOSEPH, GILBERT M., 1977. "The Logwood Trade and its Settlement," *Belizean Studies* 5(2):1-16; 5(3):1-15.

JUDD, KAREN, 1989. *Cultural Synthesis or Ethnic Struggle? Creolization in Belize.* Cimarron 11:103-18.

KERNAN, KEITH T., SODERGREN, JOHN, and FRENCH, ROBERT, 1977. "Speech and Social Prestige in the Belizean Speech Community." In *Sociocultural Dimensions of Language Change*, edited by Ben G. Blount and Mary Sanches. New York: Academic Press.

KERNS, VIRGINIA, 1983. *Women and the Ancestors: Black Carib Kinship and Ritual.* Urbana, Chicago and London: University of Illinois Press.

KERNS, VIRGINIA, and DIRKS, ROBERT, 1975. "John Canoe," *National Studies* 3(6):1-15.

KLEIN, HERBERT S., 1967. *Slavery in the Americas: A Comparative Study of Virginia and Cuba.* Chicago: University of Chicago Press.

KNIGHT, FRANKLIN W., 1970. *Slave Society in Cuba During the Nineteenth Century.* Madison: University of Wisconsin Press.

LAWS OF BELIZE, 1980. London: Eyre and Spottiswoode.

LEON, NARDA D., 1958. "Social and Administrative Developments in British Honduras, 1798-1843." University of Oxford, unpublished B. Litt. thesis.

LE PAGE, R.B., 1975. "Polarizing Factors: Political, Cultural, Economic-Operating on the Individual's Choice of Identity Through Language Use in British Honduras." In *Multilingual Political Systems: Problems and Solutions*, edited by Jean-Guy Savard and Richard Vigneault. Quebec: Les Presses de l'Université Laval.

LEWIS, ARTHUR, 1977 *Labour in the West Indies: The Birth of a Workers' Movement* (First published in 1938). London: New Beacon Books.

LEWIS, D. GARETH, 1977. "The 1794 Register of St. John's Cathedral," *Belizean Studies* 5(3):19-26.

LEWIS, GORDON K., 1968. *The Growth of the Modern West Indies.* London: MacGibbon and Kee.

MACMILLAN, W.M., 1935. *Warning from the West Indies.* London: Faber and Faber.

MANDELBAUM, MAURICE, 1977. *The Anatomy of Historical Knowledge.* Baltimore and London: Johns Hopkins University Press.

MAURER, BILL, 1997. *Recharting the Caribbean: Land, Law, and Citizenship in the British Virgin Islands.* Ann Arbor: University of Michigan Press.

MAZZARELLI, MARCELLA, 1972. "Maya Settlement in the Cayo District, British Honduras: Nineteenth Century." Paper presented at the American Anthropological Association meetings, Toronto.

MENEZES, MARY NOEL, 1977. *British Policy Towards the Amerindians in British Guiana, 1803-1873*. Oxford: Clarendon Press.

METZGEN, MONRAD SIGFRID (ed.), 1928. *Shoulder to Shoulder, or the Battle of St. George's Caye 1798*. Belize City: Literary and Debating Club.

MINTZ, SIDNEY W., 1961. "The Question of Caribbean Peasantries: a Comment," *Caribbean Studies* 1:31-34.

——, 1967. "Caribbean Nationhood in Anthropological Perspective." In *Caribbean Integration: Papers on Social, Political, and Economic Integration*, edited by Sybil Lewis and Thomas G. Mathews. Rio Piedras: Institute of Caribbean Studies.

——, 1971. "The Caribbean as a Socio-cultural Area." In *Peoples and Cultures of the Caribbean*, edited by Michael M. Horowitz. Garden City: Natural History Press.

MINTZ, SIDNEY W., and PRICE, RICHARD, 1976. *An Anthropological Approach to the Afro-American Past: A Caribbean Perspective*. Philadelphia: Institute for the Study of Human Issues.

NASH, MANNING, 1970. "The Impact of Mid-nineteenth Century Economic Change upon the Indians of Middle America." In *Race and Class in Latin America*, edited by Magnus Morner. New York: Columbia University Press.

MOBERG, MARK, 1992. *Citrus, Strategy, and Class: The Politics of Development in Southern Belize*. Iowa City: University of Iowa Press.

——, 1997. *Myths of Ethnicity and Nation: Immigration, Work, and Identity in the Belize Banana Industry*. Knoxville: University of Tennessee Press.

NETTLEFORD, REX M., 1970. *Mirror, Mirror: Identity, Race and Protest in Jamaica*. Kingston: Collins and Sangster.

OMAN, SIR CHARLES, 1922. *The Unfortunate Colonel Despard and Other Studies*. London: Edward Arnold.

ORDE BROWNE, MAJOR G. ST. J., 1939. *Labour Conditions in the West Indies*. London: His Majesty's Stationery Office.

PATTERSON, ORLANDO, 1967. *The Sociology of Slavery: An Analysis of the Origins, Development and Structure of Negro Slave Society in Jamaica*. London: Mac-Gibbon and Kee.

——, 1975. "Context and Choice in Ethnic Allegiance: A Theoretical Framework and Caribbean Case Study." In *Ethnicity: Theory and Experience*, edited by Nathan Glazer and Daniel P. Moynihan. Cambridge, Mass.: Harvard University Press.

PENDERGAST, DAVID M., 1967. *Palenque: The Walker-Caddy Expedition to the Ancient Maya City, 1839-1840*. Norman: University of Oklahoma Press.

PETCH, TREVOR, 1986. "Dependency, Land and Oranges in Belize," *Third World Quarterly* 8:1002-1019.

PIVEN, FRANCES FOX, and CLOWARD, RICHARD A., 1971. *Regulating the Poor: The Functions of Public Welfare*. New York: Pantheon Books.

POST, KEN, 1978. *Arise ye Starvelings: The Jamaican Labour Rebellion of 1938 and its Aftermath*. The Hague: Martinus Nijhoff.

——, 1981. *Strike the Iron: A Colony at War-Jamaica, 1939-1945*, 2 vols. Atlantic Highlands: Humanities Press.

REED, NELSON, 1964. *The Caste War of Yucatán*. Stanford: Stanford University Press.

RODNEY, WALTER, 1981. *A History of the Guyanese Working People, 1881-1905*. Baltimore and London: Johns Hopkins University Press.

ROGERS, E., 1885. "British Honduras: Its Resources and Development," *Journal of the Manchester Geographical Society* 1:197-227.

RUTHEISER, CHARLES C., 1993. "Belize: The Society and its Environment." In Tim Merrill (ed.), *Guyana and Belize: Country Studies*. Washington, D.C.: Federal Research Division, Library of Congress, pp.187-220.

SAMPSON, H. C., 1929. *Report on Development of Agriculture in British Honduras*. London: His Majesty's Stationery Office.

SANCHEZ, I.E., 1979. "Some Interesting Belizean Place-Names," *Belizean Studies* 7(3):9-12.

SHOMAN, ASSAD, 1973. "The Birth of the Nationalist Movement in Belize, 1950-1954," *Journal of Belizean Affairs* 2:3-40.

——, 1987. *Party Politics in Belize, 1950-1986*. Benque Viejo del Carmen: Cubola Productions.

SIO, ARNOLD, 1979. "Commentary" on "Slavery and Race." In *Roots and Branches: Current Directions in Slave Studies*, edited by Michael Craton, Historical Reflections 6:269-274.

SMITH, M.G., 1957. "The African Heritage in the Caribbean." In *Caribbean Studies: A Symposium*, edited by Vera Rubin. Seattle and London: University of Washington Press.

——, 1965. *The Plural Society in the British West Indies*. Berkeley: University of California Press.

——, 1984. *Culture, Race and Class in the Commonwealth Caribbean*. Mona: Department of Extra-Mural Studies, University of the West Indies.

——, 1991. *Pluralism, Politics and Ideology in the Creole Caribbean*. New York: Research Institute for the Study of Man.

SOBERANIS, ANTONIO, and KEMP, L.D., 1949. *The Third Side of the Anglo-Guatemala Dispute*. Belize City: Commercial Press.

SQUIER, E.G., 1858. *The States of Central America*. New York: Harper and Brothers.

STATISTICAL OFFICE, 1982. *1980 Population Census*. Belmopan: Central Planning Unit.

STONE, DORIS ZEMURRAY, 1932. *Some Spanish Entradas 1524-1695*. New Orleans: Tulane University Press.

SULLIVAN, PAUL, 1978. "The Founding and Growth of Bullet Tree Falls," *Belizean Studies* 6(6):1-22.

TAMBIAH, STANLEY J., 1989. "Ethnic Conflict in the World Today." *American Ethnologist* 16:335-49.

TANNENBAUM, FRANK, 1946. *Slave and Citizen: The Negro in the Americas*. New York: Knopf.

THOMPSON, E.P., 1963. *The Making of the English Working Class*. New York: Vintage Books.

THOMPSON, J. ERIC S., 1938. "Sixteenth and Seventeenth Century Reports on the Chol Mayas," *American Anthropologist* 40:584-604.

——, 1939. *Excavations at San José, British Honduras*. Washington: Carnegie Institution.

——, 1970. *Maya History and Religion*. Norman: University of Oklahoma Press.

——, 1977. "A Proposal for Constituting a Maya Subgroup, Cultural and Linguistic, in the Petén and Adjacent Regions." In *Anthropology and History in Yucatán*, edited by Grant D. Jones. Austin: University of Texas Press.

TOPSEY, HARRIOT W., 1987. "The Ethnic War in Belize." In *Belize: Ethnicity and Development*. Belize City: Society for the Promotion of Education and Research, pp.1-5.

TUCKER, ROBERT C. (ed.), 1972. *The Marx-Engels Reader*. New York: W. W. Norton.

VILLA ROJAS, ALFONSO, 1945. *The Maya of East Central Quintana Roo*. Washington: Carnegie Institution.

WADDELL, D.A.G., 1961. *British Honduras: A Historical and Contemporary Survey*. London, New York and Toronto: Oxford University Press.

WEST INDIAN CENSUS 1946, 1948. *Census of British Honduras, 9th April 1946*. Belize: Government Printer.

WILK, RICHARD R., 1986. "Mayan Ethnicity in Belize: An Historical Review," *Cultural Survival Quarterly* 10:73-77.

——, 1991. *Household Ecology: Economic Change and Domestic Life Among the Kekchi Maya in Belize*. Tucson: University of Arizona Press.

WILLIAMS, BRACKETTE F., 1991. *Stains on my Name, War in my Veins: Guyana and the Politics of Cultural Struggle*. Durham: Duke University Press.

WILLIAMS, ERIC, 1944. *Capitalism and Slavery*. Chapel Hill: University of North Carolina Press.

WINZERLING, E.O., 1946. *The Beginning of British Honduras, 1506-1765*. New York: North River Press.

WOOD, E.F.L., 1922. *West Indies and British Guiana*. London: His Majesty's Stationery Office.

Index

Adderley, Gabriel, 184-185
Adolphus, Edwin, 118-119
Advance system, 80, 118-120, 163-164
Africans, 7, 12, 19, 22, 24, 28-29, 47, 53,
   61-63, 73, 78-96, 104, 124, 129, 200,
   204-210, 220-221, 224-225
Agriculture, 34, 51, 82, 104, 131, 138-
   139, 142, 151, 174, 207
   development of, 112-117, 121, 123,
   127, 228, 230
   milpas, 116, 139, 142-143, 148, 205
   peasant or subsistence, 43, 59, 68, 115-
   116, 120, 144
   plantation or estate, 23, 30, 50-51, 55,
   59, 68, 115-116, 120, 138-140, 144,
   151, 205-206
   swidden, 104, 112, 116, 131
   sugar, 102-106, 113, 135-136, 140,
   161, 181, 197, 200
Alcaldes. *See* Judicial system, alcaldes
Amandala, 218
Angola, 53, 84
Apprenticeship. *See* Emancipation
Aranda, Dr. Theodore, 214, 222
Armstrong, Reverend John, 75, 76, 96
Arthur, Superintendent George, 40, 46,
   47, 63-64, 69, 71-73, 80, 103, 161
Ashdown, Peter, 173, 181-182, 191, 218
Austin, Lieutenant Governor John, G.,
   109, 117, 122, 126, 139
Ayuso, L.P., 182
Bacalar, 18, 27-28, 71, 102, 105-107,
   113, 118
Balderamos, Arthur, 182, 184-185
Barbados, 53, 63, 93, 94, 202
Barlee, Governor Frederick, 141-142, 145
Barnett, James, 176, 183
Barrow, Dean, 214, 216
Barrow, Superintendent Thomas, 39
Bastide, Roger, 94
Belize Billboard, 187-188, 212
Belize Estate and Produce Company. *See*
   Companies, Belize Estate and Produce
   (British Honduras)
Belize Town or City, 34, 42, 53, 78-95,
122-123, 136-137, 140, 163-165, 169,
172-187, 205-208, 212-217
Belize Town Board, Belize City Council,
   173, 176, 178, 183-189, 211, 214, 216
   elections, 189, 214, 216
   hurricanes, 167, 172, 174-176, 207
   riots, 167, 169
   unemployment, 172, 174, 176, 178-
   179, 183, 188, 190, 192, 207-208, 212
Benque Viejo, 140-145, 148, 150
Bermuda, 52, 76
Betson, Clifford E., 187-190, 211-212
Bight of Benin. *See* Niger delta
Blassingame, John W., 51
Brathwaite, Edward, 42
Brazil, 23, 46, 89, 94
British Guiana, Guyana, 76, 80, 132, 149,
   200, 213, 222-223
British Honduras Company. *See*
   Companies, Belize Estate and Produce
   (British Honduras)
British Honduras Federation of Workers
   Protection Association, 185, 189, 194
British Honduras Independent Labour
   Party, People's Republican Party, People's
   Nationalist Committee, 185-189, 212
British Honduras Unemployed Association,
   179-181, 185
British Honduras Workers and Tradesmen
   Union, 172, 184, 186-188, 211
British settlers, Baymen, 48, 43, 52, 55-
   56, 62-64, 67, 69-73, 80, 86, 92, 94,
   102, 104, 108, 121, 124, 132, 161,
   163, 204
   settler oligarchy, 37, 43, 45, 52, 160-
   163, 205
British Trades Union Congress, 191
Browne, Major Orde, 168-169
Burdon, Governor Sir John Alder, 101,
   167-168
Burnaby's Code, (Admiral Burnaby), 25,
   36, 48
Burns, Governor Alan, 169, 179-181,
   183-184, 191, 193
Caddy, John Herbert, 78-79, 104
Caiger, Stephen, 25, 101-102
Cain, Herbert Hill, 186, 193

Cairns, Governor William, 140
Campbell, Joseph, 185, 189, 194
Campeche, 19-20, 42, 52, 106
Can, Juan, 133, 137
Canul, Marcos, 108-109, 122-123, 133, 138, 206
Caribbean, 22, 25, 29-30, 50, 52, 59, 61, 69, 73-74, 160, 172, 200-203, 220-221, 223
Caribbean Labour Congress, 186, 194
Caribs. *See* Garifuna
Catholic Church. *See* Religion, Catholic
Central America, Central Americans, 176, 188, 208-209, 213, 215, 220-221
Chan, José Justo, 140-141
Chan, Rafael, 109, 133, 138
Chetumal, 18, 129
Chicle. *See* Forest industry, chicle
China, Chinese, 206
Christian Democratic Party, 213
Christian Social Action Group, 187-190, 211-212
Christmas holiday, 62, 83, 87-92, 94, 96, 118, 126, 164
Citizens' Political Party, 182
Clarion, 176, 190
Codd, Superintendent, 71, 77
Cohn, Bernard, 128
Colonial Office, 40, 48, 72, 63, 131-132, 141, 144-145, 147-148, 151, 163, 183, 185, 189, 191, 195
Colonialism, 1, 2, 5-9, 13, 81-82, 85, 91-113, 125-147, 180-181, 194-195, 206
Companies, Belize Estate and Produce (British Honduras), 150, 162, 169-170, 174, 178, 186-188, 195
Young, Toledo and Company, 106, 140, 162
Congo, 53, 83-84, 90
Consolidated Slave Law of Jamaica, 64, 69
Constitution, 17, 30, 45, 48, 174-175, 185, 192, 212-213
of 1854, 40, 161-162, 205
of 1871, 122-123, 152
of 1936, 182, 188-190
Independence, 1981, 214

Convention of London. *See* Treaty, Convention of London
Convention Town. *See* Belize Town or City
Corozal, 18, 109, 113-114, 118, 129, 137, 144, 148, 181-182, 184-185, 187, 205, 209, 211
Cortés, Hernán, 18, 129
Courtenay, Harrison, 188
Coxen, Captain, 19
Craig, Alan, 19
Craig, Susan, 191
Creoles, 53, 78-79, 82, 91, 94, 96, 117, 119, 137, 145, 205-220
culture of, 84-96, 199, 204, 209
middle class, 182-183, 186
origins of, 53, 83-84, 204
Creolization, 51, 79, 84-85, 91-95, 210
Crowe, Frederick, 53, 78, 83, 85, 90, 123
Crown Colony, 123, 152, 162
Crown Lands, 122, 139, 141-143, 148, 163, 206
Ordinances, 122, 139, 142, 206
Cuba, 31, 50, 202
Dangriga (Stann Creek Town), 169, 178, 180-184, 205, 208
Davey, Captain, 27
Dávila, Alonso, 18
Debt, 66, 80, 118-122, 136, 164, 169
Delgado, Father, 18
Demographic history, 204-205, 208-209
Despard, Superintendent Edward Marcus, 29, 32-39, 41-42, 47, 52, 161
Dialectical theory, 128
Districts, 32-34, 39, 121, 181, 211
Belize, 95, 101, 191, 209, 216
Cayo, 18, 148, 184, 191, 208-209, 215-216
Corozal, 144, 148, 209, 216
Northern, 82, 105, 113-116, 133, 209
Orange Walk, 19, 209, 216
Stann Creek, 180, 208-209, 216
Toledo, 18, 144, 155, 180, 206, 208-209, 213, 216
Western, 82, 122, 139, 145, 148
Dobson, Narda, 152, 192
Dollar (Belize), devaluation of, 173, 188-189, 212

Downer, Robert T., 120
Dzuluinicob, 129
Economy, 78, 173-175, 192, 200-201, 221
  in eighteenth century, 22, 43, 51-52, 82, 204
  in nineteenth century, 51, 116, 122, 139, 152, 162-163, 172, 206-207
  in twentieth century, 167-168, 172, 175, 181, 183-184, 192, 207-208
  See also Agriculture; Forest industry
Education, schools, 63, 92, 163, 166, 170, 190, 205
  and cultural diversity, 205, 209-210, 217-219
Ek, Asunción, 107-110, 133, 137-138, 141, 148, 152
Elections, 37, 148, 150, 182, 216
  Belize City, 189, 214, 216
  general, national, 212-216
  local, 213-216
El Salvador, 204, 208, 219
Emancipation, 53-55, 65, 78-82, 90-94, 119, 159, 161, 164, 170, 180
  apprenticeship, 67, 80, 159, 220
  compensation, 68, 76
Emigration, 207-208, 220
Encalada, Pablo, 106
Esquivel, Manuel, 178, 213-216, 222
Ethnohistory, 84, 95, 128, 153
Exports, 22, 112-113, 117, 161-162, 167, 173-174, 208, 220
Fancourt, Superintendent St. John, 106
Farriss, Nancy M., 129, 149
Folklore, 84, 91-92
Forest industry, 19, 167-168, 186
  chicle, 144, 167, 174, 188, 192
  exports, 21-22, 51, 112-113, 117, 124, 139, 144, 161-162, 167, 173-174, 208, 173-174, 207
  logwood, 19-23, 30-34, 50-52, 56-57, 79-80, 120, 131, 161, 170, 204
  mahogany, 21-23, 31, 38, 52, 56, 112, 120, 161, 167, 174, 188, 192, 204
  and suppression of agriculture, 34, 82, 174
Fowler, Henry, 141, 145-147, 154
Franchise, 37, 162, 183, 211, 216

Francis, Lionel, 186, 188
Free blacks and free coloured, 30, 32, 34, 48, 54, 62-67, 71, 73, 80, 87, 90, 92-95, 111, 164
  and civil rights, 43
  and conflict with white settlers, 29 culture of, 84-86, *See also* Creoles
Fuensalida, Bartolomé de, 18
Furnivall, J.S., 201
Garifuna, 129, 138, 154, 182-184, 206-211
  culture of, 89, 217-218, 223
  origins of, 82, 205
Garvey, Marcus, 186, 194, 217-218
General Workers Union, 170, 173, 182, 186-192, 211-212
Gibbs, Archibald Robertson, 24, 62, 88, 90, 96, 121-124, 126, 152
Glenelg, Lord, 131, 166
Goldson, Philip, 187, 190, 213
Goldsworthy, Governor Roger, 149
Gombay. *See* Music and dance, gombay
Gomez. *See* Soberanis, Antonio
Government, 26, 36, 52, 146-147, 160-162, 175, 182, 185, 192, 212-213
  executive authority, 36, 64
  local, 131, 150-152, 206
  See also Constitution; Judicial system; Legislature; Public Meeting
Grant, C.H., 152, 173, 210
Great Britain, 17, 52, 79, 110, 205
Great Depression, 172, 174, 207
Green, William A., 78, 160
Guatemala, 17, 79, 101, 129, 206, 208
Guatemalan claim, 188, 213-215, 220
Guerra de Castas, 82, 105-106, 101, 113-114, 123-124, 133
Gutman, Herbert G., 51
Guyana. *See* British Guiana
Hamill, Don, 191
Hamilton, Superintendent Alexander, 39
Harley, Governor Robert, 109-110
Hellinger, Marlis, 92
Henderson, Captain George, 22-24, 42, 53, 55-59, 67-68, 73, 76, 83, 88, 103, 111-112
Hill Bank, 105
Historical sociology, 82, 128

Honduras, 19-25, 33, 45, 72-73, 193, 219

Humphreys, R.A., 30, 110, 126

Hunter, Governor Sir John, 169, 186

Hunter, Superintendent Peter, 28, 37, 39

Hurricanes. *See* Belize Town or City, hurricanes

Hyde, Evan X, 218

Hyde, George, 73

Hyde, James, 162

Ibo or Eboes, 53, 83, 90, 94

Immigration, 188, 208, 213, 220

Imports, 38, 161, 167, 188
    import duties, 123, 152

Independence, 188-192, 212-214

India, Indians (East), 206, 209

Jamaica, 22, 24, 26, 27, 29, 32, 52, 53, 61, 64, 69, 70, 74, 80, 89, 93, 94, 96, 123, 182-183, 185-186, 195, 202, 212

John Canoe, Jonkonnu, 89

Jones, Grant D., 114, 127, 128, 131, 132, 138, 140, 144, 153

Jones, Joshua, 35, 36, 43

Judd, Captain W., 27

Judicial system, 17, 152
    alcaldes, 108, 121, 128-138, 140, 144-153, 206
    magistrates, 25, 33-40, 47, 70, 118-119, 140, 145-148, 152, 161, 165-167, 181
    Slave Court, 64
    Supreme Court, 64, 181

Kaxiluinic, 149

Kekchi. *See* Maya, Kekchi

Kemp, L.D., 184-186, 188-190, 193-194

Kittermaster, Governor Harold, 176-178

Klein, Herbert, 50

Knight, Franklin W., 50

Labour,
    conditions, 56, 62, 68, 74, 84, 166-169, 173, 186-187, 190
    control, 74, 78, 80, 119, 121-125, 159-170, 174
    Department, 191, 194
    disturbances, 62, 160, 165, 167-170, 173, 178-188
    division of, 57-60, 74, 114, 217

laws, legislation, 118, 159-160, 164-170, 172, 195
    seasonal demand for, 41, 56, 78, 87-88, 164, 177, 192
    strikes, 165-166, 168, 178, 180, 183-184, 187, 219
    unemployment, 167-168, 171-172, 174-180, 183-184, 188-194, 207, 212

Labourers and Unemployed Association, 169-170, 172, 176-186, 188, 207

Lahoodie, John, 176, 179-181, 184-185

Land,
    laws, 68, 80, 139, 142, 161-162
    ownership of, 32, 34, 52, 80, 161-163, 206
    reservations, 122, 128-132, 138-139, 142-144, 155, 206, 218
    taxes, 122-123, 152
    tenure, 23, 49, 56, 67, 127, 144, 218
    use, 47, 115-117, 127, 162
    See also Crown Lands

Language, 210, 218
    Creole, 91, 209, 218
    and education, 218
    English, 137, 206, 209, 213, 220
    Garifuna, 206, 210, 218
    German, 208, 210
    Maya, 137, 141, 206, 210, 218-219
    Spanish, 96, 137, 205-6, 209-210, 220

Lawrie, James Pitt, 34, 42

Legal system. *See* Constitution; Judicial system

Legislative Assembly, 122-123, 133, 152, 162, 212

Legislative Council, 162, 169, 173, 175, 178, 181-182, 185-192, 211-212

See also Constitution; Public Meeting

Lewis, Arthur, 172

Lewis, Gordon K., 37

Locations or works, 23, 30-35, 43, 49, 56, 70, 73, 10, 105-107
    location laws, 161-163

Logwood. *See* Forest industry, logwood

Longden, Lieutenant Governor James R., 115, 122, 139-140

Lynch, Governor, 19

Magistrates. *See* Judicial system, magistrates

Mahogany. *See* Forest industry, mahogany

Manumission. *See* Slaves, slavery, manumission

Maroons, 46, 70, 72, 82, 95-96

Matthews, Superintendent, 179-180

Maya, 17-19, 41, 52, 70, 78-79, 82, 96, 101-155, 182, 184, 204-211, 217-220

   ancient, 78, 219

   Chichanhá, 106-108, 121, 132, 137, 149

   Icaiché, 107-111, 122, 132-133, 138, 141, 149

   Kekchi, 142, 206, 209, 218-219

   Lochhá, 106, 108

   Manche Chol, 18, 129

   Mopan, 206, 209, 218-219

   San Pedro, 107-111, 121, 137-139, 145, 149-150, 205-206

   Santa Cruz, 105-110, 116, 132, 137, 139, 145

   Tipú, 18, 103-104, 107-108, 111, 125, 131

   Toledo Maya Cultural Council, 217-219

   Xkanha, 106

Meighan, R.T., 184-186, 189

Menezes, Mary Noel, 132, 149

Mennonites. *See* Religion, Mennonites

Merchants, Belize, 35, 42, 45, 102, 405, 113, 122-123, 152, 169, 177-178, 181

   London, 20, 26, 161-162

Mestizos, 82, 114, 116-118, 148, 182, 206-207, 209-210, 218, 220, 222

   immigration of, 79, 113-114, 117, 138

Mexico, Mexicans, 18-19, 105-107, 110, 129, 132-133, 137, 141, 149, 208, 211

Middleton, Henry A., 189-190

Militia, 27, 29, 62, 77

Mintz, Sidney W., 78, 85, 93, 95

Modyford, Governor, 19

Mosquito Shore, 29, 31-39, 47, 73

   evacuees, 32-33, 35, 38-39, 42-43, 80, 125

   Indians, 52-53, 78, 125

Moyne Commission, 184, 191

Music and dance, 62, 219

   of Garifuna, 29, 218

   gombay, 62, 86

   of slaves and Creoles, 62, 84-89, 218

National Independence Party, 213

Nationalism, 101, 192, 199-200, 211

   national unity or integration, 212

   nationalist movement, 170-173, 185, 187-183, 200, 211-212, 218, 221

Natives First Independent Group, 182, 187-188, 211

Niger delta, Nigeria, 53, 84, 86

Obeah. *See* Religion, obeah

Open Forum, 188-189

Orange Walk Town, 82, 109, 114, 120, 133, 148, 181, 193, 206, 223

Panama, 184, 186

Parry, Admiral, 25

Patterson, Orlando, 42, 64, 75

Peasants, 78, 80, 116, 127, 163

Pech, Santiago, 110, 133, 138, 141, 149

People's Committee, 182, 185-189, 212

People's Group, 186, 188

People's United Party, 170, 173, 185, 187-190, 207, 211-216

Petén, 71-72, 104, 107, 140, 142

Phillips, Denbigh, 178-179

Plural Society, 201-203, 210, 217, 219-223

Police, 25, 170, 134, 137-138, 145-148, 150, 163, 177-180, 184, 191, 193, 219-220

Pollard, Nicholas, 189

Population, 18, 37, 39, 41-42, 54, 55, 79-80, 93

   birth and death rates, 55, 204, 207

   censuses, 40-41, 53, 65, 67, 80, 82-83, 94-95, 114, 171, 205, 207-210

   foreign-born, 53, 83-84, 94, 204-205, 208

   occupations of, 42-44, 80, 82, 114, 137, 161, 171

   racial/ethnic composition of, 18, 37, 53-54, 64, 70, 80, 82, 84, 95, 101, 141, 148, 201, 205, 207, 209

   size, 113-114, 121, 139, 178, 181, 207

   See also Demographic history

Price, George Cadle, 187, 189-190, 211-216, 222

Price, Superintendent, 137-138

Progressive Party, 186

Public Meeting, 17, 23, 33, 37-38, 40, 43, 45, 48, 63, 70, 161, 166
Punta Gorda, 223
Race, racism, 39, 83, 199-212, 217, 219-220
Refugees, 79, 82, 103, 133, 135, 140, 205
   Central American, 209, 219-220
   Yucatecan, 113-119, 124, 139
Religion, 201, 205, 209-210, 212
   African, 62-63, 84, 86, 92-93, 95
   Anglican, 63, 86, 92-93, 166, 210
   Baptist, 63, 92-93, 123, 166, 210
   Catholic, 28, 83, 114, 187, 190, 206, 210-212
   Islam, 86, 218
   Maya, 114, 206
   Mennonites, 208
   missionaries, 52, 63, 74, 92-93, 131-132, 166, 218
   obeah, 29, 62, 85, 90
   Wesleyan, Methodist, 63, 92-93, 166, 210
Reneau, Benjamin, 176, 179-180, 185
Rhys, Edward L., 109, 137-138
Richardson, Leigh, 187, 190
Rivers, 23-24, 27, 30-31, 33, 56, 82, 89, 92, 112, 174
   Belize, 18-19, 27, 30, 32, 34-35, 42, 46, 78, 82-83, 103-105, 108-109, 112, 127, 140, 142, 204
   Bravo, 105, 108, 133
   Hondo, 23, 27, 30-31, 46-47, 52, 71-72, 103, 105-107, 110, 117-118, 139
   Labouring Creek, 108, 137
   New, 18-19, 224, 26, 30, 41, 103, 105, 109, 117, 133, 139
   Roaring Creek, 30, 41, 103, 108
   Sibun, 23, 30-32, 41, 46, 52, 59, 71-72, 77, 80, 103, 139
Roads, 24, 82, 143, 148, 174, 180, 183-184, 192
Rodney, Admiral, 25, 27
Ruatan, 31-32
Rum, 22, 85, 113, 115
Saint Domingue, 62, 70
St. George's Cay, 21, 25, 2-28, 30-31, 42, 47, 79-80, 102
   Battle of, 21, 25, 28, 31, 47, 80, 102

St. John's College, 187, 189, 211, 220
St. Kitts, 172
San Antonio, 114, 142-143, 145, 148, 193, 206
San Estevan, 114
San Ignacio, 79, 82, 104, 108, 184, 209, 211, 215, 223
San José, 107, 109-110, 133, 139, 145, 149-150
San Pedro, 107-111, 114, 121, 137-139, 148-150, 205-206
Seymour, Superintendent Frederick, 107-108, 112-113, 121, 133-137
Shoman, Assad, 45, 75, 153, 194
Sio, Arnold, 75
Slaves, slavery, 17, 23, 25, 29, 38, 50-75, 82, 90, 92, 95
   culture, 24, 29, 50, 53, 61-63, 85-86, 91-92
   demographic characteristics, 24, 35, 41, 54-55, 74, 80
   escapes, runaways, 24, 27-29, 31-32, 46-47, 55, 71-73, 106, 119, 129, 205
   families, 39, 51, 60-61, 66, 90-91
   laws, 29, 37, 42, 64, 159, 166, 170
   manumissions, 41, 55, 64-65, 67
   occupations, 23, 25, 56-60, 74, 82
   rebellions, 26-30, 45, 62, 70, 73, 104
   register of, 59, 61, 91
   structure of ownership, 32, 42, 63, 67
   trade, 24, 53, 61, 83-84, 90, 204
   treatment of, 17, 25-26, 30, 45, 47, 51, 55, 61, 65-66, 68-70, 74, 88, 119
   value of, 26, 65-68
Smith, John, 187, 189-190
Smith, M.G., 95 201-203, 210, 220, 223
Smyth, Superintendent John, 40
Soberanis Gomez, Antonio, 168-169, 172, 176-189, 192, 211, 218
Social structure, 17-18, 35-36, 40-41, 43, 45, 91, 104, 111, 116, 162, 201, 210, 221
Socialism, 188
Succotz, 140-142, 144-145, 148
Spain, Spaniards, 17, 21, 24, 26-29, 36, 45, 54, 71, 79, 104, 106, 116-117, 129, 142

Spanish incursions, 24-25, 128-129, 131, 204
Spanish sovereignty, 21, 23, 31, 52, 161
Squier, E.G., 82-83
Staine, Calvert, 186
Stann Creek Town. *See* Dangriga
Stephen, James, 48, 131
Sterling, Reverend John, 170
Stevenson, Superintendent William, 114-115
Sugar. *See* Agriculture, sugar
Sweet-Escott, E.B., 143
Sydney, Lord, 32-33, 37-39, 43
Tamay, Gabriel, 149
Tannenbaum, Frank, 50
Taxation, 38, 40, 122-123, 152, 161, 172
Tayasal, 18
Thompson, J. Eric S., 18, 125, 129, 150
Timber extraction. *See* Forest industry
Tipú. *See* Maya, Tipú
Tom, John Alexander, 167
Trade unions, 168-173, 184-186, 190-192, 194-195, 207, 212, 219
  legalization of, 168-169, 186
See also British Honduras Workers and Tradesmen Union; General Workers Union
Treaties, 30, 36, 45
  Convention of London, 1786, 22, 30-36, 44, 51-52, 161
  Great Britain and Mexico, 1893, 110, 133
  Madrid, 1667, 19
  Madrid, 1670, 79
  Paris, 1763, 21, 51
  Versailles, 1783, 31, 44
Trinidad, 76, 186, 202-203, 213
Truck system, 80, 118-120, 163-164, 168
Turton, Robert S., 182, 184-185, 187
Tzuc, Luciano, 106-108, 132-133, 138
United Black Association for Development, 217-218
United Democratic Party, 213-216
United States of America, 23, 51, 53, 68, 83, 176, 200, 207-208, 212, 217
Universal Negro Improvement Association, 186, 194, 217-218
Uring, Nathaniel, 22

Usher, E.S., 185
Waddell, D.A.G., 24, 38, 75
Wages, 80, 112-116, 119-124, 140, 163-169, 172, 175, 177, 179-183, 186, 190, 192, 205, 218-220
Walker, Patrick, 78-79, 104
West India Regiments, 123, 29, 84-85, 90, 103, 175
West Indies (British or Commonwealth Caribbean), 24, 74, 78, 84, 159-160, 163, 166, 169-170, 172, 182, 190-191, 201, 213
White, Robert, 20, 22
Wilk, Richard R., 218
Williams, Eric, 50
Wilson, Governor David, 143
Wodehouse, Superintendent Philip, 106
Wood, E.F.L., 182
Women, 31, 40-41, 54-55, 57-61, 65, 85, 91-92, 107, 138, 175-179, 182, 207
Yalbac Hills, 105, 107-108, 110, 133, 138, 144, 149, 152, 205
Young, Aaron, 35-36
Yucatán, 19, 24, 27-28, 71, 79, 82-83, 104-107, 110-119, 124, 129, 131-132, 140, 205